Addressing the Fog of COG:
Perspectives on the Center of Gravity in US Military Doctrine

By Select Faculty of
US Army Command and General Staff College

Celestino Perez, Jr., Ph.D.
General Editor

Combat Studies Institute Press
US Army Combined Arms Center
Fort Leavenworth, Kansas

Preface

The Combat Studies Institute continues its mission of publishing CGSC Faculty scholarship and adding to the public discourse the learned thoughts of these distinguished professors and practitioners. These analyses on the concept and application of Center of Gravity are thought provoking while at the same time illustrative of the depth of the professional unrest with the concept. As military professionals set out to do their work, the planning done prior to beginning operations is crucial; and, if that planning hinges on identifying the center of gravity (or centers of gravity if you are so inclined to believe) how the concept is used, or not, could be paramount. Readers are invited to join the professional dialogue.

CSI – The Past is Prologue!

                                          Roderick M. Cox
                                          Colonel, US Army
                                          Director, Combat Studies Institute

Foreword

Nearly twenty years ago, as a new student in the Army's Command and General Staff Officer's College, Infantry Branch officers introduced to me the relatively newly codified doctrinal term "center of gravity." Throughout the "best year of our lives" as students, we wrestled with how to apply or integrate center of gravity with the Military Decision Making Process. We read Clausewitz' *On War*. I marked every reference he made to center of gravity. We consumed Army Field Manual 100-5 AirLand Battle. I dog-eared the few center of gravity references it had. Some of us stayed at mother Leavenworth for a second year and studied even more Clausewitz, even more Field Manual 100-5, and studied the application of center of gravity in Operations Desert Shield and Desert Storm. After two years of studying, thinking, talking, and writing about center of gravity, it was time to apply this new concept while assigned to a combat unit.

A few weeks later as a Division G3 Planner, I led the staff through several planning exercises and developed Division level operations orders that were intended to be training aids for Brigade Combat Teams which were preparing to deploy to the National Training Center. The staff included enemy and friendly centers of gravity in the written orders. The G3 and Division Commander were duly impressed. They were impressed when the staff identified the enemy and friendly centers of gravity in an operations order for a US-Russian tactical exercise. Trouble emerged in 1995 when the Commander asked his staff what the enemy and friendly centers of gravity were in the developing situation in Bosnia-Herzegovina. This peace enforcement operation did not fit the mold of scenarios that had been discussed and debated in Fort Leavenworth or within the Commander's headquarters.

Initially I was not involved in the Stabilization Force planning, so it was safe to throw darts at the wall to determine the unit or headquarters or personality which might be the enemy center of gravity; but we didn't really have a focused enemy, or, depending to whom you spoke, everyone was our enemy. It was then that it dawned on me; there was no logical process to identify a center of gravity. There was no principle or criteria available for testing the validity of a proposed center of gravity. Furthermore, there was no procedure or process included in our doctrine to coherently discern how to "attack" the enemies' center of gravity in this peace enforcement mission.

Luckily for me, I had a civilian friend who was an Engineer. Just by chance, while discussing his systems analysis processes, he unknowingly clarified a way to determine the center of gravity. When the Army temporarily assigned me to United States Army Europe to complete the SFOR planning, much smarter officers had already determined centers of gravity and methods to address them, which could lead to our success. This was very fortunate for the US Army.

As concepts go in the US Army, those that are useless fall to the way side, while the useful ones tend to grow in importance. Tactics, techniques and procedures addressing these useful concepts are shared until the Army incorporates them into doctrine. Once they are written in doctrine, the Army addresses these concepts more fully in all of its relevant Professional Military Education.

Joint and Army doctrine provides a common language and defines the terms used in our profession. It is sound military advice prepared collectively, and to be used as a common framework for planning and executing a range of military operations. Doctrine is founded in previous and successful applications of tactics, techniques and procedures, but also guides modernization and budgeting programs to shape future applications. It also sets fundamental principles to guide the employment of future forces and facilitate organizing future forces for specific operations.

Over time, the definition for center of gravity in Army and Joint doctrine matured and grew more similar. Through experience and experimentation, methods emerged to better and more thoroughly analyze the environment which enables commanders and their planners to more accurately identify an adversary's center of gravity. Furthermore, this analysis, if properly applied and integrated into the Military Decision Making Process or Joint Operational Planning Process, helps a commander and his staff to identify several ways to attack the adversaries' center of gravity directly or indirectly, or to protect one's own center of gravity. Through the years commanders and staff officers became more comfortable in their comprehensive preparation of the environment, even when the environment was wickedly complex, through Design.

When developing Contingency Operations and Campaign plans for NATO's military operations in Libya, OPERATION UNIFIED PROTECTOR (OUP), I comfortably contributed to the analysis that identified the enemy center of gravity upon which NATO focused its operations. Subsequently, as the Chief of the Combined Joint Task Force UP's Operations Cell, I observed how essential it was for the commander and staff to continue to focus on the center of gravity analysis and its products during the conduct of the operation. Historians may tell a different story of the successes and failures in this operation, but from my foxhole, the center of gravity remained a focal point for the Commander and the operations that the staff directed, which ultimately led to NATO victory.

Interestingly enough, through the insistence of NATO senior mentors and NATO colleagues, NATO planning staffs became comfortable with applying the same analysis with other key players in today's complex environment, and not just criminal or terrorist organizations. We applied the same analysis to UN organizations in the theater of operations, or other international organizations, non-governmental organizations, civil organizations and the local society at large, etc. This analysis helped us to identify the element that gave these organizations the power to achieve their objectives. It also helped us to identify where these organizations might have problems. Our analysis helped us to identify where our efforts merged or intersected with the efforts of these other organizations; and, furthermore, helped us to anticipate their requests for assistance and their possible points of failure.

Soon after this NATO experience, I found myself back in the Fort Leavenworth schoolhouse and responsible for shaping the educational environment and preparing curriculum. My responsibilities included leading the very experienced faculty to achieve the school's mission—to educate and prepare our future leaders to win our nation's current and future wars and conflicts. When the center of gravity became the focal point for discussion amongst the faculty, it was déjà vu all over again. Although the discussion was conducted at a much higher aptitude than 20 years before, and positions were staked out with more precise definitions and even principles, the positions taken by the various interlocutors were similar to the viewpoints of 20 years ago. These viewpoints were: it's an irrelevant concept for today's complex environment; the definition is insufficient; the definition is sufficient, but the methods provided for analysis are too narrow; descriptions of how to apply the analysis are incomplete; we can apply better analysis processes and procedures; center of gravity analysis is relevant only in a traditional force-on-force scenario; etc.

At the conclusion of this rather heated and professional debate, several faculty members agreed to put their "pen-to-paper." Maybe, they thought, they could induce a larger audience to join them in the debate and persuade them to proliferate their ideas throughout the Army. They are passionate about this subject, and believe their view of center of gravity is most appropriate for the future of the US Army. Therefore, we have this terrific collection of articles in this pamphlet focused on the center of gravity and driven by various opinions on the concept's utility today and tomorrow, and on how to improve or replace it. The various authors poured their enthusiasm into the enclosed articles, which is quite evident. Moreover, they provide some limiting stakes to their arguments…all you have to do is to read the articles, stake out your own position, and then enter the debate.

The anticipated intellectual discussion on this subject will be healthy for the Army. It will most likely stimulate relevant criticism as well as produce some current and recent vignettes—both positive and negative—on the center of gravity, the use of center of gravity analysis, and ways to directly or indirectly apply that analysis. The authors of these articles hope you are as excited about this topic as they are. They look forward to your comments and suggestions, and anticipate professional dialogue. The joint force and the Army might possibly benefit from your insights and contributions to this discussion.

Regardless of how current doctrine addresses center of gravity, you can contribute to its modification to help ensure doctrine remains relevant to conducting operations in future complex and undefined environments. The time to engage is now.

                                      John C. Buckley, II
                                      Colonel, US Army
                                      Director, Command and General Staff School
                                      Fort Leavenworth, Kansas

Contents

page

Preface iii

Foreword v

Chapter 1
Behind the Mosaic: Insurgent Centers of Gravity and Counterinsurgency
by Jonathan Klug.. 1

Chapter 2
Center of Gravity: A Quest for Certainty or Tilting at Windmills?
by Kurt P. VanderSteen 33

Chapter 3
Exploring Outside the Tropics of Clausewitz: Our Slavish Anchoring to an Archaic Metaphor
by Christopher R. Paprone and William J. Davis, Jr. 65

Chapter 4
Center of Gravity Analysis—the Black Hole of Army Doctrine
by Stephen L. Melton.. 81

Chapter 5
Thoughts on Clausewitz, Strategy, and Centers of Gravity:
When Jargon Meets Reductionism
by John T. Kuehn 101

Chapter 6
Center of Gravity: Right Idea, Wrong Direction
by Phillip G. Pattee 113

Chapter 7
Modernizing the Center of Gravity Concept—So It Works
by Colonel (Ret) Dale C. Eikmeier 133

Figure Contents   *page*

Figure 1. COG Schooner..65

Figure 2. Various Computations of COG. 67

Figure 3. Without Reflection - Metaphoric Displacement of Meanings......68

Figure 4. Center of Gravity Systems Slide...92

Figure 5. Center of Gravity Analysis Example...145

Figure 6. Revised Center of Gravity Analysis. 146

Figure 7. Center of Gravity Identification and Analysis. 148

Figure 8. Systems Analysis, Netwrok Analysis Diagram. 150

Figure 9. Lines of Effort. 161

Figure 10. Center of Gravity Sources...164

Chapter 1
Behind the Mosaic: Insurgent Centers of Gravity and Counterinsurgency
by Jonathan Klug

"For every human problem there is a solution that is simple, neat and wrong."
—H.L. Mencken[1]

Counterinsurgency has defined the United States conventional military experience from the summer of 2003 to the present.[1] During this period American military forces faced multiple insurgencies in Afghanistan, Iraq, the Philippines, and other areas.[2] These operations brought heightened military and academic interest in counterinsurgency history, theory, and doctrine, precipitating efforts to update counterinsurgency doctrine.[3] The US Army and Marine Corps counterinsurgency manual, or Field Manual (FM) 3-24,[4] is the most well known part of these doctrinal efforts. This rapidly produced counterinsurgency doctrine sparked debate on how to execute effective counterinsurgency operations. Unfortunately, misunderstanding of the concept of centers of gravity and the content of FM 3-24 led to the mistaken notion that "the people are the center of gravity." As a consequence, some units conducting counterinsurgency operations incorrectly determined centers of gravity, which led to unnecessary expenditure of time, blood, and treasure. This manuscriptmonograph examines centers of gravity, particularly in counterinsurgency operations in the context of multiple insurgent groups operating in one area of operations and insurgent groups using localized approaches. This manuscript argues that rather than one static, monolithic center of gravity, there are multiple operational and tactical centers of gravity in counterinsurgency that vary by insurgent political purpose, location, approach, and phase.

United States forces have conducted counterinsurgency throughout their past and there will be a requirement for them to conduct counterinsurgency in the foreseeable future, which makes examining centers of gravity as part of counterinsurgency campaign planning and operations worthwhile. First, analyzing centers of gravity in context will help leaders articulate the nature, costs, opportunities, and risks of conducting counterinsurgency operations to policy makers. Second, clarifying this key element of operational art will aid in campaign planning, thereby likely improving the execution and probability of success of counterinsurgency operations.[5]

This manuscript examines multiple insurgent areas of operation and the dynamic and varied nature of multiple insurgent operational centers of gravity, recognizing and accounting for the notion that insurgency can form a complex, shifting mosaic. More specifically, many insurgencies conduct different types and combinations of operations at the local or tactical levels. For example, in one area an insurgency can be weak and consequently conducting small-scale operations, where forces of the same insurgency in an adjacent area can be strong and conducting larger-scale operations. From a macro or theater perspective, these variations form a mosaic not of small colored tiles, but of areas of varying insurgent efforts. This contextual understanding of the mosaic nature of most insurgencies and their multiple operational centers of gravity facilitates equally nuanced and tailored efforts to effectively counter insurgency. Similarly, conducting effective counterinsurgency depends on recognizing when there are multiple insurgencies operating in the same area.[6]

The first section of this manuscript is a review of key literature on centers of gravity, insurgency, centers of gravity in counterinsurgency, and the independent variables used in the case studies. The second section of the manuscript consists of two case studies. The conclusion is the final section of the manuscript and provides a summary of insights into centers of gravity in counterinsurgency.

Carl von Clausewitz's discussion on a center of gravity appears relatively late in *On War*.[7] Clausewitz stated that: "[O]ne must keep the dominant characteristics of both belligerents in mind. Out of these characteristics a certain center of gravity develops, the hub of all power and movement, on which everything depends."[8] Based on this statement, each belligerent has a center of gravity, and a center of gravity must be determined in relative opposition. In other words, each side's center of gravity emerges depending on its political aims in opposition to the opposition's political aims. Thus, Clausewitz explicitly supports the notion that multiple centers of gravity vary by time, space, and purpose.

While Clausewitz's key statement on a center of gravity defines a single center of gravity, he allowed for multiple centers of gravity. He stated that it was a goal or ideal to analyze back to the fewest number or, preferably, to one center of gravity. Clausewitz outlined two aspects important when attempting to isolate a single center of gravity. The first was to examine the distribution of political power. For example, an alliance may have only one center of gravity if the members of that alliance only loosely share political interests. The second analytical aspect was the situation in the theater of war. "[T]he effect that events in a given theater will have elsewhere can only be judged in each particular case. Only then can it be seen how far the enemy's various centers of gravity can be reduced to one."[9] Clausewitz added, that when an enemy's "resistance cannot be reduced to a single center of gravity...two almost wholly separate wars have to be fought simultaneously."[10]

Clausewitz felt that centers of gravity simultaneously cause the greatest impact on the enemy and are a target for the enemy. Thus, centers of gravity are a concentration of combat power; a concentration of combat power that can attack or be attacked. Clausewitz felt that force should be concentrated to strike a cohesive army and excess mass in striking a less coherent force is a waste and is part of the tension between dispersing forces to control territory and massing forces to strike. This major battle is often "a collision between two centers of gravity; the more forces we can concentrate in our center of gravity, the more certain and massive the effect will be."[11] Thus, centers of gravity clashing in a major battle will have an effect on the entire theater.

Cohesion was another key consideration for centers of gravity. Fighting forces have unity through cohesion, and "[w]here there is cohesion, the analogy of the center gravity can be applied."[12] Clausewitz also drew a distinction between the cohesion of a single army and an allied force. The former naturally has more cohesion than the latter, as one represents a single body politic and the other separate political groups. Clausewitz said that in coalitions political unity varies by degree between how each coalition member pursues independent interests or if there is dominant leader. Further, if defeating one foe will break the coalition, this one foe is the center of gravity. This is one of the exceptions where it is not "realistic to reduce several centers of gravity to one."[13]

According to Clausewitz there were several possibilities for centers of gravity. In most cases he said that the center of gravity was the army; however, for a small country with a protector nation, the center of gravity may be the army of the protector. The center of gravity for alliances is shared interest amongst the members of the alliance or, in other words, what holds it together and working towards common goals and interests. Finally, Clausewitz said, "in countries subject to domestic strife, the center of gravity is generally the capital."[14]

Clausewitz discussed centers of gravity in the chapter, "The People in Arms." As Clausewitz linked his notion of centers of gravity to strength and concentration, he felt armed civilians were not a center of gravity. Armed civilians, however, could attack the invader's center of gravity. Clausewitz recommended that armed civilians only "nibble at the shell and around the edges"[15] and must not concentrate to avoid destruction. The resistance of the armed civilians would set the example that would "spread like a brush fire,"[16] spurring further resistance and eroding the invaders' strength and will. Clausewitz clearly felt the prospects of armed civilians succeeding alone were low, and that armed civilians should support a regular army.[17]

Retired Israeli Reserve Brigadier General Shimon Naveh wrote extensively on operational art and systemic operational design, and this subsection provides a short examination of his operational theory, including his discussion of centers of gravity. Additionally, this subsection very briefly surveys Soviet operational history and theory, as they are the basis of Naveh's work.

The Soviet operational pioneers included Svechin, Tukhachevsky, Triandafillov, Isserson, and others. Retired US Army Colonel David Glantz and Dr. Harold Orenstein provided key Soviet contributions to the theory and practice of operational art in a two volume work: *The Evolution of Soviet Operational Art, 1927-1991*.[18] In his summary of the Soviet theorists, Glantz pointed out that the Soviets viewed military art as "the theory and practice of preparing for and conducting military operations."[19] More importantly, the Soviets subdivided military art into the interrelated fields of strategy, operations, and tactics.[20] These fields, or levels as current doctrine refers to them, have distinct standards of mission, scale, scope, and duration.[21]

An extensive study of the history and theory of operational art underpinned Naveh's work. Naveh believes that before the Napoleonic Wars was the "age of the *strategy of the single point* [emphasis original],"[22] where commanders sought a single, decisive battle. However, warfare began to change during the Napoleonic Wars. Based on this historical study, Naveh asserted that the drastic growth of nineteenth-century military forces, which in turn expanded operations in time and space. The integration of operations distributed in time and space distributed operations into a coherent whole in the hallmark of operational art. Similarly, simultaneous and successive operations are the "heart of operational art."[23]

Soviet theorist G. K. Isserson's study of warfare led him to conclude that modern operations "*must be ready to overcome the entire depth* [emphasis original]."[24] With these three points in mind, a single battle could not be decisive; only a series of battles that attacked in depth could be decisive.[25] This fact led to the expansion of warfare in time and space precipitated the genesis of abstract concept of operational art. Naveh provided the arguably best explanation of operational theory and operational art. He felt that, "The essence of [the operational] level, as the intermediary field between strategy and tactics, is the preparation, planning, and conduct of military operations in order to attain operational objectives and strategic aims."[26] Naveh articulates that operational campaigns occur within a theater and accomplish strategic goal within a framework of time and space. Naveh also noted that an independent command conducts a campaign.[27]

Systems theory is at the core of Naveh's explanation of operational art, and his use of this approach is arguably Naveh's key contribution to operational theory. Naveh uses systems theory to demonstrate that operations exist in a framework between two belligerent systems to attempt to achieve their objects. In fact, this framework is itself a system. As each belligerent attempts reach its ends, their efforts disturb the overall system. The overarching system and its components attempt to overcome these disturbances and maintain system equilibrium. As each belligerent's operations attempt to disturb the system, they cause violent clashes with their contending systems, which are part of the larger system.[28]

Naveh felt that using centers of gravity "must involve cunning, which is the essence of operational art, at its best."[29] To Naveh centers of gravity played a vital role within the larger framework of the theater, war plans, and campaigns and that there were three elements for centers of gravity. First, planners must identify the points of strength and weakness in the opposing system. Second, the friendly force must create vulnerabilities in the opposing system. Third, maneuver strikes must exploit such vulnerabilities. These three elements combined both physical and cognitive operational vulnerabilities.[30]

Naveh implicitly supports that notion that multiple centers of gravity vary by time, space, and purpose. First, he points out that a campaign has an aim, or purpose, and a defined framework of time and space. Second, Naveh continually stresses that the operational field of war is dynamic and that successful operational art must be equally dynamic. Third, he believes that operational art must address the ubiquitous factor of randomness and chaos, as the various elements within the system have a dynamic interaction. Fourth, Naveh's use of systems theory inherently distributes multiple centers of gravity in space and purpose. Fifth, Naveh explicitly mentions that centers of gravity are dynamic. Finally, he repeatedly points to the importance of synchronization, which arranges activities in time, space, and purpose. This implicitly demonstrates the dynamic nature of warfare in general and centers of gravity specifically.[31]

Dr. Joe Strange is an influential recent interpreter of Clausewitz's work on centers of gravity. In fact, US joint doctrine adopted key aspects of his thought on centers of gravity. Strange's most important work is his 1996 monograph *Centers of Gravity & Critical Vulnerabilities*,[32] where Strange promulgated his centers of gravity methodology and provided instruction on how to determine centers of gravity at each level of war. The "CG-CC-CR-CV" concept is the core of his work. This concept consisted of centers of gravity (CG), critical capabilities (CC), critical requirements (CR), and critical vulnerabilities (CV). This concept provided depth and breadth to determining centers of gravity and, therefore, facilitated understanding the operational environment and informed planning. Strange's concept also supported his assertion that centers of gravity are not characteristics, locations, or capabilities, but they are moral, political, and physical entities that either posses characteristics and capabilities, or benefit from a given location or terrain. Most importantly for this manuscript, Strange explicitly supports that multiple centers of gravity vary by time, space, and purpose.[33]

Strange subdivided centers of gravity into moral and physical types. Moral centers of gravity could include leaders and popular support, and physical centers of gravity could include military forces, economic power, and large populations. Strange also emphasized that centers of gravity are dynamic, meaning they vary with time and by context.

Strange defined critical capabilities as the primary abilities which make a center of gravity as such in the context of a given scenario. Strange's examples of CCs were to remain alive, stay informed, communicate, and remain influential. As they are something that the center of gravity does, critical capabilities are normally verbs. The third aspect was critical requirements, which are conditions, resources, or means for a CC fully effective. An example of a CR was the support of the people and powerful national leaders. CRs are normally nouns. Finally, critical vulnerabilities are deficient or vulnerable CRs or CR components; thus, one can exploit CVs in order to attack an enemy center of gravity. Strange also emphasized that a center of gravity cannot be a critical vulnerability at the same time. Like CRs, CVs are normally nouns.[34]

Dr. Milan Vego provided contemporary discussion on joint operational warfare and operational art. According to Vego, destruction of a center of gravity will have a decisive affect on a belligerent's ability to achieve an objective and that an effective plan therefore relies on the proper determination of the friendly and enemy centers of gravity. Determining centers of gravity are therefore essential to operational art and improves the chances of a short and effective military effort. Vego also very aptly points out that "tactical actions are useful only when linked together as part of a larger design framed by strategy and orchestrated by operational art."[35] As center of gravity analysis is essential to successful operational art, it is vital to ensure that tactical and operational efforts contribute to attacking the enemy operational and tactical centers of gravity and protecting friendly operational and tactical centers of gravity. Vego also mentioned that modern ground forces are smaller and more dispersed than during World War II; thus, land combat is growing more like air and naval warfare—forces are more dispersed yet have massed effects.[36]

Vego differentiated centers of gravity into nonmilitary and military types. The former could include the will to fight, a key leader, an ideology, or a government's legitimacy. The latter could be a military force or function, such as an elite formation or command and control. Vego made a vital observation that an enemy is not fully defeated until the relevant mass of power—the relevant center of gravity—is defeated. Vego began his analytical concept for centers of gravity with the key point that centers of gravity cannot be determined in a vacuum. He asserted that, the objective is a principal factor to determine the center of gravity and the solution to any military problem. When conducting center of gravity analysis, one must examine the belligerents' objectives in relative opposition to each other, which implicitly means that centers of gravity vary by time, space, and purpose.[37]

To accomplish the military end state, Vego asserted that there is a required set of military and nonmilitary aspects of the situation, and he referred to these aspects as critical factors. The three types are critical strengths, critical weaknesses, and critical vulnerabilities. Critical strengths are an essential capability required to accomplish an objective. For the strategic level, the leader of a nation, coalition, insurgency, or extremist group is typically the most important critical strength. Vego's second type is critical weaknesses. Critical weaknesses are a source of power necessary to achieve an objective, but the capability is not adequate for the requirement. For example, an insurgency's critical weakness could be the population's waning support of their cause. Finally, Vego examines critical vulnerabilities. These are military or nonmilitary sources of power that are vulnerable to attack, control, leverage, or exploitation. As an example, Vego stated that the US aversion to casualties helped weaken US resolve during the Vietnam War.[38]

Vego believed that the higher the level of war, the more static the centers of gravity. In other words, there are less frequent shifts among strategic centers of gravity than operational centers of gravity and, similarly, frequent shifts in tactical centers of gravity relative to shifts in operational centers of gravity. Thus, Vego believes that centers of gravity are fluid, underscoring that there are often multiple centers of gravity at each level of war that vary depending on time, space, and purpose.[39]

Vego provided several key insights into insurgent centers of gravity. First, the strategic objective is predominantly nonmilitary and is often ideological in nature. As an example, ideology is a critical strength of al Qaeda. For the government fighting an insurgency, the strategic objective is predominantly nonmilitary and is often how the population views an insurgency's or a government's legitimacy. Insurgents will seek to attack the government's strategic center of gravity—its legitimacy. Consequently, the government must seek to protect and improve its legitimacy. Legitimacy is a critical strength based on how the population views the justness of the government's actions. As the insurgents often seek to undermine and, consequently, exploit poor government legitimacy, those conducting counterinsurgency must protect and bolster government legitimacy. Second, insurgents conducting guerrilla warfare will rarely present a physical operational center of gravity, as their forces will normally remain dispersed to avoid destruction. Instead, insurgent commanders and forces will often be tactical centers of gravity, although if these forces concentrate they could be an operational center of gravity.[40]

Dr. Antulio Echevarria is a Clausewitzian scholar and has written several pieces on Clausewitz's center of gravity concept. Echevarria believes that it remains valid and useful. He suggests that, "the concept's advocates have perhaps been too optimistic, and its critics too skeptical."[41] Echevarria draws a distinction between these efforts and what Clausewitz intended.

Echevarria examines the influence of contemporary science on Clausewitz's concept of centers gravity, as understanding the scientific concept upon which Clausewitz based his military concept provides insight into Clausewitz's military concept. Nineteenth-century physicists described a center of gravity as the point where gravitational forces converge within an object and that removal of the center of gravity should cause collapse. More importantly for this manuscript, Clausewitz's approach mirrored that of science:

successfully striking a center of gravity would shatter the object, or, in a military setting, lead to victory.[42] Echevarria also showed that a scientific center of gravity is not an individual's source of strength, but is concerned with balance.[43] Second, a "center of gravity is not a weakness, per se, though it can be weak, or vulnerable if it is exposed."[44]

According to Echevarria, many have misunderstood Clausewitz's center of gravity concept, and Echevarria explored what he suggests Clausewitz really meant. First, one can apply Clausewitz's concept wherever there is unity, connectivity, and interdependence with respect to enemy forces and the space occupied. Echevarria provides a long quotation from Clausewitz that is worth repeating here:

> Just as the center of gravity is always found where the mass is most concentrated, and just as every blow directed against the body's center of gravity yields the greatest effect, and—more to the point—the strongest blow is the one delivered by the center of gravity, the same is true of war. The armed forces of every combatant, whether an individual state or an alliance of states, have a certain unity and thus a certain *interdependence* or *connectivity* (*Zusammenhang*) [emphasis Echevarria's]; and where such interdependence exists, we can apply the center of gravity concept. Accordingly, there exist *within* [emphasis Echevarria's] these armed forces certain centers of gravity which, by their movement and direction, exert a decisive influence over all other points; and these centers of gravity exist *where* [emphasis Echevarria's] the forces are most concentrated. However, just as in the world of inanimate bodies where the effect on a center of gravity is at once limited and enhanced by the interdependence of the parts, the same is true in war.[45]

Thus, Echevarria believed that Clausewitz's center of gravity concept was "a focal point...where energies came together to be redirected and refocused elsewhere,"[46] and Echevarria provides a plausible example that al Qaeda's strategic center of gravity may be its ideology. Furthermore, Echevarria's example supports the notion that, center of gravity refers "less to the concentrated forces than to the actual element that causes them to concentrate and gives them purpose and direction."[47] Echevarria also stated that centers of gravity have spheres of effectiveness or spheres of influence; thus, a moving center of gravity will draw in forces as they come into its sphere of influence. Echevarria states that, "[i]n short, Clausewitz's centers of gravity draw energy and resources to themselves, and then redirect them elsewhere: they possess centripetal...force, which they can convert into a centrifugal...power."[48] This means that a Clausewitzian center of gravity is more than just a powerful entity that strikes a blow or friendly forces must protect; it is a powerful entity that provides unity to forces at a specific level of war. Finally, Echevarria's interpretation implicitly demonstrates that centers of gravity vary by time, space, and purpose.

Echevarria believes that his views on centers of gravity resonate with today's counterinsurgency. First, he states that "the personalities of key leaders, a state's capital, or its network of allies and their community of interests might perform the centripetal or centralizing function of a focal point."[49] Similarly, finding a center of gravity depends on the enemy's political connectivity, which is also useful in analyzing an insurgency's centers of gravity; however, the enemy may have insufficient unity to have a specific center of gravity emerge or that "an adversary might not have a [center of gravity], or at least one we can attack."[50] Similarly, there may be multiple centers of gravity, although Clausewitz stressed attempting to trace this back to one.[51] Echevarria made a superb point in that opposing centers of gravity may be different in that a physical center of gravity may be opposing a moral one. His example is an army pitted against public opinion. Not only can this asymmetry prove difficult in execution, but it can also bring disproportionate effects.[52] Finally, "Centers of gravity are more than critical capabilities...[which] if attacked...bring about the complete collapse of an opponent."[53]

Contemporary insurgents continue to use revolutionary warfare to attempt to reach their desired goals. Experts see Mao Tse-tung as a key revolutionary warfare theorist, even referring to him as "the founder of protracted revolutionary warfare."[54] Some contemporary analysts further opine that Mao's approach remains the "most sophisticated form of revolutionary warfare."[55] Mao's approach, however, did not materialize overnight. Years of struggle, many Chinese lives, and the Japanese invasion of China formed a crucible for Mao's theory,[56] allowing him to form "a synthesis between guerrilla warfare and mass organization."[57]

Mao's theory had several key points. First, his thesis for winning the revolutionary war in China was to "uphold the strategy of protracted war and campaigns of quick decision."[58] Four characteristics of the war in China framed Mao's thesis: China was a vast, semi-colonial country; the enemy was large and powerful; communist military forces were comparatively small and weak; and a close relationship of communist leaders and peasants existed. The relatively weak position of the Chinese Communist Party (CCP) required protracted war to husband and slowly build strength while simultaneously eroding enemy strength. To successfully change their relative strength through a protracted effort, the communists had to understand the situation and use an appropriate approach of cyclic strategic retreat, strategic counteroffensive, or strategic offensive. Mao expected that success would require multiple iterations of retreat, counteroffensive, and offensive. This cycle demonstrated that Mao implicitly understood that centers of gravity vary by time, space, and purpose; furthermore, Mao's theory took advantage of this notion to concentrate to attack the enemy's centers of gravity and disperse to protect the friendly centers of gravity. He believed that campaigns of quick decision were required to execute these efforts to conserve manpower, fiscal resources, and military strength. Mao also emphasized the importance of the support of the peasantry to support the weak communist military forces. According to Mao, political unity is a key advantage of the CCP, the communist military forces, and the people.[59]

Mao advocated studying experience and history in context, as "each historical stage has its special characteristics, and hence the laws of war in each historical stage have their special characteristics and cannot be mechanically applied in another stage."[60] Thus, Mao wrote his theory for a specific place and time: China in the late 1930s. The success of the Chinese fight against the Japanese and then the CCP's defeat of the Nationalist Chinese also support his theory. His theory, however, is broadly applicable to revolutionary warfare, demonstrated by many insurgent groups having used or been influenced by Mao's theory; however, some of these groups have blindly applied Mao's theory for revolutionary warfare in China.[61] These groups ignored Mao's caution against copying "exactly without the slightest change in form or content, we shall be 'cutting the feet to fit the shoe' and be defeated."[62]

Mao improved this theory with subsequent additions and refinements, including the thought of Sun Tzu and ideas from Clausewitz's "The People in Arms" chapter in *On War*.[63] In this way Mao used both practice and theory—experience fighting the Nationalist Chinese and Imperial Japanese and melding military theory from the West and East Asia—to refine his revolutionary warfare theory, solidifying his work's continued relevance. The essence of Mao's theory of revolutionary warfare—using a strategy of protracted war, campaigns of quick decision, and ensuring support of the people—is still applicable and influencing insurgents today. It also demonstrates that Mao implicitly understood and accounted for multiple insurgent centers of gravity varying with time, space, and purpose.

Dau Tranh, roughly translated as "struggle," was the communist Vietnamese's formidable adaptation of Mao's revolutionary warfare theory and practice. Unlike many of other practitioners' attempts to use Mao's theory, however, the communist Vietnamese understood the context of their struggle and successfully adapted their strategy to fit the operational environment.[64] Merely calling *dau tranh* a strategy does not do it justice. Robert S. McNamara, Secretary of Defense during the Vietnam War, felt that *dau tranh*, "appeared to be an extreme and lethal form of fanaticism, and the capacity of the rebels to sustain it throughout the war would be a continuing source of fear and wonderment."[65] *Dau tranh* was a total war, using all means to conquer South Vietnam.[66] This subsection examines *dau tranh* as it is a key factor in a subsequent case study, because it is a successful example of insurgents combining political and military aspects into a holistic approach, and since it supports the notion that multiple insurgent centers of gravity vary by time, space, and purpose.

Communist military leader General Vo Nguyen Giap summarized *dau tranh* by stating, "We not only conduct an armed struggle but also have the benefit of the masses' fierce political struggle. We also attack the aggressors by recruiting troops and gaining enemy converts."[67] The communist Vietnamese attacked all of their enemies, including the United States, using all means available; thus, the communist Vietnamese type of warfare was "waged simultaneously on several fronts—not geographical fronts, but programmatical fronts."[68] Dr. George Tanham supports this by stating that, "the central theme of the Communist effort [was]...the integration or orchestration of all means—political, economic, psychological, and military—to control the people and seize political power."[69] Political *dau tranh* and armed *dau tranh* attack an enemy holistically to unleash a general insurrection, and the communist Vietnamese leaders expected this to be a long struggle. Furthermore, they adapted their military and political approach during ongoing operations, always seeking to maintain the military and political initiative. Most importantly, *dau tranh* is a mosaic approach. A mosaic is a piece of art made with many small colored pieces that, when combined, create a larger picture. A mosaic insurgent approach is where insurgents in one area may be using conventional warfare, in another area using guerrilla warfare, and in a third area using propaganda and terrorism. Furthermore, the local approach would shift depending on the local situation. Again, this supports the notion that multiple centers of gravity shift by time, space, and purpose, especially at the tactical level.[70]

According to historian Douglas Pike, there are two major forms of *dau tranh* armed struggle or violence program: regular force strategy and protracted conflict. The communist Vietnamese used these two forms in combination depending on the situation, including regressing to lower levels of violence depending on the relative capabilities of the insurgents and counterinsurgents. Regular force strategy consisted of high technology warfare and limited offensive warfare. Giap used high technology warfare, matching their opponents' technology, and the communist Vietnamese first used this form of regular force strategy in the 1972 Easter Offensive. In response to the failure of the Easter Offensive, the communist Vietnamese used the limited offensive form of warfare, which included the 1975 campaign.[71]

Protracted conflict was *dau tranh's* second form of violence and divided into classic, or Maoist, guerrilla war and neo-revolutionary guerrilla warfare. In Mao's revolutionary warfare, the conflict progresses through three phases. However, the communist Vietnamese felt that elements of the Mao's theory were not as relevant in their contemporary context, mostly due to advances in technology. Partly based on this, Giap's conception was that the third phase, or the counteroffensive, would consist of a general people's insurrection, which differs from Mao.[72]

Political *dau tranh* was a broad spectrum of nonmilitary efforts: political, diplomatic, psychological, ideological, sociological, and economic. Like armed *dau tranh*, Pike outlined components of political *dau tranh*. *Dich van* was action among the enemy, *binh van* was action among the military, and *dan van* was action among the people. First, *Dich van* focused on the Vietnamese population controlled by the government of South Vietnam as well as the American population. Second, *binh van* undermined the morale of enemy troops, causing desertion or eroding combat effectiveness. Third, *dan van* focused on political indoctrination and administration in "liberated areas" in South Vietnam or, in other words, areas of South Vietnam under communist control. *Dan van* was essentially the communist use of the counterinsurgency oil spot technique; thus, the insurgents created ever-expanding areas of control. Overall, political *dau tranh* was a mix of disinformation, propaganda, agitation, uprisings, terror, and subversion.[73]

If armed *dau tranh* defeats the counterinsurgent forces, the insurgents win. Conversely, if the counterinsurgents defeat the insurgents militarily, the insurgents merely revert to the strategic defense to build political and military strength. Thus, the counterinsurgents must defeat the insurgents both militarily and politically to succeed. This success over the insurgents will normally only be temporary if the core grievances that caused and sustained the insurgency remain unresolved. If these core grievances are not resolved, insurgency may reemerge, which it did time and time again in South Vietnam.[74]

The population is not a center of gravity at any level of war by definition and by Strange's methodology. More specifically, the population cannot be the insurgent center of gravity using Echevarria's interpretation of Clausewitz, nor is the population a center of gravity using Strange's methodology. First, Echevarria's interpretation of Clausewitz shows that a center of gravity is something that draws together or unifies something. In the case of an insurgency, a charismatic leader, such as the Peruvian insurgency Shining Path's leader Abimael Guzmán, and the ideology that underpins an insurgency, such as Guzmán's fierce mix of the thought of Marx, Lenin, and Mao with strong historical appeals to the Incan past, are examples insurgent strategic centers of gravity.[75] Second, the historical example of Guzmán's as an insurgent charismatic leader demonstrates that by Strange's methodology the population is not a strategic center of gravity. Using Strange's methodology, Guzmán needs the population to support him to reach his end state, and Guzmán's ideology is a key aspect of gaining this support; thus, support of the population is not in itself a center of gravity.

Although not a center of gravity, support of the population is a critical aspect of operational art in counterinsurgency. Support of the population is often an insurgent critical requirement and a critical vulnerability. As a hypothetical example, a charismatic leader who is a strategic center of gravity has several CCs, including the ability to mobilize the population and the ability to generate resources. Support of the population is essential to mobilize the population and generate resources, so support of the population is a CR for both of these CCs. As the counterinsurgents can contest the insurgency's control of the population, these CRs are also CVs.[76]

In the hypothetical example above, support of the population is both a CR and CV for the insurgents. The same methodology applies for the counterinsurgents. Thus, achieving support of the population in the hypothetical example is a *strategic, operational, and tactical objective* for both belligerents. In other words, support of the population is very important in most cases, but it is definitionally and methodologically inconsistent to refer to the population as the center of gravity.[77] In fact, if counterinsurgents treat the population as a center of gravity, it is very likely that they will waste resources and, worst case, the insurgents will win.

The operational level and operational art are context for operational centers of gravity. The key tenets of operational art apply in insurgency and counterinsurgency; however, one must adapt these tenets to account for the differences in relative force, time, space, and will.[78] In counterinsurgency insurgents tend to avoid battles. Instead, insurgents often keep their forces dispersed to avoid the normally more militarily powerful and mobile counterinsurgency forces. Insurgents normally have the advantage when protracting the conflict, as Clausewitz noted, "Both belligerents need time; the question is only which of the two can expect to derive *special advantages* from it in light of his own situation."[79] Insurgent groups also use different approaches based on their relative strength to their opponents.[80]

Schneider posited that key characteristics of modern operational art were field armies and distributed logistics, campaigns, operations, maneuver, and battlefields. While insurgents normally do not have field armies, they normally have distributed logistics, campaigns, operations, maneuver, and battlefields. Schneider's statement that the "hallmark of operational art is the integration of temporally and spatially distributed operations into one coherent whole"[81] and that simultaneous and successive operations are the crux of operational art apply for insurgent efforts as well; however, these efforts are normally also smaller and distributed further in time. In other words, the insurgents' normal military inferiority forces them to protract their wars, campaigns, and major operations. Finally, Isserson's point that modern operations "*must be ready to overcome the entire depth* [Isserson's emphasis]"[82] also applies to counterinsurgency. In other words, counterinsurgents should strive to overcome insurgent efforts—both operational and tactical—throughout the entire depth of the theater.

Strachan claimed that "the center of gravity was at the confluence of strategy and tactics,"[83] illustrating the importance of operational centers of gravity on both the operational level and operational art. Before conducting center of gravity analysis proper, there are two key steps. First, analysis of the strategic context and strategic centers of gravity frame operational center of gravity analysis. Second, operational objectives and the nature of each belligerent determine operational centers of gravity, as an opponent's operational centers of gravity resist their foe achieving threat objectives and friendly operational centers of gravity facilitate achieving friendly objectives.

An insurgency may disperse to avoid having an operational center of gravity destroyed by counterinsurgent forces, yet an operational center of gravity, such as a key insurgent leader, may exist. "Creating sub-[centers of gravity] is artificial, unless our opponent is too dispersed or decentralized to have one [center of gravity]."[84] Mao's third stage is an exception. In this case, an insurgency's operational center of gravity is able to draw operationally significant forces together and employ them to strike the enemy, forming a center of gravity in line with Strange's model. In the first two stages of Mao's theory, an operational center of gravity instead will conduct efforts through tactical centers of gravity and tactical centers of critical capabilities.

Joint Publication 3-0 defines the tactical "level of war at which battles and engagements are planned and executed to achieve military objectives assigned to tactical units or task forces. Activities at this level focus on "the ordered arrangement and maneuver of combat elements in relation to each other and to the enemy to achieve combat objectives."[85] The tactical level of war in counterinsurgency is normally a protracted series of small engagements where the insurgents try to erode the counterinsurgents' capabilities and will and the counterinsurgents attempt to defeat the insurgents.

The mosaic nature of many insurgencies, such as how the Vietnamese insurgents used *dau tranh* in South Vietnam, tends to focus attention on the tactical level. In fact, the frequent lack of an assailable insurgent operational center of gravity emphasizes tactical areas of operation and tactical activities. Clausewitz noted that "all parts of the whole are interconnected and thus the effects produced, however small their cause, must influence all subsequent military operations and modify their final outcome to some degree, however slight."[86] The lack of assailable operational insurgent centers of gravity further emphasizes the tactical actions in counterinsurgency.

This manuscript's four independent variables are insurgent political purpose, location, approach, and phase. These independent variables are key contextual components that determine centers of gravity at every level of war, and centers of gravity are dependent variables. Not only do the independent variables determine centers of gravity, changes in the independent variables determine when a center of gravity changes. As previously discussed, there are often multiple centers of gravity for each level of war. Given the typical "mosaic" nature of counterinsurgency, there are typically more centers of gravity at the tactical level of war in counterinsurgency and the independent variables at the local level impact their corresponding tactical centers of gravity.

There are three general insurgent political purposes: change, overthrow, and resistance. Seeking political or economic change on a government is a basic end that most insurgencies share. Second, an insurgency may seek to overthrow and replace a government. Resisting a foreign invader's occupation is a third basic insurgent political purpose. An insurgency may combine these ends and these ends may change depending on the strategic context. In terms of operational art, ends are some of the conditions that make up the insurgent's desired end state. Additionally, the core grievances that underpin the ends are also important to consider for an insurgency's political purpose. Perceived core grievances—which may include identity, religion, economy, corruption, repression, foreign exploitation or presence, foreign occupation, and inadequate essential services—are the basis of insurgency.[87]

Insurgent centers of gravity vary by location or space. Competent insurgents use space to wear down their opponents' will and tailor local efforts to suit the tactical situation. They often attempt to exploit areas in which counterinsurgents are relatively weak. Insurgents tend to operate fluidly and thereby react quickly to changing conditions. They often have the tactical initiative and can consequently avoid counterinsurgent efforts to decisively engage them. Porous international borders are also key aspects of space. When insurgents can exploit these political boundaries, the borders create sanctuaries. This affords the insurgency a space where they are difficult or impossible to assail, thereby allowing the insurgency to further capability to retain the operational initiative. Finally, single insurgencies may operate alone in an area, but there may be multiple insurgencies operating in the same location. In the case of multiple insurgencies operating in the same area, different insurgent groups may cooperate, ignore, or fight each other depending on their group's ends.[88]

Insurgent approaches include conspiratorial, military-focused, terrorism-focused, identity-focused, protracted popular war, and subversive. The conspiratorial approach involves a small group seizing power and then normally focuses on quickly gaining support of key groups and the population. The military-focused group attempts to reach its ends by acting against the opposing security forces. A terrorism-focused insurgent uses terror to gain and maintain power, and they may focus their efforts on the population, the opposing government, and/or the opposing security forces. Insurgents who use an identity-focused approach based on common identity, such as clan, tribe, religion, or other group identity. Insurgents may use many variations of protracted popular war to erode counterinsurgent physical and psychological strength. Insurgents may also focus on subversion and use relatively less violence to support its subversive efforts. Additionally, insurgencies may use a composite approach or several insurgencies using difference approaches can form a coalition.[89]

Insurgent phasing and timing play a key role in determining insurgency centers of gravity. First, insurgents can normally afford to be patient. While they are normally materially inferior to their opponents, they often have a superior strength of will. This often allows them to erode their opponents materially and psychologically over time. From a perspective of phasing and timing, one can view insurgents as being on the defensive, at equilibrium, or on the offensive. Insurgent operations while on the defensive normally can include subversion, terrorism, and guerrilla warfare. These operations often continue during equilibrium, but increase in size and may include some convention warfare. The offensive phase will often include more conventional warfare and the overall conflict will often become more properly viewed as a civil war. The insurgent phasing and timing does not have to be the same on all levels of war simultaneously. For example, an insurgency may be on the strategic defensive, on the operational defensive in one area, and on the tactical offensive in one small area.[90]

American involvement in Vietnam followed a long tradition of Vietnamese resistance to outsiders, most recently the Japanese during the Second World War and the French attempt to reassert their control of Vietnam after the Second World War. The communists defeated the French, which led to the partition of Indochina into Laos, Cambodia, North Vietnam, and South Vietnam. Second, the Vietnam War was a complex war in that it was both an external and internal war. It was external as North Vietnam and its communist supporters fought South Vietnam and its American partners. The Vietnam War also was an internal war as the National Liberation Front (or Viet Cong) fought an insurgency against the forces of South Vietnam and its supporters.

Some strategic context is required for a discussion of operational and tactical centers of gravity before, during, and after the Tet Offensive. There are four broad phases in the Vietnam War from the US perspective. The initial phase was US security force assistance to the Diem government of South Vietnam. The second phase began with the assassination of President Ngo Dinh Diem in November 1963 and included growing US involvement in South Vietnam.[91] The third phase began with the introduction of US ground forces in 1965 ends with the Tet Offensive and other attacks of 1968. The fourth phase was the after the communist offensives of 1968, included the American Vietnamization effort, and ended with the Paris Peace Accords of 1973.

The type of war—limited or unlimited—that each of the belligerents fought impacted the overall conduct of war. While in practice all wars have limits on the means used,[92] the willingness of a belligerents is important, especially when there is a distinct asymmetry between the belligerents as there was in the Vietnam War. Similarly, Clausewitz wrote, "the value of this object must determine the sacrifices to be made for it in *magnitude* and also in *duration* [emphasis original]."[93] To America the Vietnam War was a limited war within the framework of the Cold War. American policy was to maintain a non-communist South Vietnam while avoiding touching off a larger, more destructive war. Consequently, the US strategy in Vietnam had to strike a balance between achieving the desired end state and risking the direct Chinese or Soviet intervention. To South Vietnam the war was total. If South Vietnam could not defeat communist conventional and insurgent forces, South Vietnam would cease to exist. Because of previous assistance of the United States, however, South Vietnam did not fully appreciate this existential threat until after US support drastically waned during the Ford administration. To the communist Vietnamese the war was a total war for national unification under communist rule, although the communists portrayed the war as an effort against outsiders and the outsiders' puppets.[94] From their perspective, the communist Vietnamese desire to reunite Vietnam stemmed from interest and honor. More importantly for this manuscript, the core grievances of the insurgent narrative were nationalism, anti-colonialism, and social justice,[95] although the communist ideology was a key component of the narrative as well.

The asymmetry between belligerents also impacted how the war evolved. As Clausewitz stated, "the degree of force that must be used against the enemy depends on the scale of political demands on either side."[96] Over the course of the Vietnam War, the communist Vietnamese were willing to escalate means and maintain the use of these additional means more readily than the United States. Nevertheless, this case study focuses on the operational and tactical centers of gravity before, during, and after the Tet Offensive.

Throughout the Vietnam War, the communist Vietnamese used *dau tranh* to attack their foes politically and militarily; however, the communist Vietnamese insurgents always fought first politically and second militarily. The Americans, however, used a strategy of attrition, feeling that it "offered the Army the prospect of winning the war quickly, or at least more quickly than with traditional counterinsurgency operations."[97] The issue was that there were insufficient enemy forces exposed to attrition.

Instead of massing battalions conveniently for American attritional efforts, the communists would cycle though the tactical offense, equilibrium, and defense, as appropriate to the situation, and maintain military and psychological pressure on the Americans and South Vietnamese. The communist response to American firepower and advanced technology was to disperse their forces. By dispersing, the communists controlled the tempo of attrition and, consequently, the "long war in Vietnam [was] fought almost exclusively on the tactical level."[98]

The communists tailored their approach to fit the local conditions, using both North Vietnamese regular forces and South Vietnamese insurgent forces. These regular and insurgent forces focused on executing small, well-planned precision strikes and mounting multiple daily attacks, thereby varying their tactical approach by location and time. While these tactical iterations eroded both sides, the communist Vietnamese were more willing to accept this tactical protracted attrition to hold the village and hamlets. The intent of these methods was to erode military strength and, more importantly, undermine the enemy's morale. The steady escalation of these efforts was to culminate in a major attack, such as Dien Bien Phu, that would impact enemy military and political will. Additionally, the Viet Cong were very adept at capturing and disseminating tactical lessons, where the Americans and South Vietnamese were not.[99]

By mid-1967, the American commitment of ground troops hindered communist progress. While the mosaic approach of *dau tranh* was slowly proceeding at the operational and tactical levels, the Vietnamese communists viewed the war as strategic stalemate. Despite the apparent stagnation of their strategic approach, the communist Vietnamese felt they were in a position to attempt to spark a general uprising in South Vietnam. They planned to seize the strategic, operational, and tactical initiative, and they scheduled their offensive to begin during the Tet holiday of 1968—the Tet Offensive.[100]

Before the Tet Offensive there were no operational insurgent centers of gravity in South Vietnam, nor were there many operational communist conventional centers of gravity in South Vietnam. Insurgent forces remained dispersed down to the tactical level to avoid detection and destruction. The sanctuaries just over the Cambodian, Laotian, and North Vietnamese borders were operational centers of gravity; however, America and South Vietnam did not allow conventional land forces to attack across these borders. The communist forces that attacked Khe Sanh were an operational center of gravity; however, the efforts of these forces were merely a shaping operation for the actual Tet Offensive. More specifically, the attacks on Khe Sanh were a deception effort designed to convince the Americans and South Vietnamese that the main offensive would come on the periphery of South Vietnam and not the urban areas of South Vietnam.[101]

In addition to Khe Sanh, the communists planned multiple operational and tactical efforts that were supporting efforts to the larger deception operation. Communist conventional forces conducted a tactical attack on the border town of Song Be near the Cambodian border, and communist insurgents conducted a similar attack at Loc Ninh, another border town and provincial capital. Giap's final shaping operation was an operational-level attack—four conventional regiments—in the Dak To region. Unfortunately for the communists, these battles did not draw enough US forces away from the communist objectives for the Tet Offensive.[102] Nevertheless, these efforts demonstrate that the communists formed multiple operational and tactical centers of gravity that varied by purpose, location, and phase.

The communist Vietnamese had three objectives for the Tet Offensive. The most important was to spark the aforementioned general uprising amongst the people of South Vietnam. Second, this offensive was to defeat the armed forces of South Vietnam and America. Third, the Tet Offensive was to convince the Americans that communist victory was inevitable. The plan called for a three-pronged offensive to bring about a popular uprising. Supporting operations in outlying regions were to draw forces and attention away from the urban areas, the actual objectives of the offensive. Second, the main effort was a countrywide attack on cities, key units, headquarters, communications, and air bases. In order to conduct these attacks, the communist Vietnamese would concentrate formerly dispersed forces, forming conventional and insurgent operational and tactical centers of gravity. Third, the communists executed a massive *binh van*—action among the military—effort to get South Vietnamese forces to flip to support the communist Vietnamese. Additionally, major communist efforts in May and August 1968 followed the Tet offensive.[103]

The military results of Tet were horrendous for the communist Vietnamese. From a communist perspective, "after the summer campaign of 1969 a major portion of our main force army was forced to withdraw...to regroup...the strength of our local forces was seriously eroded."[104] From an American point of view, "for once we could find him...and the cost to him was enormous militarily."[105] The communist guerrilla forces in South Vietnam never recovered, and North Vietnamese regular forces did much of the fighting for the remainder of the war. The Tet Offensive, however, had a more important political impact: "The confidence of the American people had been badly shaken."[106] Not only did Tet end General Westmoreland's tenure as the American military commander in Vietnam, but President Johnson chose not to run for another term and the South Vietnamese government believed that the US was losing its resolve to continue the war.[107]

The American approach changed significantly in early 1969 due to the Tet Offensive. For the Americans, the "One War" concept and Vietnamization came to the fore. While Vietnamization was an American policy decision, the "One War" concept permeated all three levels of war, although it had profound impacts on the operational level of war. The "One War" concept linked military efforts with pacification. Additionally, the Americans and South Vietnamese placed more emphasis on the Phoenix Program. After Tet, Phoenix more effectively attacked the Vietnamese insurgent infrastructure.[108]

The failure of Tet required the communists to adapt their military efforts. The insurgent effort had lost many of its personnel and its underground infrastructure. As a result, the communists reverted back to dispersing their forces, thereby changing their operational and tactical approaches. After several months of experimentation and development, the communist Vietnamese began to use neo-revolutionary guerrilla warfare in some areas. The underpinning notion was to remain at stage two of classic guerrilla warfare, thereby avoiding concentrating forces. Elite guerrilla forces would again take up the routine of precision strikes and mounting multiple daily attacks. They coupled this approach with increased operations by North Vietnamese conventional forces in South Vietnam. Many communist leaders, however, felt that this approach would never generate enough momentum to lead to victory. In fact, communist Vietnamese leaders vowed to never again risk all of their military forces.[109]

Despite their earlier vow, the communist leaders did plan and execute a major offensive in 1972. This Easter Offensive, however, did not have to contend with American ground forces. Due to Vietnamization, only South Vietnamese ground forces and American advisors remained. Thus, the communist Vietnamese concentrated conventional forces, which formed an operational center of gravity. In fact, the communist forces staged major attacks in three separate areas simultaneously. South Vietnamese forces fought well, albeit with many American advisors and ample American air support. However, the communist Vietnamese were still more willing to sacrifice more than their South Vietnamese foes.[110]

After the 1972 failed Easter offensive, the North Vietnamese Central Committee examined it strategy to defeat South Vietnam and its supporters. Communist forces had recovered from previous operations and, with the withdrawal of American ground forces and American difficulty with direct intervention, were growing stronger than their South Vietnamese foe's military forces; however, some party members were concerned that a major offensive with Soviet and Chinese support could backfire and draw direct American intervention. The committee consequently compromised. They decided to shift from primarily focusing on the political to focusing on the military aspect of dau tranh and continue to erode South Vietnamese military and psychological strength. This strategy quickly began to affect the South Vietnamese, whose military forces struggled in 1973 and 1974. This strategy so weakened the South Vietnamese psychologically, that they rapidly collapsed in 1975. In fact, the speed of the final offensive campaign that toppled South Vietnam even surprised the communist Vietnamese.[111]

The complexity of the Vietnam War was the genesis of the concept of "mosaic warfare." Both before and after the Tet Offensive, local circumstances drove the communists' tactical purpose, approach, and phase. Thus, North Vietnamese conventional forces could be conducting offensive operations in a South Vietnamese province adjacent to an area where communist insurgents were mobilizing the population of a South Vietnamese hamlet and avoiding combat. While this approach was successful at the tactical level before and after Tet, lack of strategic progress led to the communists to attempt to foment a general uprising with the Tet Offensive as an operational catalyst. The analysis of the insurgent centers of gravity before and after the Tet Offensive demonstrates that there were multiple insurgent strategic, operational, and tactical centers of gravity that varied by insurgent political purpose, location, approach, and phase.

This case study does not address the invasion of Iraq. Rather, the analysis concentrates on the period of insurgency after the spring and summer of 2003. However, the invasion itself and subsequent occupation acted as core grievances of many of the insurgent groups. This case study examines multiple insurgent operational and tactical centers of gravity before and after the US change in theater strategy, commonly known as "The Surge." The Iraq case study is different from the Vietnam case study in that multiple insurgent groups were operating in Iraq where there was a single insurgent group operating in Vietnam.

When the United States invaded Iraq in 2003, the existing regime and its security apparatus fractured and subsequently seemed to dissipate like so much vapor.[112] This was partly due to coalition combat operations, coalition informational efforts, Iraqi design,[113] and the centralized nature of the Iraqi government. In the years following 2003, the Iraq War was multifaceted and often difficult for non-Iraqis to fathom. The Iraq War has several key points: a change in strategic center of gravity, examples of unbalanced counterinsurgency approaches (including both enemy-focused and population-centric approaches, the previous discussion of the initial American approach in the Philippines is an example of an unbalanced population-centric approach), and a mosaic nature similar yet more complex than that of the Vietnam War.

After the fall of Saddam Hussein's Ba'athist regime, the United States chose to remain in Iraq rather than treat the operation as a punitive expedition.[114] Thus, the United States forced regime change in Iraq.[115] Despite establishing a transitional military authority,[116]6a tremendous power and governance vacuum existed after the fall of the Iraqi central government. The task of working on post-invasion Iraq fell to Jay Garner. Garner led the Office of Reconstruction and Humanitarian Assistance (ORHA).[117] For reasons beyond the scope of this manuscript, this civilian transitional military authority was not capable of accomplishing its mission.[118] The failure of ORHA meant squandering the "golden window" of post-conflict termination: the first year after hostilities.[119] In fact, Iraq was in a state of anarchy or, as Metz aptly stated, "It was 'Lord of the Flies' on a monumental scale."[120] The meager resources—insufficient numbers of security forces and insufficient reconstruction capability and capacity—allowed several future threat groups to gestate, which included several proto-insurgencies to coalesce.[121] In more traditional insurgency terms, these groups were in the latent and incipient phase of insurgency.[122]

When forces of the United States occupied Baghdad, they occupied a strategic objective thereby collapsing a strategic center of gravity.[123] As mentioned previously, if a strategic center of gravity falls, the enemy should collapse at that level of war. In this case, the Iraqi nation and military did indeed collapse after Baghdad fell. In addition to Baghdad, there was another strategic center of gravity: Saddam Hussein. This second strategic center of gravity, however, went into hiding while his nation shattered.[124] Although he remained at large, he no longer had a tangible operational center of gravity. Because of continued survival, the Ba'athist resistance would later re-emerge. Overall, the initial US campaign is an example of the collapse of one enemy strategic center of gravity—Baghdad—and the severing of a second strategic center of gravity—Saddam Hussein—from its operational centers of gravity. The lull in enemy efforts and apparent lack of capabilities appeared to indicate a Coalition strategic victory; however, this lull was merely a period where new centers of gravity emerged.

During the period immediately after the fall of Baghdad, there were no operational centers of gravity, as there are no operational centers of gravity for an emergent insurgency that is in the latent and incipient phase. The insurgency is normally too small and lacks sufficient capability and capacity to act on the operational level of war. Instead, a latent and incipient insurgency has emerging tactical centers of gravity. These may be early insurgent leaders and associated nascent underground infrastructure. Instead, small groups of guerrilla fighters coalesced during this period.

There were several emergent insurgent groups in 2003 in Iraq. Although there were other smaller groups, On Point II listed seven major groups of insurgents: Sunni Arabs, secular ideologues, Sunni tribes, religious groups, ultra radical Salafis and Wahhabis, Shia groups, and Al-Qaeda and other foreign groups. These multiple groups emerged and grew quickly given the security and power vacuum. Each of these groups had their own goals and approaches; however, elements of these major groups had different approaches depending on local conditions. For example, local conditions dictated if a group was conducting offensive guerrilla warfare or if a group had to remain hidden and terrorize the local population. While these groups often fought each other, the Coalition was a common foe.[125] Consequently, the Coalition attempted to stabilize the situation in an environment that included a confusing array of multiple groups with multiple emerging tactical centers of gravity.

Local tactical commanders took unique approaches in their areas of operation to counter the emerging enemy tactical centers of gravity, which is appropriate given this shifting mosaic of insurgents and irregular actors. The real challenge for each unit was finding the right balance of aggressive counterguerrilla operations with stability operations given the operational environment and resources. When the 4th Infantry Division relieved the Marines in Tikrit, they used an enemy-focused approach that some historians view as heavy-handed; however, the division used a multifaceted approach, although initially the approach was likely too aggressive. Similarly, some historians feel the 82nd Airborne

Division used an overly enemy-centric approach; however, the division task force defined its overall objective as winning the support of the Iraqi people. The 101st Airborne Division's used a less-enemy centric approach than the 4th Infantry Division or the 82nd Airborne Division, but this approach was appropriate for the area of operations and given the 101st Airborne Division's combat power in relation to area of operations, the size of the Iraqi population, and the local threat. The 1st Armored Division took an approach that focused on fighting for intelligence or fighting based on intelligence. While the division performed well, the growing threat, however, meant that the division lacked the combat power to deal with the emerging insurgent forces and instability.[126] Ultimately, there were insufficient Coalition forces to deal with multiple enemies, each of which "is a hydra with numerous heads and no single center of gravity."[127]

The three years that followed the emergence of multiple insurgencies were bloody and chaotic. The fighting, however, reached a new level in 2006 when Sunni extremists attacked the al-Askari Mosque. The Sunni destruction of this key Shia mosque unleashed a new, unprecedented wave of sectarian violence. Thus, insurgent groups and other irregular actors fought each other and anyone who attempted to quell the violence. If this event did not change the nature of the conflict, it certainly underscored the need to address sectarian violence. Policy makers consequently realized they had to craft a "new" strategy for Iraq.

Although it did not change the strategic ends, this "new" strategy called for changes in ways and increased means in order to decrease the risk of strategic failure. This revised strategy became the so-called "Surge."[128] The increase in means came in additional military and non military resources. Importantly for this case study, the key military component of "The Surge" was to increase ground forces. The new ways for the strategy of "The Surge" incorporated lessons that US forces had learned in combat since 2003. The key aspect of the new ways was a change in operational approach. The additional ground forces were to clear and hold Baghdad with the objective of securing the population and, hopefully, earning the support of a greater portion of the population. From a US policy perspective, the strategy relied on improved security and support from the population to allow for an Iraqi political settlement.[129]

As the Coalition commander in Iraq as of February 10, 2003, General Petraeus oversaw the implementation of an operational approach that focused on protecting the population. As "The Surge" increased the combat power available to the Coalition by five US Army brigades and two US Marine infantry battalions, with additional military police, aviation, a division headquarters, and other enables. These additional forces and forces already in Iraq increased the tactical ground density of Coalition forces in key areas in Iraq, especially Baghdad. For the clear phase, the additional combat power allowed Coalition commanders to mass combat power and effects to achieve tactical objectives and deal with the multitude of insurgent tactical centers of gravity. For the hold phase, the additional combat power allowed dispersion of forces not involved in clearing, specifically dispersed in small outposts called joint security stations. Thus, the additional combat power allowed tactical sequencing of concentrating combat power to clear an area and then dispersing combat power to hold an area.[130]

On June 15, 2007, Coalition forces began several major operations outside of Baghdad. This was a change in the operational approach. Coalition commanders coupled successful operations in Baghdad with operations outside of the capital; thus, relative tactical combat power now allowed a change in operational art: simultaneity instead of sequencing. The point was to conduct simultaneous tactical operations to prevent terrorists to simply move from point-to-point away from Coalition pressure and thereby gain an operational effect on the enemy.[131] More specifically, the Coalition approach undermined the enemy's tactical flexibility to choose its purpose, approach, and phase by location. Instead, the Coalition had the combat power to seize and retain the operational and tactical initiative. The insurgent groups, however, would regenerate and fight in other areas, such as Anbar province.[132]

The surge efforts were successful in the short- and medium-term, as they created some breathing space in the violence, a vital condition for potential political negotiations. While "The Surge" gets most of the credit for creating this breathing space, there were many other military and nonmilitary efforts that contributed to the reducing the violence.[133] One area that is often sadly neglected is the Iraqis themselves. Not only was the population weary of the violence, Iraqis joined their new nation's security forces in the thousands. Like the additional "Surge" forces, these forces also added combat power to fight the insurgent groups and help reduce sectarian violence, although building the capacity of the Iraqi security forces pre-dated "The Surge." However, some also speculate that the declining sectarian violence had more to do with the completion of sectarian cleansing; nevertheless, the overall efforts reduced the level of insurgent and sectarian violence in Baghdad.[134]

At the time of writing this manuscript, insurgent and sectarian violence continues in Iraq. The United States continues to maintain military forces in Iraq; however, the future of these forces is open to speculation. Currently, there is no political agreement between the US and Iraq to keep US forces in Iraq after December 2012. However, it is unclear if all US forces will depart. If some US forces remain, the size of the US forces in Iraq is unclear. The US forces that stay would likely conduct security force assistance, primarily as trainers and advisors supporting Iraqi security forces.

The Iraq War was a "perfect storm" of circumstances and initial mistakes followed by rapid tactical and operational adaptation.[135] The Coalition's "Surge" was a strategic effort that attempted to institutionalize field adaptations, increase the means available in theater, and to better nest theater ends, ways, and means. The analysis of the insurgent centers of gravity before and after "The Surge" demonstrates that there were multiple insurgent strategic, operational, and tactical centers of gravity that varied by insurgent political purpose, location, approach, and phase; thus, Clausewitz's centers of gravity concept proves useful.

This manuscript's literature review examined Clausewitz's original center of gravity concept, interpretations of Clausewitz's concept, key insurgent theory, and centers of gravity in counterinsurgency. The centers of gravity in counterinsurgency subsection also explained the vital point that the population is not a center of gravity; rather, the support of the population is often a critical requirement/critical vulnerability. The cases studies in this manuscript validated the hypothesis that there are multiple centers of gravity in counterinsurgency that vary by insurgent purpose, location, approach, and phase. However, the case studies also outlined the difficulties of affecting insurgent operational and tactical centers of gravity if insurgents vary their efforts by local conditions. This challenge becomes more acute if there are multiple insurgent groups and other violent actors in the same area of operations. Overall, this underscores the difficulty of directly acting against an insurgent operational center of gravity and thereby achieving decisive results.

Centers of gravity continue to be relevant; however, leaders and planners need to place them in their proper context for understanding and planning counterinsurgency operations. By placing them in context, understanding there are often more than one at any level of war, and understanding they vary by insurgent purpose, location, approach, and phase, previous material on centers of gravity is useful for counterinsurgency. Center of gravity analysis from the proper point of view can support effective counterinsurgency campaign planning and help avoid the historical conceptual planning issues, such as improperly focusing on just the insurgents or just protecting the population.

As mentioned previously, the population is not a center of gravity. Rather, operational leaders and planners should understand that the support of the population is often a critical requirement and a critical vulnerability. As a likely insurgent and friendly critical requirement and critical vulnerability, the support of the population is often an objective for insurgents and counterinsurgents. This is also true on more than one level of war and for both the insurgents and counterinsurgents. Regardless of approach, insurgents are often dependent on a portion of the population for resources, such as food and shelter, and for protection, often in the form of early warning and concealment. Counterinsurgents, especially foreign forces conducting counterinsurgents, are often dependent on a segment of the population for human intelligence. Consequently, the support of the population should be a strategic, operational, and tactical objective for both insurgents and counterinsurgents.

The approach should fit the environment. In other words, there must be a proper balance between countering the actual insurgency and protecting the population; this is not binary or an "either/or" question. Instead, it is a question of balancing enemy-centric and population-centric activities given the current environment. Proper center of gravity analysis will determine an initial balance from which forces can quickly adapt.

Treating the population as a center of gravity will often skew the balance between attacking insurgent centers of gravity and efforts to protect and positively influence a critical requirement/critical vulnerability. Leaders and planners involved in counterinsurgency must look for the actual centers of gravity and properly treat the support of the population as an objective. Clausewitz, Strange, and Echevarria's works would point to the notion that centers of gravity will form to attack or defend this objective. While this may seem overly nuanced or superfluous, treating the people as the center of gravity will naturally result in an approach that overemphasizes protecting the people at the potential price of ceding the insurgents the operational initiative. Conversely, not protecting the people leaves a critical vulnerability open to insurgent activities and, more importantly, the possible second-order effect of center of gravity destruction and the cascading third-order effect of friendly collapse. Overall, proper balance between will improve the probability of counterinsurgent success.

The two case studies demonstrated that counterinsurgency often occurs in a complex operational environment. Consequently, countering an insurgency requires understanding the operational environment, which the manuscript often refers to as a mosaic. Not only should leaders and planners understand that the operational environment is a mosaic—insurgents vary their purpose depending on the circumstances, use localized approaches in multiple areas of operations, and change over time. Multiple insurgent groups operating with or near other violent actors only add to the complexity and difficulty of counterinsurgency operations. Nevertheless, this complexity carries both risk and opportunity. Normally counterinsurgents are relatively strong compared to insurgents, and insurgents normally disperse their forces to avoid destruction. Savvy counterinsurgents can take advantage of this to seize the operational initiative, much like the Coalition forces did in Iraq 2007; however, this requires a sufficient relative combat power advantage to allow the feasible balance between protecting the population and conducting offensive operations directly against the insurgency.

United States land forces have continuously conducted counterinsurgency operations for nearly a decade. These operations have occurred in several countries, but most importantly in Iraq and Afghanistan. Looking to the future, it almost seems inevitable that the US will either conduct counterinsurgency operations or at least support another host nation government to conduct counterinsurgency. Naturally, the American military must be able to quickly and effectively adapt to effectively fight insurgent foes, and it is essential that the US military services capture and internalize the hard-won lessons of the past decade. While there are many areas to capture these lessons, future joint and service doctrine must capture what has been learned with respect to enduring fundamentals and successful tactics, techniques, and procedures, thereby continuing the to improve on the key doctrinal effort of FM 3-24/MCWP 3-33.5.

Planning and conducting counterinsurgency campaigns and major operations are key aspects of operational art in counterinsurgency operations. More importantly, the US military must capture the operational art lessons of the recent wars and internalize these lessons. Understanding centers of gravity in counterinsurgency at the operational and tactical levels is a vital part of these efforts. Centers of gravity point to several key ideas and concepts that aid in conducting counterinsurgency as a whole and at each level of war. However, "[i]f everything is a center of gravity, nothing is."[136] The population is clearly not a center of gravity. Instead, support of the population is normally essential for US involvement in counterinsurgency and important for most insurgent approaches—a critical requirement/critical vulnerability for both sides.

This manuscript examined centers of gravity, particularly in counterinsurgency operations in the context of multiple insurgent groups operating in one area of operations and insurgent groups using localized approaches. The two case studies demonstrated that rather than one static, monolithic center of gravity, there are multiple operational and tactical centers of gravity in counterinsurgency. Fighting an insurgency or multiple insurgencies is fighting a mosaic war, and centers of gravity determine the nature of tactical areas of operation—or, to continue the metaphor, each piece of the mosaic—and these centers of gravity vary by insurgent political purpose, location, approach, and phase. Quantitative study and additional qualitative analysis could further underscore that the independent variables—purpose, location, approach, and phase—cause multiple operational and tactical centers of gravity to shift. More importantly, this additional study may facilitate better understanding and practice of operational art in counterinsurgency operations.

Notes

1. Donald P Wright and Timothy R. Reese, *On Point II: Transition to the New Campaign: The United States Army in Operation IRAQI FREEDOM: May 2003-January 2005* (Fort Leavenworth, KS: Combat Studies Institute Press, 2008), 87. Wright and Reese discuss that units arriving during the spring and summer of 2003 were confronted by insurgency.

2. For Iraq see Gregory Fontenot, E. J. Degen, and David Tohn, *On Point: The United States Army in Operation Iraqi Freedom: Through 01 May 2003* (Fort Leavenworth, KS: Combat Studies Institute Press, 2004). For Afghanistan see Donald P. Wright et al., *A Different Kind of War: The United States Army in Operation ENDURING FREEDOM, October 2001-September 2005* (Fort Leavenworth, KS: Department of the Army, 2010). While there has not been a book length study of Operation Enduring Freedom–Philippines, articles are available. See Eric P. Wendt, "Strategic Counterinsurgency Modeling," *Special Warfare* 18, no. 2 (September 2005): 2-12. Also see Peter Brookes, "Flashpoint: No Bungle in the Jungle: Operation Enduring Freedom-Philippines is Getting Results," *Armed Forces Journal* (September 2007), http://www.armedforcesjournal.com/2007/09/2926516 (accessed June 4, 2011).

3. Counterinsurgency operations in Iraq, Afghanistan, and the Philippines set in motion the rewriting or writing of several doctrinal manuals. New manuals included: FMI 3-07.22, *Counterinsurgency Operations*; FM 3-07.1, *Security Force Assistance*; FM 3-24, *Counterinsurgency*; FM 3-24.2, *Tactics in Counterinsurgency*; JP 3-24, *Counterinsurgency Operations*; and JP 3-26, *Counterterrorism*. Updated manuals included: FM 3-0, *Full Spectrum Operations*; FM 3-07, *Stability Operations*; and FM 5-0, *The Operations Process.* Manuals that were subsumed by FM 3-24 and FM 3-24.2 included FM 90-8, *Counterguerrilla Operations* and FM 7-98, *Operations in a Low-Intensity Conflict*.

4. US Department of the Army, Field Manual (FM) 3-24, *Counterinsurgency* (Washington, DC: Government Printing Office, 2006).

5. The White House, National Security Strategy (Washington, DC: Government Printing Office, 2010), 14; US Department of the Army, Field Manual (FM) 3-0, *Operations*, Change 1 (Washington, DC: Government Printing Office, 2011), 7-5.

6. FM, 1-8; Kyle Teamey and LTC Jonathan Sweet, "Organizing Intelligence for Counterinsurgency," *Military Review* 86, (September-October 2006): 24; Phillip B. Davidson, *Secrets of the Vietnam War* (Novato, CA: Presidio Press, 1990), 20. The literature review section will examine mosaic warfare in more detail.

7. Carl von Clausewitz, *On War*, 1st ed., (Princeton: Princeton University Press, 1989).

8. Clausewitz, 595-596.

9. Clausewitz, 617-618.

10. Clausewitz, 623.

11. Clausewitz, 248, 486-487, 489, 583, 596.

12. Clausewitz, 486.

13. Clausewitz, 596-597.

14. Clausewitz, 596, 633.

15. Clausewitz, 480.

16. Clausewitz, 481.

17. Clausewitz, 481-482.

18. David M. Glantz, ed., *The Evolution of Soviet Operational Art, 1927-1991: Volume I, Operational Art, 1927-1964*, trans. Harold S. Orenstein (Portland, OR: Frank Cass and Co., 1995). The second volume covers 1965 to 1991.

19. Glanz, xvi..

20. David M. Glantz, *Soviet Military Operational Art: In Pursuit of Deep Battle* (New York: Frank Cass and Company, 1991), 12-13.

21. Glantz, *The Evolution of Soviet Operational Art, 1927-1991: Volume I*, Operational Art, 1927-1964, xvi.

22. Shimon Naveh, *In Pursuit of Military Excellence: The Evolution of Operational Theory* (New York: Frank Cass Publishers, 1997), 75, 181-183; James J. Schneider, *Vulcan's Anvil: The American Civil War and the Foundations of Operational Art* (Fort Leavenworth, KS: Command and General Staff College, 1992), 1.

23. James J. Schneider, "The Loose Marble--and the Origins of Operational Art," *Parameters*: 19, (March 1989): 87.

24. Richard Harrison, *Architect of Soviet Victory in World War II: The Life and Theories of G. S. Isserson* (Jefferson, NC: McFarland and Company, Inc., 2010), 109; Naveh, 230.

25. Harrison, 147.

26. Naveh, 9-10.

27. Naveh, 13.

28. Naveh, 15.

29. Naveh, 19.

30. Naveh, 19.

31. Naveh, 10, 13, 167, 232, 308-309.

32. Joe Strange, *Centers of Gravity & Critical Vulnerabilities*, Perspectives on Warfighting No. 4 (Quantico: Marine Corps University, 1997).

33. Strange, 43-48.

34. Strange, 43-51, 74.

35. Milan Vego, *Joint Operational Warfare: Theory and Practice* (Newport, RI: US Naval War College, 2007), VII-13, I-3.

36. Milan, VII-13.

37. Milan, VII-13 to VII-14.

38. Vego, VII-17 to VII-19.

39. Vego.

40. Vego, VII-15, VII-20.

41. Antulio J. Echevarria, *Clausewitz and Contemporary War* (New York: Oxford University Press, 2007), 177.

42. Echevarria, *Clausewitz and Contemporary War*, 179-180; Antulio J. Echevarria, "Clausewitz's Center of Gravity: Changing our Warfighting Doctrine--Again!" (Monograph, Strategic Studies Institute, US Army War College, 2002), 5-6. Here Echevarria underscores how Clausewitz's concept was closer to the physics analogy. See also, Antulio J. Echevarria "Clausewitz's Center of Gravity: It's Not What We Thought!," *Naval War College Review* 56, (Winter 2003): 10-110.

43. Echevarria, *Clausewitz and Contemporary War*, 179-180; Echevarria, "Clausewitz's Center of Gravity: Changing our Warfighting Doctrine--Again!," vi, 8; Echevarria "Clausewitz's Center of Gravity: It's Not What We Thought!," 112-113.

44. Echevarria, *Clausewitz and Contemporary War*, 179-180; Echevarria, "Clausewitz's Center of Gravity: Changing our Warfighting Doctrine--Again!," 8.

45. Echevarria, *Clausewitz and Contemporary War*, 180-181. The quotation is originally from Clausewitz, 485, although Echevarria has added italicized emphasis and included on parenthetical referencing the original German word. Echevarria is also using a different translation than the Michael Howard and Peter Paret translation. See also, Echevarria, "Clausewitz's Center of Gravity:

Changing our Warfighting Doctrine--Again!," vi, 10; Echevarria, "Clausewitz's Center of Gravity: It's Not What We Thought!," 112-113.

46. Echevarria, *Clausewitz and Contemporary War*, 181. As mentioned previously, Vego also believes that al Qaeda's ideology is its strategic center of gravity. See Vego, *Joint Operational Warfare: Theory and Practice*, VII-15.

47. Echevarria, *Clausewitz and Contemporary War*, 181.

48. Echevarria, *Clausewitz and Contemporary War*, 181; Echevarria, "Clausewitz's Center of Gravity: Changing our Warfighting Doctrine--Again!," 11-12, 19; Echevarria, "Clausewitz's Center of Gravity: It's Not What We Thought!," 113-114.

49. Echevarria, *Clausewitz and Contemporary War*, 182; Echevarria, "Clausewitz's Center of Gravity: Changing our Warfighting Doctrine--Again!," vii; Echevarria, "Clausewitz's Center of Gravity: It's Not What We Thought!," 114.

50. Echevarria, "Clausewitz's Center of Gravity: Changing our Warfighting Doctrine--Again!," 5.

51. Echevarria, *Clausewitz and Contemporary War*, 183; Echevarria, "Clausewitz's Center of Gravity: It's Not What We Thought!," 115.

52. Echevarria, *Clausewitz and Contemporary War*, 184.

53. Echevarria, *Clausewitz and Contemporary War*, 185; Echevarria, "Clausewitz's Center of Gravity: Changing our Warfighting Doctrine--Again!," 12-13.

54. John J. McCuen, *The Art of Counter-Revolutionary War* (1966; repr., St. Petersburg, FL: Hailer Publishing, 2005), 27.

55. Thomas A. Marks, *Maoist Insurgency since Vietnam* (Portland, OR: Frank Cass, 1996), 2. This subsumes the refinements others have made to Mao's original theory, such as the Vietnamese approach to revolutionary warfare.

56. Mao Tse-tung's early life included working on a farm, education, and interest in politics, including joining the Chinese Communist Party. Mao led an abortive uprising in Hunan, resulting in retreat to an isolated mountain village. In 1934, CCP leaders decided to abandon their base due to relentless Nationalist pressure, leading to a year-long march where the vast majority of marchers perished. After this march, Mao found himself in "swirling levels of...debate and analysis." To meet this internal challenge, he read voraciously and wrote several short works. See Jonathan Spence, *Mao Zedong* (New York: Penguin Group, 1999), 1-5, 42, 73-75, 80-83, 93.

57. Marks, 8.

58. Mao Tse-tung, "Problems of Strategy in China's Revolutionary War," in *Selected Military Writings of Mao Tse-tung* (Peking, China: Foreign Languages Press, 1967), 96-97.

59. Mao, 94-96, 113-114, 130-131, 144. The fourth characteristic is paraphrased to clarify and summarize Mao. Clausewitz's discussion of modifications in practice, that war is never an isolated act, and erosion and protraction on the defense all clearly influence Mao's thought. Clausewitz, 78, 93, 479. Clausewitz's *On War* permeated communist military and revolutionary thought, including his chapter "The People in Arms." While indirectly influenced by Clausewitz from communist military thought, Mao read Clausewitz in 1937. Beatrice Heuser, *Reading Clausewitz* (London, United Kingdom: Pimlico, 2002), 47.

60. Mao, 79.

61. An illustrative list includes Vietnam, Thailand, Philippines, Sri Lanka, and Peru. Marks, 1, 19, 83, 174, 253.

62. Mao, 78.

63. Mao, 84, 88, 115; Clausewitz, 479-487.

64. Davidson, *Secrets of the Vietnam War*, 18; Douglas Pike, *PAVN: People's Army of Vietnam* (New York: Presidio Press, 1986), 214; George K. Tanham, *Communist Revolutionary Warfare:*

From the Vietminh to the Viet Cong, rev. ed. (Westport, CT: Praeger, 2006), 2-3. This case study uses "Communist Vietnamese" in reference to both the North Vietnamese and communist insurgents in South Vietnam.

65. Robert S. McNamara, *Argument Without End: In Search of Answers to the Vietnam Tragedy* (New York: PublicAffairs, 1999), 162.

66. Davidson, *Secrets of the Vietnam War*, 20.

67. Vo Nguyen Giap, *Banner of People's War, the Party's Military Line* (New York: Praeger Publishers, 1970), 23.

68. Phillip B. Davidson, *Vietnam at War: The History 1946-1975* (New York: Oxford University Press, 1988), 25.

69. Tanham, xi. See also Max G. Manwaring and John T. Fishel, *Uncomfortable Wars Revisited* (Norman, OK: University of Oklahoma Press, 2006), 13-14.

70. Vo Nguyen Giap, *People's War, People's Army: The Viet Cong Insurrection Manual for Underdeveloped Countries* (1962; repr., Honolulu: University Press of the Pacific, 2001), 29. See also Giap, *Banner of People's War, the Party's Military Line*, xvii; Davidson, *Vietnam at War*, 25; Davidson, *Secrets of the Vietnam War*, 18, 20-21; Robert Thompson, *No Exit from Vietnam* (New York: David McKay Company, Inc., 1969), 48-49; Pike, 226..

71. Davidson, *Vietnam at War*, 26-27; Davidson, *Secrets of the Vietnam War*, 19; David M. Toczek, *The Battle of Ap Bac, Vietnam: They Did Everything But Learn from It* (Annapolis, MD: Naval Institute Press, 2001), 48-49; Pike, 229.

72. Pike, 212, 215-216; Davidson, *Vietnam at War*, 26; Giap, *Banner of People's War, the Party's Military Line*, xix.

73. Pike, 212, 216, 224, 236-246; Davidson, *Vietnam at War*, 27-28; Davidson, *Secrets of the Vietnam War*, 19. For more on the oil spot technique, see Robert B. Asprey, *War in the Shadows: The Guerrilla in History: Two Thousand Years of the Guerrilla at War from Ancient Persia to the Present* (New York: William Morrow and Co, 1994),153-155, 481, 672, and 711. Page 711 draws an analogy between Che Guevara's *foco insurreccional* with the oil spot.

74. Pike, 227; Davidson, *Vietnam at War*, 25-26; Ben Connable and Martin C. Libicki, "How Insurgencies End" (Monograph, RAND Corporation, Santa Monica, 2010), 20. See also US Department of Defense, Joint Publication (JP) 3-24, *Counterinsurgency Operations* (Washington, DC: Government Printing Office, 2009), III-3 to III-4; Angel Rabasa et al., *Money in the Bank: Lessons Learned from Past Counterinsurgency (COIN) Operations* (Santa Monica, CA: RAND Corporation, 2007), 71-72; Stephen T. Hosmer and Sibylle O. Crane, *Counterinsurgency: A Symposium, April 16-20, 1962* (Santa Monica, CA: RAND Corporation, 1963), 143.

75. Asprey, 1114-1115; Jeremy M. Weinstein, *Inside Rebellion: The Politics of Insurgent Violence* (New York: Cambridge University Press, 2007), 84.

76. Strange, 43-45.

77. Strange, 74-75.

78. JP 3-24, II-4.

79. Clausewitz, 597.

80. David Galula, *Counterinsurgency Warfare: Theory and Practice* (New York: Praeger Publishers, 1968), 43-62.

81. James J. Schneider, "The Loose Marble--and the Origins of Operational Art," 87-90.

82. Harrison, *Architect of Soviet Victory in World War II*, 109. Isserson conducted this study in the 1930s.

83. Hew Strachan, *Clausewitz's On War* (New York: Atlantic Monthly Press, 2007), 132.

84. Echevarria, "Clausewitz's Center of Gravity: Changing our Warfighting Doctrine--Again!," 20.

85. US Department of Defense, Joint Publication (JP) 3-0, *Joint Operations*, Change 2 (Washington, DC: Government Printing Office, 2010), GL-28.

86. Clausewitz, 158.

87. JP 3-24, II-4 to II-7.

88. JP 3-24, II-4.

89. JP 3-24, II-20 to II-21.

90. JP 3-24, II-4, II-13 to II-16.

91. Graham A. Cosmos, *MACV: The Joint Command in the Years of Escalation, 1962-1967* (Washington, DC: Government Printing Office, 2005), 95-106.

92. Donald J. Mrozek, *Air Power & the Ground War in Vietnam* (New York: Pergamon-Brassey's, 1989), 167.

93. Clausewitz, 92.

94. John Lewis Gaddis, *We Now Know: Rethinking Cold War History* (New York: Oxford University Press, 1997), 155-163. See also Maurice Matloff, ed., *American Military History* (Washington, DC: Center of Military History, 1988), 619; Wray R. Johnson, *Vietnam and American Doctrine for Small Wars* (Bangkok: White Lotus, 2001), 23-24; Andrew J. Birtle, *US Army Counterinsurgency and Contingency Operations Doctrine: 1942-1976* (Washington, DC: Center of Military History, 2006), 223; H. R. McMaster, *Dereliction of Duty: Lyndon Johnson, Robert McNamara, the Joint Chiefs of Staff, and the Lies That Led to Vietnam* (New York: HarperCollins Publishers, 1997), 23; Davidson, *Secrets of the Vietnam War*, 20.

95. Austin Long, "On 'Other War': Lessons from Five Decades of RAND Counterinsurgency Research" (Monograph, RAND Corporation, Santa Monica, 2006), 36; John A. Nagl, *Learning to Eat Soup with a Knife: Counterinsurgency Lessons from Malaya and Vietnam* (Chicago: University of Chicago Press, 2005), 117; Ronald H. Spector, *After Tet: The Bloodiest Year in Vietnam* (New York: The Free Press, 1993), 90-91; Stanley Karnow, *Vietnam: A History*, 2nd ed. (New York: Penguin Books, 1991), 474-479.

96. Clausewitz, 585, 605-606.

97. Andrew F. Krepinevich, *The Army and Vietnam* (Baltimore, MD: Johns Hopkins University Press, 1986), 164.

98. Clayton R. Newell, "On Operational Art," in *On Operational Art*, ed. Clayton R. Newell and Michael D. Krause (Washington, DC: Center of Military History, 1994), 12.

99. Davidson, *Secrets of the Vietnam War*, 19-20; Jeffrey Race, *War Comes to Long An: Revolutionary Conflict in a Vietnamese Province* (Berkley, CA: University of California Press, 1972), 148-149; Thompson, 33, 50-54; Long, 37; Nagl, 133; Bernard B. Fall, *Street Without Joy: The French Debacle in Indochina* (1961; repr., Mechanicsburg, PA: Stackpole Books, 1994), 351; Pike, 226-227; Tanham, 78-80, 85-93, 102-108.

100. James H. Willbanks, *The Tet Offensive: A Concise History* (New York: Columbia University Press, 2007), 9. For more information on the general uprising aspect of *dau tranh*, see Toczek, 51-52; Pike, 218-219; Sam C. Sarkesian, *Unconventional Conflicts in a New Security Era* (Westport, CT: Greenwood Press, 1993), 87.

101. Davidson, *Vietnam at War*, 468.

102. Davidson, 468-469; Willbanks, *The Tet Offensive*, 15-22.

103. Willbanks, *The Tet Offensive*, 10-13, 66-68; Davidson, *Vietnam at War*, 442-443; Davidson, *Secrets of the Vietnam War*, 98; Spector, 25.

104. The Military History Institute of Vietnam, *Victory in Vietnam: The Official History of the People's Army of Vietnam, 1954-1975*, trans. Merle L. Pribbenow (Lawrence, KS: University Press of Kansas, 2002), 246.

105. Robert Komer, "Robert Komer Recalls Tet's Impact," in *Major Problems in the History of the Vietnam War*, ed. Robert J. McMahon (New York: Houghton Mifflin, 2003), 327.

106. Clark M. Clifford, "Clark M. Clifford Remembers His Post-Tet Questions (1968), 1969," in *Major Problems in the History of the Vietnam War*, ed. Robert J. McMahon (New York: Houghton Mifflin, 2003), 329. See also Karnow, 538-565.

107. Am C. Sarkesian, *America's Forgotten Wars: The Counterrevolutionary Past and the Lessons for the Future* (Westport, CT: Greenwood Press, 1984), 207; Lewis Sorely, ed. *Vietnam Chronicles: The Abrams Tapes 1968-1972* (Lubbock, TX: Texas Tech University Press, 2004), xviii; Spector, 299, 311-316; Karnow, 594, 578-581.

108. Sorely, 19-20; Thompson, 145-161. The one war concept essentially viewed the Vietnam War as one effort, not a conventional effort and a pacification effort conducted separately. Robert W. Komer, *Organization and Management of the 'New Model' Pacification Program-1966-1969* (Santa Monica, CA: RAND Corporation, 1970), 257; Robert W. Komer, *Bureaucracy Does Its Thing: Institutional Constraints on US-GVN Performance in Vietnam* (Santa Monica, CA: RAND Corporation, 1972), 104-105; William Colby, *Lost Victory: A Firsthand Account of America's Sixteen-Year Involvement in Vietnam* (New York: Contemporary Books, 1989), 271-272. For more information on Operation Phoenix, see Dale Andrade, *Ashes to Ashes: The Phoenix Program and the Vietnam War* (Lexington, KY: Lexington Books, 1990), 71-98; Mark Moyar, *Phoenix and the Birds of Prey: Counterinsurgency and Counterterrorism in Vietnam*, 2nd ed. (Omaha, NE: University of Nebraska Press, 2007), 242-244; Thomas L. Ahern, *Vietnam Declassified: The CIA and Counterinsurgency* (Lexington, KY: The University Press of Kentucky, 2010), 318-320; Colby, 331-334; Karnow, 617-618.

109. Pike, 227-229; Neil Sheehan, *A Bright Shining Lie: John Paul Vann and American in Vietnam* (New York: Random House, 1988), 732-733; Richard A. Hunt, *Pacification: The American Struggle for Vietnam's Hearts and Minds* (Boulder, CO: Westview Press, 1995), 218; James H. Willbanks, *Abandoning Vietnam: How America Left and South Vietnam Lost Its War* (Lawrence, KS: University Press of Kansas, 2004), 67.

110. Willbanks, *Abandoning Vietnam*, 122-155; Karnow, 654-658, 673-674.

111. Willbanks, *Abandoning Vietnam*, 196-198, 256-258; Karnow, 676-684.

112. Bruce R. Pirnie and Edward O'Connell, Counterinsurgency in Iraq (2003-2006) (Santa Monica, CA: RAND Corporation, 2008), 9.

113. Pirnie and O'Connell, 7.

114. Steven Metz, *Iraq & The Evolution of American Strategy* (Washington, DC: Potomac Books, Inc., 2008), 121; Steven Metz, "Decisionmaking in Operation Iraqi Freedom: Removing Saddam Hussein by Force" (Monograph, Strategic Studies Institute, US Army War College, 2010), 47.

115. Wright and Reese, 27-29, 41-42.

116. Department of the Army, Field Manual (FM) 3-07, *Stability Operations* (Washington, DC: Government Printing Office, 2008), 5-2.

117. Dale R. Herspring, *Rumsfeld's Wars: The Arrogance of Power* (Lawrence, KS: University Press of Kansas, 2008), 125-127.

118. Metz, *Iraq & The Evolution of American Strategy*, 132-134, 152-153; Michael R. Gordon and General Bernard E. Trainor, *Cobra II: The Inside Story of the Invasion and Occupation of Iraq* (New York: Pantheon Books, 2006), 472; Wright and Reese, 149-153.

119. James Stephenson, *Losing the Golden Hour: An Insider's View of Iraq's Reconstruction* (Washington, DC: Potomac Books, 2007), 36,155.

120. Steven Metz, "Decisionmaking in Operation Iraqi Freedom: The Strategic Shift of 2007" (Monograph, Strategic Studies Institute, US Army War College, 2010), 1.

121. David C. Gompert and John Gordon IV, "War by Other Means: Building Complete and Balanced Capabilities for Counterinsurgency" (Monograph, RAND Corporation, Santa Monica, 2008), 37-40. For additional information on proto-insurgencies, see Daniel Byman, *Understanding Proto-Insurgencies* (Santa Monica, CA: RAND Corporation, 2007), 1-6.

122. US Department of Defense, JP 3-24, II-14; US Department of the Army, Field Manual (FM) 7-98, *Operations in a Low-intensity Conflict* (Washington, DC: Government Printing Office, 1992), 2-13 to 2-17.

123. Gordon and Trainor, 432-433.

124. Gordon and Trainor, 434.

125. Wright and Reese, 87, 105-110. For more information on the emergent Iraqi insurgent groups, see Ahmed S. Hashim, *Insurgency and Counter-Insurgency in Iraq* (Ithaca: Cornell University Press, 2006), 17-124, 347-348; Thomas R. Mockaitis, *Iraq and the Challenge of Counterinsurgency* (Westport, CT: Praeger, 2008), 103-107; Thomas R. Mockaitis, *The Iraq War: Learning from the Past, Adapting to the Present, and Planning for the Future* (Carlisle: US Army War College, 2007), 25-31; Bing West, *The Strongest Tribe: War, Politics, and the Endgame in Iraq* (New York: Random House, 2008), 9-13, 18-20, 28-36; Carter Malkasian, "Counterinsurgency in Iraq: May 2003-January 2007," in *Counterinsurgency in Modern Warfare*, ed. Daniel Marston and Carter Malkasian (New York: Osprey Publishing, 2008), 241-242; Metz, *Iraq & The Evolution of American Strategy*, 147-148, 151-152; Thomas E. Ricks, *Fiasco: The American Military Adventure in Iraq* (New York: The Penguin Press, 2006), 190-191, 197, 215-216; Peter R. Mansoor, *Baghdad at Sunrise: A Brigade Commander's War in Iraq* (New Haven, CT: Yale University Press, 2008), 28.

126. Wright and Reese, 113, 199, 121-123, 127-129, 322-325; Gordon and Trainor, 447-448; Malkasian, 243-244; Ricks, 228-234.

127. Mockaitis, *The Iraq War: Learning from the Past, Adapting to the Present, and Planning for the Future*, 26.

128. Quotations are used here as many authors argue convincingly that "The Surge" did not represent a real shift in US strategy for Iraq. See Metz, *Iraq & The Evolution of American Strategy*, 184.

129. Malkasian, 257-259; Metz, *Iraq & The Evolution of American Strategy*, 173-174; David Kilcullen, *The Accidental Guerrilla: Fighting Small Wars in the Midst of a Big One* (New York: Oxford University Press, 2009), 128-130. The nonmilitary aspects of "The Surge" are beyond the scope of this monograph.

130. Dale Andrade, *Surging South of Baghdad: The 3d Infantry Division and Task Force Marne in Iraq, 2007-2008* (Washington, DC: Center of Military History, 2010), 8, 16-22, 101-102; Kilcullen, *The Accidental Guerrilla: Fighting Small Wars in the Midst of a Big One*, 119-122, 128-129, 135-141; Pirnie and O'Connell, 15-19; Metz, "Decisionmaking in Operation Iraqi Freedom: The Strategic Shift of 2007," 4-5; Linda Robinson, *Tell Me How This Ends: General David Petraeus and the Search for a Way Out of Iraq* (New York: PublicAffairs, 2008), 25-45, 88-89; Malkasian, 258; West, 228-229.

131. Kilcullen, *The Accidental Guerrilla*, 144-145; West, 273-274.

132. Andrade, *Surging South of Baghdad*, 209; West, 250.

133. Malkasian, 255-256; Metz, *Iraq & The Evolution of American Strategy*, 186-190; Kilcullen, *The Accidental Guerrilla*, 141-143; Andrade, *Surging South of Baghdad*, 199-208; West, 27, 250-251.

134. Malkasian.

135. Andrade, *Surging South of Baghdad*, 211; West, 222-223, 248-251.

136. Echevarria, *Clausewitz and Contemporary War*, 185.

Chapter 2
Center of Gravity: A Quest for Certainty or Tilting at Windmills?
by Kurt P. VanderSteen

Introduction

Don Quixote, the aging man of La Mancha, was filled with bookish enthusiasm for a model of chivalry that did not exist from history, nor was present in the everyday lives of his fellow Spaniards. Nonetheless, he mounted his old horse, Rocinante, and with his worldly companion, Sancho, began his quest to impose a model of chivalric code on everyone he met. He soon learned that his model of chivalry did not accord with the real world, and he found himself in multiple misadventures that eventually led to disillusionment and renunciation of what he once saw to be true.

Is the military tilting at windmills by imagining centers of gravity with similar preconceptions that clash with reality? Since its doctrinal inception, iscenter of gravity became a lightning rod for how we conceptualize doctrinal terms that have ambiguous meaning and doubtful application. Many of the early arguments focused on definition and process that soon became a cornerstone for methods and techniques, giving rise to a sense of certainty from the results of analysis. Over time, arguments began to look like "you-have-your-peanut-butter-in-my-chocolate" in that they failed to see the unifying aspect of centers of gravity in their relationship to other elements of war.

There are many reasons why these arguments emerged, but most revolve around metaphysical ideas of how we come to know what is true, how we reason about what is true, and what we see as being real, or merely a shadow on the wall of a cave. If indeed centers of gravity are critical to war plans, then it is an important concept to study. But we should have no illusions—like gravity, our definitions can only be rough outlines for how we see forces operating in nature. We cannot see a center of gravity as a specific, physical property; rather, it's an abstract concept that enables us to think about what is real. Centers of gravity help us to understand what governs the underlying processes in war.

Thinking about centers of gravity is like trying to visualize how individual pieces fit as part of a 100,000 piece puzzle. We have a picture on the box to guide us, but it's hard to start with one piece when we don't know how the other pieces fit in. Piece by piece, images begin to emerge, but we have a long way to go before completion. Throughout, we always keep the picture on the box in mind, but we look to the individual pieces to see how they fit with the whole. That is the quest for this monograph: to understand why centers of gravity are difficult to grasp as a concept based on its pieces, and to see how centers of gravity fit with the whole of war.

Invitation to Conceptual Controversy

> *The art of war deals with living and with moral forces. Consequently, it cannot attain the absolute, or certainty; it must always leave a margin for uncertainty, in the greatest things as much as in the smallest.*[1]
>
> —Carl Von Clausewitz

It's understandable why center of gravity as a usable concept in operational art continues to be a source of controversy in the military community. Clausewitz was not deeply studied by the American military community prior to his inclusion in doctrine, perhaps because his translated writings were considered dense and uninspiring, or perhaps because other thinkers held sway over the body of knowledge practitioners referred to in trying to understand war.[2] Once center of gravity was introduced to American doctrine, seemingly endless debates about its definition, methodology, and practical uses continues to appear in books, journals, and especially in the staff and war colleges where it is taught. Conceptual confusion can also be attributed to translations from the original German, Clausewitz's use of dialectical reasoning, and arguments over the comprehensive nature of *On War*. Despite those shortcomings, military thinkers increasingly turned to Clausewitz and his ideas about the nature of war. Following strategic defeat in Vietnam and challenges of facing down Soviet power in Western Europe, doctrinal writers looked to a "curious mixture of Clausewitz and Jomini" for explanatory power and sparked renewed interest in operational art and the operational level of war.[3]

US Army doctrine had its origin in regulations concerning unit drill and was mostly concerned with the tactical level of war, but in 1986 the Army's capstone doctrinal manual for warfighting, Field Manual 100-5 *Operations*, defined centers of gravity for the first time, including a greatly expanded theoretical treatment of operational art based upon "AirLand Battle" development first seen in the 1982 manual.[4] The introduction of operational art concepts—including center of gravity—invited controversy and criticism from the start. A *Military Review* article from 1986 anticipated problems with the soon-to-be-released manual intended to be read as a textbook, and an Army expecting to use the operational art concepts prescriptively.[5]

Military thinkers took to the pen to argue their points of view, and soon a large body of knowledge emerged that unknowingly contributed to further doctrinal confusion. There was recognition that centers of gravity were important to operational art, but writers diverged on several key points of contention. Inevitably, each military service and a multitude of theorists proposed their own definitions and methodologies for determining the "elusive" concept. Joint doctrine had a definition that reflected service disagreements and used language meant to appease all parties.[6] Rather than resolve the issue, it provided an additional source of disagreement, but over time critics of the joint definition paradoxically agreed on one thing: the joint definitions were flawed. Typical of many articles were those that questioned the relevancy of the concept to the modern conduct of war. One writer came to grips with the ambiguous nature of centers of gravity by asking the question: Center of gravity or center of confusion? [7]

Since its doctrinal inception, the concept has undergone numerous changes in definition, description, and prescriptive uses. Although originally derived from *On War*, center of gravity was seen as a tactical and operational tool to attain campaign objectives or to strike at enemy weaknesses rather than as a theoretical concept nested in an overall understanding of the nature of war as Clausewitz originally intended. Theorists took one concept out of the whole of Clausewitz's thinking in an attempt to extract concrete usefulness from abstraction. In doing so, how we think about center of gravity devolved from what should be a relational and holistic understanding to thinking about its parts, and from its parts to thinking in terms of a methodology, and from methodology to technique.

The first use of center of gravity doesn't appear in *On War* until Book 6, which is a discussion of defense, and specifically in chapter 27, "Defense of a Theater of Operations." Clausewitz began by describing factors and characteristics of the defense of a theater of operations with a sequence of actions that contribute to victory. This sequence of actions includes "blows" against concentrated enemy forces that

> leads us to an analogy that will illustrate it more clearly—that is, the nature and effect of a center of gravity. A center of gravity is always found where the mass is concentrated most densely. It presents the most effective target for a blow; furthermore, the heaviest blow is that struck by the center of gravity. The same holds true in war. The fighting forces of each belligerent—whether a single state or an alliance of states—have a certain unity and therefore some cohesion. Where there is cohesion, the analogy of the center of gravity can be applied.[8]

Although he had more to say about centers of gravity in Book 6, Clausewitz concludes his thoughts in *On War*'s final book, in chapters 4 and 9. Discussing the relationship of the defeat of the enemy to the military objective in chapter 4, Clausewitz provided a basis for action: "One must keep the dominant characteristics of both belligerents in mind. Out of these characteristics, a certain center of gravity develops, the hub of all power and movement, on which everything depends. That is the point against which all our energies should be directed."[9] This description of a "hub of all power and movement" is cited most often in the literature about the concept, but it is an analogy created by Paret and Howard. The literal translation is a "center of power and movement."[10] Although Paret and Howard provide the reader with a superior visual analogy, they also introduce another reason for subsequent misunderstandings. From this definition, Clausewitz identifies likely centers of gravity that are conditional based on certain characteristics: "In countries subject to domestic strife, the center of gravity is generally the capital. In small countries that rely on large ones, it is usually the army of their protector…alliances…community of interest… in popular uprisings…personalities of the leaders and public opinion."[11] After outlining priorities of effort against the army, capital, and principal ally, he provides a caveat about the nature of conflict related to assumptions about finding a single center of gravity: if there is more than one center of gravity, it's likely that there are two wars to consider.[12] In his final chapter (according to his text, Clausewitz intended to write a chapter on "supreme command" following chapter 9), he describes centers of gravity related to war planning with respect to a particular description for overthrowing an enemy:

> The first principle is that the ultimate substances of enemy strength must be traced back to the fewest possible sources, and ideally to one alone….In short, the first principle is: act with utmost concentration….From this it follows that the concept of separate and connected enemy power runs through every level of operations, and thus the effect that events in a given theater will have elsewhere can only by judged in each particular case. Only then can it be seen how far the enemy's various centers of gravity can be reduced to one. The principle of aiming everything at the enemy's center of gravity admits only one exception—that is, when secondary operations look exceptionally rewarding. But…only

decisive superiority can justify diverting strength without risking too much in the principal theater....The first task, then, in planning for war is to identify the enemy's centers of gravity, and if possible trace them back to a single one.[13]

Most of the criticisms about centers of gravity begin with one of the descriptions listed above. Some critics relate the concept to other ideas in *On War*, but many writers are content to begin their analysis on this basis. A review of the literature reveals several common themes related to critiques of Clausewitz. Some struggle with his use of dialectic thinking or the fact that *On War* is generally considered incomplete. Others take issue with Clausewitz's conflicting definitions, and the fact that it does not provide an effective method for determining centers of gravity, that he was a linear, nineteenth-century thinker using outdated mechanistic explanations, and that he only thought in terms of state-on-state warfare that is irrelevant to twenty-first-century concerns.[14] There are some writers who reject his conception altogether and prefer to start with their own ideas and definitions about centers of gravity.[15]

After *On War* was published in 1832, there were several translations into English that formed the basis for many of the disagreements about the definition of center of gravity. The current translation by Peter Paret and Michael Howard is considered to be the best translation to date, but it also contributes to hermeneutic confusion. Although the Paret and Howard translation recognized Clausewitz's own thoughts about writing consistency, which emphasized "clarity of expression" rather than his confining himself to strict definitions of terms, they nonetheless standardized the center of gravity concept from different terms found in the text.[16] Although their translation likely provides a more accurate understanding of Clausewitz's thought and intent, their standardization of center of gravity and its acceptance as a standard of reference frustrates attempts at doctrinal application.

In Book 6, Clausewitz uses *centra gravitates* and *schwerpunkt* to describe essentially the same concept. The first term, translated from Latin as "center of gravity," is clearly used as an analogue from Newtonian science. *Schwerpunkt* has several related meanings. A literal interpretation is "heavy point." It can also mean "focal point," "highlight," "emphasis," "heavy emphasis," "grave emphasis," or even "center of gravity."[17] The key determination for which term applies is context, but because Clausewitz was more concerned with understanding the dynamics of war rather than providing precise definitions more applicable to doctrinal uses, it becomes easier to understand modern ambivalence and rejection of center of gravity as a conceptual tool. Newton also declined to be precise about definitions of gravity. He explained in *Principia Mathematica* that, although he could observe its effects, he did not have the conceptual tools at the time to be exact about its nature.[18] The center of gravity literature is replete with discussions about the misuse of *schwerpunkt*, with some key arguments hinging on the proper use of the term.[19]

Historians and other biographers of Clausewitz's life and writings investigated *On War*'s completeness or lack thereof. Clausewitz began his inquiry into the nature of war early in his life, and he spent the remainder of it adding and revising his thoughts. Because Clausewitz claimed that he was generally satisfied with Book 1, chapter 1, but not with the remainder of his manuscript, many writers adduced that an understanding of his concepts introduced elsewhere in the manuscript are subject to skepticism about the completeness of his thoughts. There can never be complete certainty in this line of inquiry because his archived material was destroyed near the end of World War II.[20] Nonetheless, a more recent biography of Clausewitz and *On War* written by historian Hew Strachan makes the case that not only did Clausewitz revise some of his key concepts based on later understandings of the nature of war, but he also intended to conduct a complete rewrite of the majority of his manuscript.[21] It is clear from letters he wrote in 1827 and what is presumed to be 1830, shortly before his death, that Clausewitz was generally unhappy with the overall thrust of his arguments.[22] The impetus for rewriting his theories on war was based on his insight later in life about the overarching political nature of warfare, thus elevating the discussion above merely military considerations into the sociopolitical realm of discussion.[23] Strachan highlights an important point about understanding Clausewitz: if we limit ourselves to specific descriptions in *On War*, we exclude other considerations within the comprehensive nature of Clausewitz's thought that can only be detrimental to making conclusions about some aspect of his thinking.

Clausewitz did not provide a prescriptive center of gravity methodology that campaign planners could reference. Soon after its introduction to doctrine, center of gravity became part of the planning process. Timothy Keppler, as a member of a US Army War College project that attempted to "operationalize" the concept in the early 1990s, observed that discussions of center of gravity's usefulness to planning placed participants in two camps: champions of a logical approach, and those who thought that discerning centers of gravity could be reflected only in the genius of the operational art practitioner.[24] He further quotes two officers who thought that a methodology was needed:

Students and practitioners of operational art often find themselves guided by little more than intuition. While intuition certainly has its place, a modicum of logic should guide our thinking about the important relationships between the fundamental concepts of operational art and the application of the military element of power for strategic purposes.[25]

Keppler is indicative of a trend toward seeking ways to place the concept in the context of planning. A problem arises when implicit understandings of centers of gravity are at odds with the explicit process for discovering them. As an illustration of an attempt to merge the center of gravity concept with planning, editor Eliot Cohen, writing in the *Gulf War Air Power Survey* series, sought to understand how operational concepts that included center of gravity were integrated into the planning for Operation Desert Storm. He noted from the beginning that there were several disagreements concerning the identification of centers of gravity.[26] Colonel John Warden, the air operations planner, had his own ideas about centers of gravity based on his five-ring model, with strategic leaders occupying the "bullseye" of the model. Subsequently, target sets evolved from an analysis of several centers of gravity within categories, ranging from leadership through key production or system essentials, infrastructure, population, and fielded forces.[27] These general categories are universal sets of targets for any conflict and form the conceptual basis for a drive toward certainty in planning. This makes his model attractive for planners who want to get beyond arguments over centers of gravity and continue with operational planning.

Players in an Ongoing Debate

Over time, debates within the military began to coalesce after Dr. Joe Strange and the USMC War College published *Centers of Gravity & Critical Vulnerabilities*. Later, Strange and Colonel Richard Iron published articles that criticized the joint doctrinal definition at the time, and they also provided a simplified methodology for determining and analyzing centers of gravity that became very influential throughout the military. Reactions to his publications took on two strains: those who saw his methodology as a way out of doctrinal incoherency, and those who saw his thinking as conceptually flawed from the start. Strange is joined by Dale Eikmeier and Jack Kem, both currently instructors at the US Army Command and General Staff College, in their agreement that centers of gravity are analyzed by determining their critical capabilities, critical requirements, and critical vulnerabilities. Eikmeier and Kem have also influenced a generation of officers in the Army and throughout the joint community with their versions of Strange. The negative reaction to Strange is exemplified by Dr. Antulio Echevarria, who is currently the director of research for the Strategic Studies Institute and the US Army War College. Eikmeier and Echevarria have written extensively on the subject over the course of more than a decade, and they are both adamant about their particular understandings of centers of gravity. They tend to represent the poles of the same argument, a sort of "unity of opposites," which will be discussed further in the monograph.

Strange does not reject Clausewitz; in fact, he defends him against well-known critics John Keegan and Martin van Creveld.[28] Strange sees himself a defender of a body of knowledge that should not be removed from military canon but modified to suit the times. The problem he originally identified following his reading of the joint definition in *Perspectives on Warfighting*, and one that he emphasizes in an article cowritten with Colonel Iron in "What Clausewitz (Really) Meant by Center of Gravity," is that "many hours are thereby wasted in fruitless discussion and argument; hours that could be better spent on planning....It's all supposed to be so much simpler than this."[29] This expression is common to many planners and students of warfare. They are frustrated with constant bickering over a concept they see having little overall utility to planning. The attraction of the Strange approach is found in the ease with which planners can reduce complexity to a simple methodology of finding either moral or physical sources of strength in order to "solve" problems in planning. Look for the sources and find the greatest source that is a "dynamic and active agent."[30]

Strange takes his understanding of center of gravity from *On War* in Book 6 and the "clash of armies," thereby rejecting subsequent descriptions found in Book 8.[31] He analyzed all relevant center of gravity passages from *On War*, provided an analysis for each part, and described these as "what Clausewitz really meant," with the further goal of ensuring that center of gravity had only one meaning that applied to all levels of war.[32] His solution was to redefine center of gravity in light of its critical capabilities, critical requirements, and critical vulnerabilities (CG-CC-CR-CV).[33] The Strange definition for centers of gravity is "primary sources of moral or physical strength, power and resistance." Critical Capabilities are "primary abilities…in the context of a given scenario, situations, or mission." Critical Requirements are "essential conditions, resources and means for a CC to be fully operative," and Critical Vulnerabilities are "critical requirements or components thereof which are deficient or vulnerable."[34]

Strange's method of analysis begins once a moral or physical center of gravity is identified. He does not propose a method to logically infer centers of gravity from their critical capabilities, although it is implicit in his proposition that physical centers of gravity are composed of certain capabilities that have an ability to *do something*, which he explained in his refined definition: "They are dynamic and powerful physical and moral agents of action or influence with certain qualities and capabilities that derive their benefit from a given location or terrain."[35] This became the standard of reference for subsequent theory and doctrine. His explanatory power is evident, especially with his detailed descriptions for each part of a center of gravity related to *On War* and historic case studies at the operational level. Strange based his descriptions on a comprehensive reading of *On War*. He also identifies the importance of placing centers of gravity within an adversarial conception, and the fact that centers of gravity can only be found as a result of a "clash of wills." But he caveats its strategic relevance by insisting that centers of gravity are equal regardless of the level of war, and his method of analysis begins with *first* identifying centers of gravity rather than understanding the context of how centers of gravity may emerge in war, which is a critical a priori requirement.

His dualism of moral and physical centers of gravity separates an irreducible property of war into two spheres; instead of looking for one, we have to search within two realms: the tangible and the intangible. Is there any case in which both are instantiated into one rather than two? Might we say that Jerusalem is a center of gravity that holds both moral and physical characteristics for Israelis and Palestinians? It is moral in that Jerusalem is a cultural-religious symbol as a seat of power, and physical in its existence as a capital city. Clausewitz warned us that "military activity is never directed against material force alone; it is always aimed simultaneously at the moral forces which give it life, and the two cannot be separated."[36] The problem with a dualistic viewpoint is that there can be no reconciliation between the two poles; they are metaphysical creations that do not substantiate in the real world, where moral and physical properties *both* reside in one being, such as the moral characteristics of key leaders and the will of armies to fight. These have real effects and are not mere abstractions.

His perspective was likely tempered by the need to explain complex theoretical concepts to future practitioners at Marine Corps University, a dilemma all war and staff college instructors have to address. Students often demand clear concepts that have direct application to problems they face in the operational environment. They are not interested in theory that is contradictory and ambiguous, and provides no clear answer. The Strange method solves their problem at the operational level, but his reductionist and dualistic construct largely fails to provide convincing evidence for its use at the strategic level of war. Skepticism about the relevance of center of gravity in campaign planning was largely abolished by Strange for most students of war, especially related to its targeting potential, but doubts about it properly reflecting Clausewitz's conceptual thinking persists.

Dale Eikmeier continues to be a consistent contributor to center of gravity theory since his 1999 master's thesis, "The Center of Gravity Debate Resolved."[37] Eikmeier teaches at the Army's Command and General Staff College. His theory enjoys wide influence, and his method-turned-technique is popular with students. He also shares Strange's quest for certainty and the need to get on with planning as evident in the title to his monograph. He solved the theoretical dilemma; the debate must end.

Eikmeier's thinking about centers of gravity has changed over the years, but his central conceptualization remains. He accepts the Strange definitions but adds by incorporating the ends-ways-means construct derived from the strategically relevant Lykke model. He also changes the order for considering centers of gravity from CG-CC-CR-CV to CC-CG-CR-CV. This reflects the importance he places on indentifying centers of gravity from a menu of critical capabilities, thus rejecting moral centers of gravity—all are physical.[38] The body of his writings has similar themes in that he finds center of gravity to be a useful construct but rejects any conception based on Clausewitz's thinking. There is no discussion about the relational aspect of centers of gravity that Strange acknowledged and also found in Clausewitz's theory. He considered Clausewitz a "linear" thinker and was terse in his assessment that Clausewitz is a hindrance to conceptual understanding and should be ignored—"forget Clausewitz."[39]

Eikmeier's 2004 article identified two reasons why centers of gravity were difficult to understand. The first reason was that the joint community failed to agree on a common definition and allowed conflicting definitions to take root. The second reason was that joint doctrine did not provide a framework to "make the theory useful."[40] Eikmeier agrees with Strange that centers of gravity determination should be easy for the aspiring joint planner. He thought that centers of gravity are sources of power, at least in 2004; by 2010 he thought that "sources of power" lacked clarity.[41] His 2004 concept coincides somewhat with current joint doctrine in that a center of gravity is a source of power: "a source of power that provides moral or physical strength, freedom of action, or will to act."[42] But his current preferred definition is: "The center of gravity is the primary entity that possesses the capability to achieve the objective."[43]

At the strategic level, Eikmeier recognizes only two instruments that have the power to act, which are military and economic power. Will of the people and other instruments of power, including diplomatic and informational, are not proper sources for centers of gravity. He more narrowly defines the strategic center of gravity in conventional war as being within the economic or industrial capability of a nation (which represented Warden's second ring).[44] In the same article, he uses the analogy of a train system to explain how the does/uses criteria work in validating a chosen center of gravity.[45] Since only the locomotive is a "doer," then the remaining parts of the system are requirements. It is interesting that a systems theorist would use an analogy derived from what is essentially a linear, closed system to describe an aspect of what is inherently an open system, but it serves the purpose of reminding us that his conceptualization is focused on a part of a system rather than a holistic framework.

Perhaps he recognized deficiencies in his reasoning. For his last two articles from 2010, he included a strategic framework for identifying centers of gravity. Rather than starting with critical capabilities he originally proposed in 2004, his first step now is to identify the goal (ends), the ways (critical capabilities), and then list the means (critical requirements). From the means that have "the inherent ability (critical capability) to execute the chosen way," you will derive the center of gravity, and everything else is just a requirement.[46] He considers this formula as the most efficient and effective method for determining a center of gravity. Certainty is now more guaranteed with this method and a validation test. He concludes with an appeal to adopt Dr. Strange's definition and drop nodal analysis, replacing it with his ends-ways-means framework of center of gravity analysis for a more "logical" outcome.[47]

Eikmeier shares with Strange the notion that if the definition is fixed, problems of understanding centers of gravity will go away. Although he appreciates systems theory and a holistic approach to centers of gravity, he advocates a reductionist approach: "So as with attacking a complex problem, we can break strategic centers of gravity down into more manageable pieces. Campaigns focus on these pieces, which are operational centers of gravity."[48]

Dr. Jack Kem, also an instructor at the Army's Command and General Staff College, has similar points of understanding shared by Strange and Eikmeier, and he has similar influence in the promulgation of technique for discerning centers of gravity. His thoughts on the subject are in his *Campaign Planning: Tools of the Trade,*[49] another popular handbook often referenced by students and others. His handbook is a logical approach to campaign planning that begins with his ideas of critical thinking and creative thinking, establishes the importance of ends-ways-means for solution framing, and begins a discussion about centers of gravity before tackling concept of operations development that incorporates elements of operational art and targeting from center of gravity analysis.[50] His intent is not to spend much time on theory but to provide techniques that may be helpful for streamlining the planning process and a method that planners can use as a starting point for developing the "science of war."[51]

Kem thinks about centers of gravity from a planning perspective: where is the real power, and where can I strike a blow that will cause the enemy to culminate or knock him out? He sees only the will of the population of a country as the true strategic center of gravity or perhaps a key leader, thereby accepting examples from Strange.[52] Kem describes various strategic and operational centers of gravity that were likely in Operation Iraqi Freedom, with the observation that at the operational level, it's typically the military that is the center of gravity, which is consonant with Clausewitz's writings.[53] Where he differs from both Strange and Eikmeier is the recognition that there is little chance of consensus among planners as to what a center of gravity is, but that it is still useful for understanding the problem, regardless of what level it's being planned against. His bottom line is that a center of gravity "at the strategic, operational, and tactical levels is critical for linking plans to the end state."[54]

Now students have models and examples from which they can choose that may be the "best fit" for their particular circumstances. His thoughts on method again have us focusing on some capability that can be *targeted*. The upshot of looking to Kem for center of gravity guidance places us back to the same muddle that Eikmeier was trying to solve with his method for center of gravity certainty. His pastiche of techniques and attempts to merge them into a coherent body of praxis in search of solutions gets us answers but at the expense of understanding.

There are several other writers in the same vein. A consistent theme is the drive toward technique that will remove all confusion. Typical among other writers is the search for a "model" that planners can use. One writer saw the need for an "American Theory of War" that would provide the locus of a model for combining all joint forces under a theory that leads to operational planning success. Rather than a theory of war, his is a theory of warfare at the operational level. By overthrowing Clausewitz and his comprehensive, strategic understanding of war, we are left with buzzwords such as "strategic geometry" that misplaces the strategic value of center of gravity with a purely operational concept that joint commanders can use.[55] The *reductio ad absurdum* in the search for a methodology to replace thinking about centers of gravity can now be found in a computer program.[56]

A curious coincidence among these theorists also becomes apparent when you peer into their theories: none of them really seems to care about the political nature of war that Clausewitz saw as being central to any theory of war and its understanding. Their focus remains at the operational level, despite an occasional tip and nod toward strategic issues. And because they cause planners to concentrate on capabilities and requirements from one perspective, their views are one-sided and ultimately lack the incorporation of the reciprocal nature of war that is at the heart of any political understanding of war. Students of these techniques use centers of gravity as a "MacGuffin" to drive the plot because they are uncomfortable with ambiguity that is the essence of war and desire quick answers to continue planning. Like a Hitchcock movie, it drives the first act, but by the end of the story, it remains forgotten in the entire scheme of the war plan. The fog of war remains, despite all attempts to lift it.

Napoleon once said that the moral is to the material as three is to one.[57] Although mathematical certainty is impossible when calculating moral characteristics, it is clear from his conception that any theory of war must give greater weight to human aspects of warfare, including passion and irrational behavior, chance and probabilities, operational friction and rational miscalculation, and intuitive genius and the iron will of the commander. Instead we have methods and techniques that inevitably lead to some physical or material construct, such as found in an army, a navy, an air force, or some other physical *thing* thereof. This drive toward reification in their theories causes us to think of Clausewitz's original center of gravity conception as a *thing* rather than a theoretical visualization of a particular confluence of human energy, force, and will as part of a larger strategic framework of political understanding about conflict. You cannot separate the moral from the physical. The Japanese calculated that a knockout blow against the US Pacific Fleet in 1941 would influence the strategic calculation of the United States to withdraw in the region. This was a purely military consideration without understanding the strategic implications that would eventually manifest itself in the American trinity—disunited before the attack— now united in purpose. Paret identified in *The Cognitive Challenge of War: Prussia 1806* that Clausewitz was "writing to understand war, not to establish a doctrine for engaging it."[58] As we look to their methods for a sense of understanding about where centers of gravity fit into the entire phenomenon of war, we start with the Cheshire Cat but end up with only the grin remaining. s

Antulio J. Echevarria's body of scholarship on Clausewitz is extensive. Echevarria has authored several journal articles and books that explore strategic subjects, with many of his themes returning to Clausewitz as his muse. He can be properly called a Clausewitz scholar. Like Strange, Echevarria identified flaws in doctrine and thinks we should return to Clausewitz for our understanding about centers of gravity. But he departs from Strange and his disciples on fundamental issues that make his view on center of gravity to be greatly at odds in construction and uses.

Whereas Strange and Eikmeier sought to create new meaning for center of gravity, Echevarria returned to Clausewitz to bring original meaning back into the discussion. He analyzed the problems of translation, debunked the capabilities-based approach or references to sources of strength or power, and gave us a more comprehensive appreciation for all of Clausewitz's thinking.[59]

Starting with Clausewitz's original use of *schwerpunkt* in relation to the mechanical science analogy of center of gravity, Echevarria describes the strength of the metaphor in terms of effects of striking a blow against a concentrated mass. Theoretically, striking a blow at the center will cause the entire mass to shift or lose balance. This is where the physical science analogy is most appropriate. It's not meant in the literal sense but rather as a metaphor to describe an effect *theoretically*. But, as Echevarria observes, the thrust of previous doctrine was to think of it in a literal sense.[60]

Because we are looking for *things* we can call a center of gravity, we literally lose sight of their purpose: to provide a focus for our aims in war. As a construct of physical science, centers of gravity have focal points where the forces of gravity come together. As explained by Echevarria, when you exert force against the *center* of the forces affected by gravity, you move the entire system.[61] If the aim in war is to overthrow an opponent, you focus *all* your energies against that focal point. In Book 6 of *On War*, Clausewitz had this analogue in mind: maximum exertion for maximum gain—a throw of the "iron dice." In theory, Clausewitz saw decisive battle as a clash of forces that would decide the fight, but he knew in reality that war is a series of battles whose outcome is unsure and most appropriate for a military force as the center of gravity where chance and probabilities play out in a war. This is the aim for war in the absolute sense: to overthrow your enemy and impose your will.[62] But in Book 8, where the predominant political characteristics of the strategic level are discussed, specific relationships within an alliance, or the relationship of the capital to its people, government, and military, or some other political characteristic that is related to limited outcomes, may become the *focal point* for a campaign.[63]

Clausewitz's notes from 1827 and 1830 points to his dissatisfaction with Book 6 and his conclusions about the nature of war from his discussion of defense in a theater of operations. Book 8 was meant to encapsulate his thinking about the overall phenomenon of war. Upon completion, he intended to rewrite the previous books to ensure that his main ideas were accounted for in the text. In Book 8, centers of gravity are now seen as relating directly to human considerations and political purposes in warfare, which is why he identifies politically relevant centers of gravity, such as leaders of popular uprisings, alliances, and capitals—these are now primary focal points for strategic decision makers rather than simply the armies of opposing belligerents.[64] This does not mean that military forces cannot be centers of gravity—they often are—but they are subordinate in priority to the human and political dimensions that predominate in war. His description of centers of gravity in Book 6 was clearly thought of in terms of armies clashing. This is where Strange and Eikmeier derive their understanding and why they are limited to a purely military perspective. But by Book 8, where Clausewitz intended to explain all his ideas within an overall framework, strategic considerations are more important. This is why Echevarria properly translates *schwerpunkt* as a focal point based on his understanding of Clausewitz derived from a holistic appreciation for *On War*.

This is not overthrow or even defeat of any military force as Eikmeier's theory suggests. You may attain your strategic goals through diplomacy and information instruments by *focusing efforts* or applying more *emphasis* toward disrupting an emerging or actual alliance. Clausewitz likened this relationship to policy as taking the heavy battle sword of pure war to "a light, handy rapier—sometimes just a foil for the exchange of thrusts, feints, and parries."[65] This does not mean that decisive battle is excluded from his thinking in Book 8—far from it. Clausewitz knew that in reality war in a pure sense is decided in decisive battle, the means for attaining the goals of war: victory. But victory is conditional to rational calculations: policy. It's also conditional to reciprocal understandings of policy, in that each participant calculates his chances relative to the policy calculations of the opposing belligerent. If policy precludes absolute victory, limited ends are sought. In chapter 3 of Book 8, Clausewitz discussed the relationship between means and ends to calculations about the amount of effort required. He then relates it to his conclusions about policy. Policy is the driver for strategic considerations; the military point of view is irrelevant until considerations turning on policy are taken into account.[66] He emphasized this point in one of his "Two Letters." When a fellow general gave Clausewitz an operational level problem to solve, he protested about its lack of strategic political and policy considerations, which made the exercise moot.[67] To be grounded in reality, policy and political decisions about war must also be grounded in a proper understanding of the means required to attain the ends of war. Policy considerations are essential to any approach to understanding centers of gravity. A capabilities approach tends to focus on military capabilities, which are only the means. Centers of gravity can be considered only in relation to interrelated policies, politics, and other human characteristics between parties of war. Perhaps this is what joint doctrine and Eikmeier mean by centers of gravity being related to the objective, but objectives are not considered until a complete appreciation is formulated prior to their determination, the essence of a strategic approach. Echevarria understands this distinction; Strange, Eikmeier, and Kem—including many other writers—do not adequately consider policy or politics.

Looking for centers of gravity based on a capabilities-based approach gives us a problem the Israelis had in their fight against Hezbollah in the 2006 battle in Lebanon. Hezbollah knew that the Israelis were searching for "strategic" centers of gravity to target. The Israelis were looking for "assets" (capabilities) to use precision weapons against. Hezbollah chose not to present any materiel centers of gravity that could be targeted.[68] Echevarria warns us that in wars of this nature, centers of gravity as an analogy can fail us.[69] Clausewitz identified caveats to the analogy being applicable. If centers of gravity are not readily discernible and lack unity or cohesion, then you don't have visualization where you can provide a focus that matches reality, or you are in a different war than you anticipated in your estimates.[70] Not only must they be discernible, they must be in accordance with the political reality of the conflict.

Because the myriad interplays between policy, politics, enmity, and other considerations in war cannot be neatly reduced to exact calculations, centers of gravity determinations will always be a concept subject to error. Clausewitz was clear on our ability to be exact in light of uncertainty:

> At this point, then, intellectual activity leaves the field of the exact sciences of logic and mathematics. It then becomes art in the broadest meaning of the term—the faculty of using judgment to detect the most important and decisive elements in the vast array of facts and situations. Undoubtedly this power of judgment consists to a greater or lesser degree in the intuitive comparison of all the factors and attendant circumstances; what is remote and secondary is at once dismissed while the most pressing and important points are identified with greater speed than could be done by strictly logical deduction.[71]

Clausewitz further adds that "at the outset, then, we must admit that an imminent war, its possible aims, and the resources it will require, are matters that can only be assessed when every circumstance has been examined in the context of the whole."[72] In other words, it is futile to discuss centers of gravity without understanding war from a holistic perspective. This is one of the reasons why students of war flounder when determining centers of gravity without a complete appreciation for the contextual elements involved.

We began with a concept poorly understood from the original Clausewitzian framework and proceeded to add and subtract until the concept lost much of its meaning. Is center of gravity a source of strength? Is it a source of power? Or is it a key vulnerability? We want to guarantee certainty by relying on steps of a technique, and our reluctance to accept ambiguity intrinsic to war displays an epistemological problem of knowledge—how we know what a center of gravity is or isn't. We have problems with reasoning when we argue over metaphors and analogies and over-rationalize their meaning but fail to grasp the unitary essence of war by analyzing its parts without considering relationships within the whole phenomenon. And the unitary essence of war, the whole versus the parts, the process of thought, leads us to ontological problems of being—what is the proper relationship of centers of gravity to the whole of war?

Clausewitz always had his critics. Paret identified several who viewed the history of warfare from only a military perspective. He noted that the military lens had its strengths but also glaring gaps in understanding that "prevented its practitioners from recognizing deeper causes, which in the end could weigh more heavily than the overt operational and tactical factors they analyzed with such knowledge and understanding."[73] Paret finds the seat of Clausewitz's strength in his inquisitive nature and his "intellectual and cultural background,"[74] a background that was not necessarily dedicated to direct military application, but to other intellectual pursuits in science, philosophy, and the arts.[75] To further our understanding as to why it is difficult to create a positive doctrine for center of gravity, it's best to turn to historians, philosophers, physicists, anthropologists, and thinkers from other disciplines to gain a deeper appreciation.

Problems of Knowing, Reasoning, and Being: Unpacking Approaches to Understanding Centers of Gravity

"It is the mark of an educated man to seek precision only so far as the nature of the subject admits."

—Aristotle, *Nichomachean Ethics*

Most of the military writers who look to concepts in *On War* for practical knowledge end up making similar mistakes. Instead of asking why it's difficult to take theoretical concepts and develop practical uses for them, they soldier on and create new meanings and context. Some of their conceptualizations have real-world use, but as an overall approach there will continue to be arguments until we recognize that the theory has limits. Among other sources, Clausewitz grounded his theory in experience and readings from history, but he also knew that he had to "rise above" his own limited experience.[76] He recognized the importance of history, not with the narrative descriptions of battles, but the testing of theoretical ideas against actual outcomes. Despite limitations inherent in historical understandings, outside of real experience, there were no other means that provided a greater understanding of the nature of war. The ability to make judgments based on experiences in war assumes a priori knowledge—that which you find from theoretical observations in historical studies as a basis of comparison. This was the method of understanding Clausewitz used.[77] His search for truth about the nature of war incorporated the dialectic of thesis and antithesis as a means to test theoretical reasoning against experience. An example is to compare policy against the military imperative: to understand the tension of these opposing poles, the means used toward attainment of policy ends had to be considered.[78] We find conditional truth from an understanding of the tension. That doesn't mean that there is strict resolution in accordance with the Hegelian Dialectic, but it does serve to highlight meaning.[79] His knowledge about the reality of war was his way of reaching tentative conclusions about his observations, which are mainly found throughout Book 1. Yet he was still unhappy with his overall conclusions—for Clausewitz, truth about the real nature of war was always conditional on particulars, patterns, and relationships that he may not have fully developed in his own theoretical constructs.

When it comes to understanding and the search for truth about the essential elements of war, there are tensions represented by the twin poles of Cartesian certainties versus Aristotelian doubt. Descartes, the father of modern philosophy, sought certainty of knowledge based on use of a rational method inspired by the newly discovered mechanistic sciences and his understanding of mathematics.[80] The Cartesian method established criteria for truth. If the subject met the criteria of truth, certainty of knowledge was attained.[81] Cartesian certainty is contrasted with an Aristotelian approach of conditional certainty in knowledge, especially in the realm of human affairs.[82] The ambiguous nature of warfare is naturally subject to uncertainty of perfect knowledge, but there still is a Cartesian drive in some people to banish doubt. They seek clear and particular steps to follow that leads to an answer that "solves" the problem, and they especially respect a sort of scientific reductionism that can guarantee results every time, as long as the method is applied correctly. We see this originally with the Strange approach, and more strongly with the Eikmeier method for determining centers of gravity. As long as certain criteria are met—is it a doer? Is it a capability? Is it an entity that has an inherent capability? Is it linked to the objective? Then it's "The-Center-of-Gravity." We are left with choosing a method based on verisimilitude—which false theory is likely true? Echevarria sees probable truth rather than certain truth in how Clausewitz described centers of gravity: they are conditional on too many variables to claim perfect truth of understanding, but they provide an aim to test a theory of action, they don't always obtain in every circumstance, and you cannot build universal truth around definitions of centers of gravity. Knowledge must be grounded in concrete reality and not subject to claims of certainty that do not exist in the real world.

Along with limits to knowledge about centers of gravity, there are limits to rational methods for framing solutions to problems. Descartes may have ignited the modern philosophical drive toward rationalism, but by Clausewitz's time, and reflected in *On War*, the romantic movement sought to put brakes on the use of pure reason for understanding reality.[83] What we mainly see with Strange, Eikmeier, and, to a lesser extent, Kem are ex nihilo rationalist arguments that elevate method and technique in place of understanding. As rational men, they exchange intuitive genius with technical knowledge expressed in terms of rules and steps. Their goal is practical knowledge that can be learned by grasping their methods. The problem is expressed by Michael Oakeshott:

The heart of the matter is the pre-occupation of the Rationalist with certainty. Technique and certainty are, for him, inseparably joined because certain knowledge is, for him, knowledge which does not require to look beyond itself for its certainty; knowledge, that is, which not only ends with certainty but begins with certainty and is certain throughout. And this is what technical knowledge appears to .be…In short technical knowledge appears to be the only kind of knowledge which satisfies the standard of certainty which the Rationalist has chosen.[84]

Those with a rationalist disposition lead others to think that their methods are reliable for choosing centers of gravity over a more intuitive approach, but their conclusions cause them to commit a historical fallacy by failing to account for the underlying processes involved. As Echevarria observed, using a capabilities method might get you centers of gravity, but only by accident.[85]

The ambiguous nature of centers of gravity, the "elusive concept," brings us back to the earlier discussion Timothy Keppler provided about the two camps of thought: those who thought it should be restricted to the realm of genius and intuition, and those who argued for method. Students wrestling with centers of gravity also fall into both camps. There are those who prefer certainty, and others are comfortable with probable answers. William Perry studied learning preferences and noted that there were various gradations of comfort with learning in an ambiguous environment. It begins with absolute certainty—things are black or white—but mature learners adapt to ambiguity and reflect comfort in knowing that there is only probable certainty.[86] Until doctrine acknowledges that centers of gravity provide merely an aim and not necessarily a tangible substance subject to certain targeting, we will continue to have arguments for creating methodologies in place of intuitive judgment informed by concrete understandings.

Along with problems of knowing are problems of reasoning about centers of gravity. *On War* is rich with analogies and metaphors. Because some phenomena are difficult to explain, analogies and metaphors help to bridge our lack of definitive language. Sun Tzu used several metaphors, including his use of boulders in water and birds of prey to describe the strategic advantages of timing and focused effort.[87] Clausewitz used metaphorical reasoning and analogies to explain the whole concept of war itself. "War is a duel, war is like two wrestlers, and war is like a true chameleon."[88] In the case of metaphors, which are figures of speech, vivid imagery relates what is tangible and known to less tangible or hard to grasp concepts. Metaphors are not meant to be used as literal replacements or exact analogues to the concept they are explaining. Of course war is not really a chameleon, but it is like one in the singular property that both share, which is the ability to adapt to surroundings and circumstances. A chameleon changes its protective coloring, and war adapts to different levels of violence, calculation, and passion. Analogy is a cognitive device for understanding deep truths about a subject. It gives us a sense of relationships. In the case of a center of gravity, it is analogous to a point where forces come together and gives meaning to their relationship in a system of war.

Like Newtonian mechanics, there is a tension that arises from the push/pull of competing forces as expressed in Newton's third law of motion. Gravity cannot be seen, but it is a real force observed in the influence it has on physical substances in nature. It is real in its effects but not in its physical properties. It is both a description observed in the physical sciences, and phenomenon seen in war. It was a tool Clausewitz used to relate his theory of how forces converge that has meaning in the context of war where there are reciprocal responses. Where the analogy can falter in application is that force is not a constant in war; it is a variable that changes and adapts to its circumstances. Eikmeier sought clarity of thought about the concept, but it resists exact definition as a clarified analogy. The analogy is a generalization of similar properties.[89]

Contra Strange, it does not go too far to use the analogy in Book 8, where the description applies to political considerations. In fact, the analogy is even more relevant in that visualizing how all environmental forces come together provides us with a better understanding of how centers of gravity may emerge out of a given context rather than being some purely abstract concept that is given physical properties. The analogy gives us a picture of unity and cohesion in an observed system, much as gravity acts as force that imposes a state of being that we can recognize, such as our solar system. Cohesion and unity are necessary precepts to Clausewitz's descriptions of centers of gravity.[90] For Clausewitz, centers of gravity are based on the confluence of tangible and intangible forces, seen as both physical and moral characteristics that have cohesion and emerge out of the unique circumstances of a given war. Policy then dictates what a commander should aim for, his *focal point*, the *schwerpunkt*. Center of gravity is not an outdated concept. Despite Newtonian understanding being replaced by theories of relativity, and now quantum field and string theories, gravity as a force of nature still applies in the way we view the real world. We can still accord the same meaning for insights to twenty-first-century warfare as Clausewitz did for his nineteenth-century conception.

Historians also have problems reasoning about history because the entirety of their subject matter is by nature unavailable to them. Historian John Lewis Gaddis recognized that some subjects cannot be measured by purely rational means, nor can they be measured by intuition alone. Besides reasoning by metaphor and analogy, Gaddis saw the value of cross-discipline inquiry by thinking in terms of consilience, or "fitting things together"[91]—not synthesis, which is a product of reductionist thinking, but taking all relationships involved and seeing how other disciplinary fields would address the problem. Gaddis sees the value of reductionist science for understanding materiel properties, but reductionism fails to explain complex phenomenon that are unseen, such as quantum field theory or history for that matter. In contrast, an "'ecological approach'… considers how components interact to become systems whose nature can't be defined merely by calculating the sum of their parts."[92] Reductionist explanations of "parsimony, stability, and universality" are standard sets of rational criteria that are useful in the engineering sciences but fail to provide a more accurate description about human relationships and quantum physical properties we cannot accurately measure.[93] We recall that Strange and Eikmeier wanted it all to be simple. Clausewitz warned us that war is simple in theory, but friction from myriad occurrences and events overcomes simplicity.[94] Parsimony does not work well in explaining social systems in the real world, and because war is irreducibly complex, we cannot reduce all our understanding to a few methods that apply in every war.

Purely inductive or deductive approaches do not work in explaining complex systems such as war. When you attempt either, you are forced to recognize that parts don't inductively explain the whole and you cannot deduce the parts strictly from its properties.[95] This is why Clausewitz preferred to use experience and history for inductive inferences, and theory for deductive reasoning. Current joint doctrine describes centers of gravity by looking at the parts of the enemy using variables based on the acronym PMESII (Political, Military, Economic, Social, Information, and Infrastructure) and nodal analysis to reach conclusions.[96] This is an inductive approach. One of the problems we have with inductive reasoning is that we often forget that it is based on probabilities. It may be true in most cases, but there is always a possibility that we've left out a critical variable or failed to see the potential in a given property. If all we observe in nature are white swans, we will not understand a black swan when we see it.[97] Nonetheless, inductive reasoning is essential if we seek to understand political probabilities based on centers of gravity. We use deductive reasoning when we evaluate the character of war by understanding a center of gravity from its cohesion, its relationship to one type of war, and reciprocal, competing relationships with political and policy purposes informed by enmity and means available. A purely deductive approach won't work either: "Why should the physical world conform to the pattern of man's reasoning?"[98] Understanding centers of gravity from a holistic perspective requires both inductive and deductive reasoning. We *inductively* infer centers of gravity from all the characteristics that emerge between two opponents, but we *deductively* arrive at their meaning from their reciprocal competing relationships with politics, policy, and means available. What centers of gravity *do* is make sense of relationships within a system of conflict. It gives us an understanding of the character of the war and possible aims for our ends. That is their value and not simply a reductionist mechanism for targeting.

I have chosen not to use the acronym COG to describe the concept of center of gravity throughout this monograph. As we have seen from the previous discussion, how we think about a concept has relevancy to our understanding about its nature. COG is semantically similar to a mechanical device, *a physical thing*, which moves other pieces within a closed system (e.g., the "cog" in a machine). When you consider that this is roughly analogous to the effect we want to achieve in war—that by moving a center of gravity we create effects throughout the rest of the system—a cog is still a material device, fixed in place. It does not have unpredictable and human characteristics that comprise the actual elements of war. We see this effect by descriptions of centers of gravity as being composed only of material properties alone. The thirty spokes converge at one hub, but the utility of the cart is a function of the nothingness inside the hub.

> *We throw clay to shape a pot, but the utility of the clay pot is a function of the nothingness inside it.*
> *We bore out doors and windows to make a dwelling, but the utility of the dwelling is a function of the nothingness inside it.*
> *Thus, it might be something that provides the value, but it is nothing that provides the utility.*
>
> —Dao De Jing[99]

Understanding how we think and reason about centers of gravity leads us to questions of ontological importance: Are centers of gravity real? Where can we find meaning in centers of gravity as they apply to real war? Fortunately, Clausewitz provides us with a comprehensive way to address these questions in *On War*. Any approach to centers of gravity should consider both the whole of war and its parts: the "hermeneutic circle."[100] Jon Sumida argues in *Decoding Clausewitz* that, in its essential form, *On War* is a completed body of thought about the nature of war.[101] His theory is compelling, but knowing that Clausewitz was always trying to refine his thinking leaves some room for doubt. Nonetheless, in its comprehensiveness Clausewitz comes as close as possible to a unified theory of the nature of war. Clausewitz wanted *On War* to be a treatise about the nature of war—not necessarily how to fight one—and the arrangement of his manuscript started with the elements of war that lead to an understanding of how they are unified in a holistic body of thought. In fact, his introduction should be kept in mind when reading the remainder of his writing:

I propose to consider first the various elements of the subject, next its various parts or sections, and finally the whole in its internal structure. In other words, I shall proceed from the simple to the complex. But in war more than in any other subject we must begin by looking at the nature of the whole; for here more than elsewhere the part and the whole must always be thought of together.[102]

Clausewitz attempted to understand and evaluate war from a holistic, unified perspective. Throughout *On War* are references to understanding war as a whole.[103] Book 1 contains the constituent parts of his thinking, but Book 8 was meant to be his conclusions about the overall nature of war from his previous observations. He died before its completion, but we should evaluate center of gravity in light of its relationship to the remainder of his thinking about war, and in particular from our understanding formed in Book 8. Because the discussion in Book 6 was about a clash of armies in a theater of operations, centers of gravity were seen from the military perspective of a commander contemplating battle in light of characteristics found in the tension between offensive and defensive battle. This might be helpful from an operational perspective, but it does not give us sufficient strategic insight. Paret, quoting Clausewitz, tells us why this is so: "The emphasis Clausewitz places on strategy is reinforced by his next sentence: 'Tactical matters I regarded as merely of secondary importance, at least wherever the strategic threads ceased to be visible.' At first glance the conclusion seems paradoxical.… It disappears when we remember that for Clausewitz, it is the strategic context that renders tactical episodes comprehensible."[104] He meant to resolve his understanding in Book 8: "The last book will describe how this idea of a center of gravity in the enemy's force operates throughout the plan of war. In fact, that is where the matter properly belongs."[105] In Book 8, centers of gravity are now considered with the "paradoxical trinity" in mind and the implications for directing energies against a center of gravity based on its political character. A capital city was viewed as a potential center of gravity with regard to the relationship of the people to its government and army. An alliance points out that other trinities also have an effect on the duel of trinity versus trinity. The whole and its parts must be thought of in a unified manner. In war, individual victories don't necessarily matter; it's the end that counts, but the end depends on individual victories. This is what we lack from most of the writings about centers of gravity. They direct "their principles and systems only to physical matters and unilateral activity. As in the science concerning preparation for war, they wanted to reach a set of sure and positive conclusions."[106]

The philosopher Hegel was obsessed by unity and the ultimate harmonizing of reality. He saw unity in seemingly opposite properties, and his thought attempted to systematize all of history as an explanation for all phenomena.[107] Paret places Clausewitz in a time where it was common to think in terms of opposites, contradictions, and paradox.[108] Throughout *On War* we see references to polarity, thesis, and antithesis, and theoretical tests of rational extremes. Hegelian thought that had its origins in pre-Socratic philosophy provides the basis for our understanding of why centers of gravity as described by Clausewitz can be seen in the context of paradox and the unity of opposites.

Heraclitus of Ephesus was a pre-Socratic philosopher who developed his theory of unity of opposites to describe seemingly opposite properties that nonetheless have essential unity.[109] The unity comes from their relationship. One of the most famous Greek tragedies, the *Oresteia* by Aeschylus, was about a curse on the family of Agamemnon, the high-seated leader of the Greek war against Troy. A series of blood feuds caused the next generation to murder members of its own family. The chain of murders began with a rivalry, and each murder caused reciprocal enmity that continued until the gods ended the cycle of violence. The reciprocal nature of conflict was composed of a unity of opposites that was informed by the relationship of hate and struggle between opposing forces. The relationship was a vendetta that could be broken only by a decision of justice by the gods.[110]

Clausewitz described this unity of opposites in his opening chapter in which war is a duel and a clash of wills. His other important concepts are likewise similar in polarity and resolution, including attack and defense, war and peace, absolute and limited war, destructive means versus policy, and probably his most important in relation to his entire theory, the "paradoxical trinity." The paradoxical trinity was composed of the elements of calculation and policy, which can be represented by the government; passion and enmity, which are represented in the people; and chance, uncertainty, and action, which are represented by the destructive means held within the military. He likened any theory of war as having to consider the variability between these forces.[111] It is paradoxical in that it is composed of unity and disunity at the same time. There is always competition and tension among these forces—between policy that is supposed to guide the efforts of war and the destructive psychological and physical means to attain the ends.[112] But these elements are not important in and of themselves. The trinity finds its meaning only in its relationship with an opposing trinity. Their unity is found in the circumstances that arise from conflicts of interest and misunderstandings that lead to armed clashes and what may become full-blown wars of annihilation. Michael Handel comes to similar conclusions— that the nature of war must be defined by the interactions of belligerents composed of their unique trinities.[113]

The clash of trinities forms a unity of opposites and is the beginning of our understanding of the relationship centers of gravity have to the whole of war. It begins with the duel. Clausewitz posited that there are two types of war: absolute war in which one side or the other is completely victorious, and limited war in which, for example, occupation of territory is a goal. He further observed that the entire phenomena of war runs on a scale from total wars of annihilation to armed observation.[114] Absolute wars are characterized by the potential to escalate based on policy informed by enmity, and the reciprocal actions of destructive means that increases a tendency to extremes. If we use an analogy from quantum theory, trinities are now "entangled" in an escalating spiral of violence that policy may no longer have the ability to control. Each successive round of violence produces a desperate cycle, similar to the cycle of revenge in the *Oresteia*. Anthropologist René Girard sees this as the natural tendency to consider in all wars in that they are a part of the "hidden structure" of war, especially when destructive means are no longer limited in the nuclear age.[115]

The hidden mechanism that drives escalation is the entangled hatred that forms the relationship between the trinities. A form of mimesis takes place where mirrored hatred and action have tendencies toward cycles of unstoppable violence.[116] When this happens, it is likened to the non-severability principle in quantum field theory in which "the joint state of the whole completely determines the probability distributions of the state-dependent properties of the parts."[117] In order to break this relationship, one or the other participants must be overthrown completely. Centers of gravity now become more apparent with this relationship in mind. Complete victory must ensure a more lasting peace, which is the ultimate goal for absolute war in theory.[118] If policy differences between antagonists cannot be overcome, and political considerations based on enmity are taken into account, the final calculation for war must ensure that the means can attain their desired ends. Those ends include a lasting peace that can be attained only by overthrowing the enemy, breaking its will to fight, occupying its country, and imposing peace by violent means. At this point, discussions from Book 6 become apparent in that one country is the invader, and the other the defender. Clausewitz observed that a defender tends to have a more unified trinity in that the people, government, and military are unified by their moral claim to legitimacy of action. Among other things, this is why Clausewitz viewed defense as the stronger form of war.[119] In this type of war, decisive battle and breaking the enemy's will is the only means to victory; hence, the most important centers of gravity will likely be associated with military force, at least initially. They provide focal points for operations. Discernment as to which centers of gravity should be focal points for operations is based on Clausewitz's understanding that force must be massed to have the effects desired. His observations from experience and his study of history led him to conclude that any other use of force diluted necessary effects at the decisive point.[120]

But Clausewitz also observed that the more likely type of war over time will have limited aims and therefore limited means. The hidden mechanism is not so hidden: policy considerations on both sides will conclude that their "policy entanglement" requires limited means. If one party to war demands territory, and has the means to take it, the defending party may not be able to employ the necessary means to oppose it, based on calculations of its own trinity. Those calculations would likely include whether the population of the territory supports annexation, its military capabilities, or its potential alliances. If the defending party makes an alliance, then it would be an example of what Clausewitz meant by alliances being centers of gravity and *focal points* for the attacking party to consider. This was the case for the run-up to World War II. Hitler was able to march into the Rhineland because he knew that France and Great Britain were incapable of forming an alliance to meet a threat of limited danger to their existence. France and Great Britain also knew their populations would not support preventive war at that point. Germany's *focal point* was not directed against any military force. It was directed toward French and British politics with their people, and the potential for an alliance. For Hitler, this action was a rational calculation, despite Germany not having the military means to sustain its occupation should France have contested. Where it becomes seemingly irrational are the escalating tendencies that occur despite initial limited aims. The warning from Clausewitz is that despite initial intentions, war can grow far out of proportion than calculated policy can manage. The paradox in the opening stages of a new war was that Germany was acting in terms of a defender based on its moral claim that France was the aggressor from its imposition of unjust reprisals from World War I.[121] Rather than simply being a policy decision, enmity was fused again in a trinitarian entanglement between France and Germany. "It was thus the French desire for peace that caused the new trend towards extremes."[122] At this point, new *focal points* emerged that required one or the other participant to consider total war to attain their ends. Lasting peace could not be attained until enmity was resolved by decisive battle. In theory, total war consists of all elements of a trinity united in purpose opposing another trinity that has the same characteristics. This is what Clausewitz observed from the Napoleonic Wars and the effects of a state system that overturned previous conceptions of warfare that tended to be limited.[123] During the Napoleonic Wars, the French people, army, and government were united in purpose, and therefore total war had greater potential. At the dawn of World War II, they were thoroughly disunited.

The ability to make judgments about centers of gravity in the context of the character of any conflict requires more than a simple methodology. Clausewitz placed this understanding in the coup d'oeil (strike of the eye) of the commander, the one with the ability to grasp the essential reality of a situation. Had Clausewitz completed his chapter on supreme command, we may have been treated to a more comprehensive understanding of how centers of gravity are discerned. Rather than Newtonian metaphors, perhaps modern scientific theory would be helpful for our understanding of qualities found in a commander with coup d'oeil. Quantum field theory is composed of the bewildering observation that matter consists of waves and particles simultaneously, with particles being the reality we can observe, and waves being the potential for particles to manifest themselves in time and space.[124] David Bohm called these properties explicate and implicate orders. The explicate order is what we observe. When we are not observing, there is implicate order—this is where chance and probability play out in small and big things that cannot be determined before they happen—in short, complexity. Particles—the stuff of the explicate world—can also be waves in the implicate world, where there is infinite potentiality for expression. In his seminal article, Alan Beyerchen noted that Clausewitz intuited the implicate order with his observations of dynamical patterns found in complexity theory.[125] Centers of gravity are emergent from all the characteristics of a given conflict and constitute a property of complex systems. Like quantum waves, they exist in the abstract until observed in the context of conflict. Focal points are like particles in that they allow us to make sense of conflict related to purpose. Choosing focal points enables a theory of action for attainment of desired end states. For us to give the implicate order meaning related to what we observe in the explicate order, we have to "see" what we tangibly cannot observe and create a visualization that accords as closely as possible to reality. This can happen only in the intuitive realm because there are no physical properties available that enable us to deduce their importance—those physical properties become manifest in the future and are thus unavailable to us for direct observation. Bohm likens this to a holograph in that a holograph holds the same information as the real physical entity it is reproducing.[126] A holograph is a 3D perspective of reality. So much of what we observe in war is from a singular perspective. Coup d'oeil that takes into consideration multiple perspectives provides a more accurate "hologram" as a picture of how centers of gravity emerge and how they are related to the aims of war.

Writing about attributes of effective leaders, Roger Martin observed that rather than their actions, it's best to learn how effective leaders think through their resolution of tensions that arise from competing ideas. Besides incorporating a comprehensive assessment and a multi-perspective appreciation for a problem's causality, and appreciating problems based in a holistic sense, the best leaders are able to resolve tensions between competing ideas for creative solutions. Contrast this with a conventional approach that looks only for the obvious, analyzes causality as linear relationships, breaks problems into separate pieces, and makes a choice that is either/or or "best available option." Clausewitz's genius is comparable to the criteria listed by Martin as something done naturally by the best leaders he's observed, whom he calls "integrative leaders."[127] Comfort with ambiguity and an ability to visualize the reciprocal characteristics of the trinities are prerequisites for "supreme command." Those who want a methodology and easy answers that are universal in all circumstances are common to the conventional approach described by Martin. It takes a leader with uncommon coup d'oeil who can recognize where forces might converge at a future time and place. Intuition informed by experience and deep study is a start, but it is an intuition informed by multiple perspectives. Intuition may let us down when we make snap decisions and don't consider the complexity of data, but it becomes necessary for making choices that require meditation on complex, intangible properties and sussing out their interrelationships.[128] Pure reason alone will not give us final answers, nor will shoot-from-the-hip intuition; it requires both. Philip Tetlock saw value in combining approaches that enable "theory-driven and imagination-driven" decision making, in which the "hedgehog that knows one thing" (theory driven) shakes hands and cooperates with "the fox (imagination driven) that knows many things."[129]

How we view potential wars and centers of gravity has important strategic implication when we consider the reciprocal nature of "entangled" systems. The Cold War could be characterized as an entangled system based on competing ideologies, and the United States, with its allies, had a grand strategy of containment. With deterrence at the forefront of policy, focal points were naturally found at decision making related to nuclear weapons and armies stationed in Eastern Europe. This required more than military means to include diplomatic, economic, and informational instruments. When we think of grand strategy and an overarching approach that incorporates other strategies, what we really mean is that we perceive a unifying "entanglement" of trinities that forms a single system of conflict. Grand strategies don't work well in a multipolar environment when there are several potential focal points to consider. Similar circumstances apply to centers of gravity when there are multiple trinities and the potential for multiple centers of gravity such as in counterinsurgency. A contemporary illustration of this dynamic can be found in Afghanistan, where there are multiple relationships involved that also constitute potential and actual centers of gravity. Difficulty tracing them back to only one no doubt contributes to confusion about war aims in the region. We are all "entangled" in Afghanistan, and it is difficult to discern a single focal point to engage. Enmity, calculation, and chance are interconnected in exponential numbers of combinations that would likely leave Clausewitz scratching his head. We can start with an understanding of the Afghan trinity and recognize that any potential solutions would have to consider their relationships, especially the ongoing struggle between the Pashtun Ghilzai and Durrani tribes that have fought for legitimacy among each other, and the Pashtun relationship to the Tajiks and the remaining ethno-cultural tribes and identities.[130] That's not even taking into account other centers of gravity in the region, such as Pakistan, India, Russia, China, plus the ethnic and cultural centers of gravity that consist therein. The Taliban, Haqqani, and HiIG networks are all entwined within multiple strategic centers of gravity. And the most relevant center of gravity that is a primary focal point for regional and global interests are NATO-led coalition forces.

Knowing that there are numerous centers of gravity in a system of conflict should give us pause when thinking about the means necessary for attainment of strategic aims. In a conventional struggle between two opposing antagonists, it's easier to calculate means applied to the ends. Afghanistan is illustrative of a system of conflict that has too many centers of gravity competing for conflicting ends. Simply calling the population the center of gravity for a counterinsurgency campaign is an operational construct that fails to account for emergent strategic centers of gravity in an extraordinarily complex environment. "The population" is an abstract, bookish concept. What exactly do you focus on, emphasize, and apply main efforts to that will satisfy all the conflicting requirements in such a system? If the population is the center of gravity, why is US policy focusing on governance? Or is policy focusing on internal, US domestic considerations? Or is policy focusing on the Af-Pak relationship? What we have are operational considerations dressed up as strategy, the results of accumulated policy rather than deliberate strategic judgment. United StatesUS and NATO disunited trinities are clashing with more unified ones, and the military is placed in the position of having to pursue strategic objectives without the means to accomplish them.

Following closely on the heels of unrest in Tunisia and Egypt, Operation Odyssey Dawn was a brief, US-led operation against the Libyan regime in order to "protect the population" of the Libyan people in keeping with UNSCRs 1970 and 1973. US policy was to hand off responsibility for the final end state to NATO.[131] There was no strategic center of gravity to thereby focus on other than the speed of transferring operations to NATO. The operational imperative was to create conditions for transfer of authority, which then included tactical targeting of specific regime forces to prevent the Libyan rebels from being overrun and give time for NATO to assume operational control. This is an example in which centers of gravity did not inform strategic judgment. Where it may inform strategic judgment in the region is found in future potentials following regime change. Fighters radicalized by the war in Libya are streaming back to neighboring Mali, and based on a confluence of enmity, poor governance, and multiple bands of warring factions, another state may fall into anarchy and become another failed state.[132]

Since conceptual design was added to joint and Army doctrine, planners now seek tendencies and potentials in systems. Tendencies only account for what we see; the "particles" of an explicative view of war. Implicate perspectives look for potentials in a system, the "waves" of merging forces that are composed of will, matter, and purpose. Emergent centers of gravity might be interdicted to prevent their confluence, the essence of deterrence. For decisive action, enemy centers of gravity become focal points as they pertain to strategic goals.

Center of gravity also has a role in conflict resolution. Rather than being only a focal point in war, it can also be a mechanism for focusing efforts toward peace. Peter T. Coleman sees intractable conflicts arising from a simplification of enmity. There is nothing to differentiate between belligerents in that they share entanglements of hatred and reciprocal violence. Central to his scheme of differentiation—which is necessary to break the cycle of violence—is to understand the degree of "betweenness" for the antagonists, and to determine "central hubs of activity" and "centers of energy in the system, gateways for high-impact intervention, strategic targets for introducing conflict-inhibiting feedback and peace reinforcing feedback [that] help to focus the analysis of conflict-mapping."[133] In other words, embrace complexity to reintroduce other aspects of reality rather than allow simplified feedback loops that enable escalations of violence. Centers of gravity properly conceived as *focal points* for de-escalating violence would look to the confluence of enmity-generating forces that converge with calculation and violent means to use them. Focal points are also considered as those points of agreement or disagreement when calculating strategic moves in the classic strategy book that used game theory to explain opposing strategies in *The Strategy of Conflict*. [134]

Toward a Positive Doctrine?

Should we still include centers of gravity in doctrine? If so, who should determine them? The center of gravity concept was not central to Clausewitz's understanding of war. He used it to describe forces in nature that can be observed but not wholly defined, much as Newton found with his own discovery of gravity, which became part of his wider theory of physical mechanics. NewtonClausewitz considered the process of identifying centers of gravity to be natural and attained by sound reasoning and intuitive judgment. Because of the political character of war, operational imperatives should always be secondary to strategic considerations. Clausewitz remarked that "we must be willing to wage such minimal wars, which consist in merely threatening the enemy, with negotiations held in reserve....The art of war will shrivel into prudence, and its main concern will be to make sure...the half-hearted war does not become a real war after all."[135] We constantly see operational art considerations trumping strategic thinking. Most explanations fail to show the relational aspect of war, that it takes at least two to tango, and that centers of gravity are abstractions until they are focused upon to provide a theory of action. Centers of gravity only emerge out of the unique circumstances found in any given conflict, and our understanding of them must be grounded in this organic conception, otherwise planners may as well begin determining centers of gravity for each country and plug them into war plans for later use. Although doctrine can include theoretical discussion, such as with principals of war and operational art, much of what we see is prescriptive.

Current joint doctrine has the intelligence function determining enemy centers of gravity as part of their Joint Intelligence Preparation of the Operational Environment (JIPOE). Other staff members, typically in Operations or Plans, determine friendly centers of gravity. An obvious problem with this approach is that a holistic understanding based on essential entanglement between opposing states of being are not considered. We have stovepiped viewpoints that do not take into account the reciprocal and political nature of the war. Additionally, joint-level planners are naturally concerned with the military aspects of conflict, and their tendency is to overlook other, more strategically important tensions, tendencies and potentials in systems of conflict.

Strategic centers of gravity should be the concern of leaders who make decisions in pursuit of strategic goals. Only the president can make supreme judgments for final calculations of strategic aims after political, policy, and means considerations are brought to light and discussed. Discussing centers of gravity in this context leads to decisions about priorities and decisions about the use of strategic means. Strategic *focal points* for directing lethal and nonlethal energies are the natural province of the president and his cabinet, with the chairman of the Joint Chiefs and combatant commanders providing advice related to means and ways. The further centers of gravity determinations get from their political and policy relationships, the less effective they are as useful constructs for focusing efforts.

Other terms, such as decisive points and main efforts, are more relevant to the tactical effects desired; otherwise we face an infinite regression for each level of war activity down to squad, team, or individual level. Centers of gravity are unifying constructs that can only be considered as part of other unifying phenomenon. They do not stand alone as separate units of analysis outside the system of war that gives them their meaning.

Clausewitz did not clearly define centers of gravity, but preferred to describe their effects within his understanding of war. Based on a holistic view of the nature of conflict explained in *On War*, perhaps a doctrinal description would include the following:

From the interplay and reciprocal collisions of competing interests and goals between opposing forces, each comprised of the elemental properties of psychology, calculation, and destructive means, centers of gravity emerge that can become focal points for directing instruments of power in pursuit of strategic aims. Centers of gravity are the confluence of unified physical and moral characteristics inherent in each opposing entity. They become focal points as strategic decisions are made for a theory of action. Their relevancy to strategic decisions is a matter of political and policy considerations for both war and peace. Focused efforts directed against centers of gravity enables attainment of strategic goals and objectives. They are less effective as focal points as strategic considerations become tactical. Strategic focal points will tend to shift slowly over time depending upon political and policy considerations; operational level focal points will change based on emerging centers of gravity as campaigns progress, such as the situation following OIF 1 with the emergence of insurgent and other state centric centers of gravity.

The description above places emphasis upon the strategic nature of centers of gravity in our understanding about war. Design found in joint planning doctrine is uniquely suited for understanding the role center of gravity has in understanding the operational environment, but a similar construct needs to occur at the strategic level.

Conclusion and Recommendations

There is no one way to define and articulate centers of gravity that will please everyone. Method alone cannot provide the certainty it desires and should be suspect as the final word on such an abstract concept. Competing philosophical interpretations of reality cause problems of knowing, understanding, and reasoning about how centers of gravity fit into the overall scheme of warfighting. For too long the argument has revolved around operational level considerations rather than on placing the concept back in the strategic dimension where it accords more with reality. Because it is useful for understanding the character of particular conflicts, centers of gravity have relevance for aims in both war and peace. But it is not a construct that is helpful for all conflicts where there are too many potential focal points to consider in the absence of unified war aims. For conflicts involving multiple centers of gravity, military commanders may need to take action in the absence of clearly delineated focal points in order to resolve immediate objectives; however, centers of gravity may thereby emerge from those actions that can then provide a focus for further action tied to strategic purpose. This is what Clausewitz meant by a military being the most likely center of gravity to consider for war. You may have to remove a belligerent's military in order to further strategic aims. This is of primary value for considerations related to invasion and occupation of another state.

Joint doctrine should reflect the ambiguous nature of the concept by recognizing both its abstract nature reflected in it being composed of emergent properties that we can call a center of gravity, and its more concrete expression as a focal point in which a theory of action is executed. Doctrinally identifying centers of gravity and potential focal points should be resident in the Joint Staff, Combatant Commands, or Joint Task Force level. Any further down into the tactical realm and the concept becomes less relevant to political and policy purposes. Joint staffs should no longer stovepipe the process for determining centers of gravity. They are part of conceptual design in planning and should be considered holistically rather than as individual staff functions coming up with their own determinations.

As part of options recommendations to the president, the military should identify more than one center of gravity. Other centers of gravity are thereby linked to potential strategic options that run the range of possibilities from deterrence options to decisive combat. The president's choice becomes the focal point for the whole of government efforts and provides the basis for operational decisions.

A return to the roots of conceptual understanding about centers of gravity and their relationships to the overall phenomenon of war will allow us to wake from bookish dreams that have us tilting at windmills rather than truly knowing their place and purpose.

Notes

1. Carl von Clausewitz, *On War*, trans. and ed. Michael Howard and Peter Paret (Princeton, NJ: Princeton *University Press*, 1984), 86.
2. Stephen L. Melton, *The Clausewitz Delusion: How the American Army Screwed Up the Wars in Iraq and Afghanistan* (Minneapolis: *Zenith Press*, 2009), 15.
3. Center of Military History, *Historical Perspectives of the Operational Art,* ed. Michael D. Krause and R. Cody Phillips (Washington, DC: Dept. of the Army [Supt. of Docs., U.S. G.P.O., distributor], 2005), 14–15.
4. Walter E. Kretchik, *US Army Doctrine: From the American Revolution to the War on Terror* (Lawrence: University Press of Kansas, 2011), 211.
5. Archie Galloway, "FM 100-5: Who Influenced Whom?" *Military Review* (March 1986): 46–51.
6. Joe Strange, *Centers of Gravity & Critical Vulnerabilities: Building on the Clausewitzian Foundation So That We Can All Speak the Same Language*, 2nd ed. (Quantico, VA: Marine Corps University, 1996), iv–v. Marine doctrine no longer recognizes CVs equaling centers of gravity. Joint doctrine has undergone several changes since many of the critics wrote complaining about its definition; however, it still is defined as a source of power.
7. Seow Hiang Lee and Air University (US), *Center of Gravity or Center of Confusion: Understanding the Mystique,* Wright Flyer Paper no. 10 (Maxwell Air Force Base, AL: Air Command and Staff College, Air University, 1999). Lee makes the case that an adequate definition for center of gravity cannot be resolved, but he sees its importance as a theoretical construct that informs decisions.
8. Clausewitz, *On War*, 484–486.
9. Clausewitz, *On War*, 595–596.
10. Joseph Strange and Richard Iron, *"Understanding Centers of Gravity and Critical Vulnerabilities, Part 1,"* www.au.af.mil/au/awc/awcgate/usmc/cog1.doc (accessed 19 January 2012), 7.
11. Clausewitz, *On War*, 596–597.
12. Clausewitz, *On War*, 617–619.
13. Clausewitz, *On War*, 618–619.
14. Melton, *The Clausewitz Delusion,* 11–18. Melton argues that our lack of strategic vision for Iraq and Afghanistan is attributable to the American military embracing Clausewitz.
15. Dale C. Eikmeier, "Redefining the Center of Gravity," *Joint Force Quarterly,* 59 (December 2010): 156.
16. Clausewitz, *On War*, xi.
17. Eva Vennebusch, Horst Kopleck, and Robin Sawers, *HarperCollins German College Dictionary: German-English*, English-German (Glasgow: HarperCollins Publishers, 1996), 382, 436–437.
18. Isaac Newton, *Newton's Principia: The Mathematical Principles of Natural Philosophy* (New York: Daniel Adee, 1864), 506–507, http://www.archive.org/details/newtonspmathema00newtrich (accessed 1 February 2012).
19. Strange and Echevarria tangle over definitions based on the translated Clausewitz text. Other authors also used Book 6 as the textual hammer for arguing their definitions of centers of gravity; see James J Schneider and Lawrence L. Izzo, "Clausewitz's Elusive Center of Gravity" (1987), http://handle.dtic.mil/100.2/ADA509969.
20. Clausewitz, *On War*, 3–4.

21. Hew Strachan, *Clausewitz's "On War": A Biography,* 1st American ed. (New York: Atlantic Monthly Press, 2007), 106–108.

22. Clausewitz, *On War*, 69.

23. Strachan, *Clausewitz's "On War,"* 131–133.

24. Timothy J. Keppler, "Center of Gravity Concept: A Knowledge Engineering Approach to Improved Understanding and Application," Master of Military Art and Science Thesis, US Army Command and General Staff College, 1995, 8.

25. Keppler, "Center of Gravity Concept," 8.

26. Eliot Cohen, *Gulf War Air Power Survey, Volume 1: Operations and Effects and Effectiveness,* ed. (Department of the Air Force, 1993), 145.

27. Gulf War Air Power Survey, Volume 2: Operations and Effects and Effectiveness, ed. Eliot Cohen (Department of the Air Force, 1 January 1993), 24.

28. Strange, *Centers of Gravity & Critical Vulnerabilities,* 5.

29. Strange and Iron, "Understanding Centers of Gravity and Critical Vulnerabilities, Part 1," 7–8.

30. Richard Iron and Joseph L. Strange, "Center of Gravity: What Clausewitz Really Meant," *Joint Force Quarterly,* 35 (April 2004): 27.

31. Iron and Strange, "Center of Gravity," 21–22.

32. Strange, *Centers of Gravity & Critical Vulnerabilities,* 41.

33. Strange, *Centers of Gravity & Critical Vulnerabilities,* 43.

34. Strange, *Centers of Gravity & Critical Vulnerabilities,* 44–46.

35. Strange, *Centers of Gravity & Critical Vulnerabilities,* 17–18.

36. Clausewitz, *On War,* 37.

37. Dale C. Eikmeier, "The Center of Gravity Debate Resolved," Monograph, School of Advanced Military Studies, US Army Command and General Staff College, 1998.

38. Dale Eikmeier, "Centers of Gravity," *Marine Corps Gazette* 94, (30 November 2010): 97–105. Most of his conceptualization can be found in this article.

39. Eikmeier, "Redefining the Center of Gravity," 156.

40. Dale C. Eikmeier, "Center of Gravity Analysis," *Military Review* 84, (August 2004): 4.

41. Eikmeier, "Redefining the Center of Gravity," 157.

42. Joint Chiefs of Staff, *JP 5-0, Joint Operations Planning,* Department of Defense Washington, DC, 10 August 2012, xxi.

43. Eikmeier, "Redefining the Center of Gravity," 157.

44. Dale Eikmeier, "Centers of Gravity," *Marine Corps Gazette* 94, (30 November 2010): 99.

45. Dale Eikmeier, "Centers of Gravity," 100.

46. Eikmeier, "Redefining the Center of Gravity," 156.

47. Eikmeier, "Redefining the Center of Gravity, 158.

48. Eikmeier, "Center of Gravity Analysis," 5.

49. Jack D. Kem, *Campaign Planning: Tools of the Trade,* 3rd ed. (Fort Leavenworth, KS: Department of Joint, Interagency, and Multinational Operations, 2009).

50. Kem, *Campaign Planning,* v.

51. Kem, *Campaign Planning,* 3.

52. Kem, *Campaign Planning,* 25–26.

53. Kem, *Campaign Planning,* 27.

54. Kem, *Campaign Planning,* 31.

55. Gordon M. Wells, "The Center of Gravity Fad: Consequence of the Absence of an Overarching American Theory of War," Landpower Essay, no. 01-1 (March 2001): 61–68. Col. Wells also agrees with Eikmeier in that a center of gravity must be something tangible, and that it is

likely only relevant as a historical document rather than a body of knowledge that has insight to the essence of war. And he gets the "age of reason" incorrect for insight about how Clausewitz thought. Clausewitz was actually writing in the age of German romanticism that was a reaction against pure reason. He was influenced by Kant, Hegel, Schiller, Fichte, and others in his thinking. They were not rationalists. Newtonian physics is not a fad. We continue to use his concepts in day-to-day engineering because the latest fad, quantum field theory, does not provide many useful analogues as of yet.

56. A student wrote his thesis on using software to decide operational level centers of gravity. When you reduce the concept to military systems only, then an algorithm based on fixed variables is a logical approach. Command decisions are now a whole lot easier.

57. *Respectfully Quoted: A Dictionary of Quotations,* Bartleby.com, http://www.bartleby.com/73/1213.html (accessed 21 January 2012).

58. Peter Paret, *The Cognitive Challenge of War: Prussia 1806* (Princeton, NJ: Princeton University Press, 2009), 120.

59. Antulio J. Echevarria, "Clausewitz's Center of Gravity: It's Not What We Thought," *Naval War College Review* 56, (Winter 2003): 109–123.

60. Echevarria, "Clausewitz's Center of Gravity," 110–111.

61. Antulio Echevarria II, "'Reining in' the Center of Gravity Concept," *Airpower Journal 17,* (April 2003): 88–92.

62. Clausewitz, *On War,* 75.

63. Clausewitz, *On War,* 596.

64. Clausewitz, *On War,* 70–71.

65. Clausewitz, *On War,* 606.

66. Clausewitz, *On War,* 607.

67. Carl von Clausewitz, *Carl Von Clausewitz: Two Letters on Strategy,* trans. and ed. Peter Paret and Daniel Moran (Fort Leavenworth, KS: Combat Studies Institute, 1984).

68. Matt M. Matthews, *We Were Caught Unprepared: The 2006 Hezbollah-Israeli War* (Fort Leavenworth, KS: Combat Studies Institute, 2008), 21.

69. Echevarria II, "'Reining in' the Center of Gravity Concept," 92.

70. Clausewitz, *On War,,* 484–487.

71. Clausewitz, *On War,,* 585.

72. Clausewitz, *On War,,* 585.

73. Paret, *The Cognitive Challenge of War,* 136.

74. Paret, *The Cognitive Challenge of War,* 138.

75. Paret, *Clausewitz and the State,* 147–168.

76. Strachan, *Clausewitz's "On War,"* 40–41, 77.

77. Strachan, *Clausewitz's "On War,"* 77.

78. Strachan, *Clausewitz's "On War,"* 86–87.

79. Paret, *Clausewitz and the State,* 84.

80. *Internet Encyclopedia of Philosophy,* "René Descartes (1596–1650): Overview," http://www.iep.utm.edu/descarte/ (accessed 28 January 2012).

81. Ted Honderich, *The Oxford Companion to Philosophy,* ed. (New York: Oxford University Press, 1995), 242.

82. Richard Kraut, "Aristotle's Ethics," in *The Stanford Encyclopedia of Philosophy,* ed. Edward N. Zalta, Spring 2012, under "Intellectual Virtues," http://plato.stanford.edu/archives/spr2012/entries/aristotle-ethics/ (accessed 28 January 2012).

83. Paret, *Clausewitz and the State,* 149–150.

84. Michael Oakeshott, *Rationalism in Politics and Other Essays*, new and expanded ed. (Indianapolis: Liberty Press, 1991), 16.

85. Antulio J. Echevarria, *Clausewitz's Center of Gravity: Changing Our Warfighting Doctrine—Again!* (Carlisle Barraks, PA: Strategic Studies Institute, US Army War College, September 2002), 5.

86. Joanne Kurfiss, "Perry on Cognitive Development," http://people.ucalgary.ca/~dabrent/webliteracies/perry.htm (accessed 28 January 2012).

87. Roger T. Ames, trans., *Sun-Tzu: The Art of Warfare*, 1st ed. (New York: Ballantine Books, 2010), 120. This is by far the best translation for explaining hermeneutical concepts relevant to understanding Sun Tzu from a Chinese perspective. There are many similarities between Sun Tzu and Clausewitz in their understanding of the "implicate order" of war.

88. Clausewitz, *On War*, 75, 89.

89. G. Polya, *Mathematics and Plausible Reasoning, Volume 1: Induction and Analogy in Mathematics* (Princeton, NJ: Princeton University Press, 1990), 12–13.

90. Clausewitz, *On War*, 485–486.

91. John Gaddis, *The Landscape of History: How Historians Map the Past* (New York: Oxford University Press, 2002), 49.

92. Gaddis, *The Landscape of History*, 54–55.

93. Gaddis, *The Landscape of History*, 57.

94. Clausewitz, *On War*, 119.

95. Gaddis, *The Landscape of History*, 60–62.

96. JP 5-0, *Joint Operations Planning*, 22–25. Note: JP 2-01.3 JIPOE goes into more detail but is unavailable to the general public. JP 5.0 specifically places enemy center of gravity identification squarely in the intelligence arena. Decisions about focus should be resident only in the commander for operational decisions, which is found in the design process. The J2 can help with military aspects, but because of the political nature of war, commanders need a broad range of disciplines to assist his thinking.

97. Nassim Nicholas Taleb, *The Black Swan: The Impact of the Highly Improbable*, 1st ed. (New York: Random House, 2007).

98. Morris Kline, *Mathematics and the Physical World* (Mineola, NY: Dover Publications, 1981), 470.

99. Roger T. Ames, *Dao De Jing* (New York: Ballantine Books, 2003), 91.

100. Ramberg and Gjesdal, "Hermeneutics," in *The Stanford Encyclopedia of Philosophy*, ed. Edward N. Zalta, Summer 2009, under "Beginnings of Hermeneutics," http://plato.stanford.edu/archives/sum2009/entries/hermeneutics/ (accessed February 2, 2012).

101. Jon Sumida, *Decoding Clausewitz: A New Approach to "On War"* (Lawrence: University Press of Kansas, 2008), xi.

102. Clausewitz, *On War*, 75.

103. Clausewitz, *On War*, 75, 91, 95, 158, 177, 184, 231, 484, 501, 582, 606, 607. Just to name a few. Clausewitz is clearly seeking unity in the phenomena he studied.

104. Peter Paret, *Understanding War: Essays on Clausewitz and the History of Military Power* (Princeton, NJ: Princeton University Press, 1992), 204.

105. Clausewitz, *On War*, 486.

106. Clausewitz, *On War*, 134. Throughout On War, Clausewitz hammered contemporary theorists, especially Bülow and Jomini, who failed to take into account the human and complex aspects of war.

107. Honderich, *The Oxford Companion to Philosophy*, 339.

108. Paret, *Clausewitz and the State*, 150.

109. Honderich, *The Oxford Companion to Philosophy,* 349–350.

110. Richard Seaford, "Aeschylus and the Unity of Opposites," *The Journal of Hellenic Studies* 123 (1 January 2003): 141–163.

111. Clausewitz, *On War*, 89.

112. Herberg-Rothe, "Clausewitz's 'Wondrous Trinity' as a Coordinate System of War and Violent Conflict," *International Journal of Conflict and Violence* 3 (2009): 205–219.

113. Michael Handel, *Masters of War,* 3rd rev. and expanded ed. (London: Routledge, 2005), 106–107.

114. Clausewitz, *On War*, 69.

115. René Girard, *Battling to the End: Conversations with Benoît Chantre* (East Lansing, MI: Michigan State University Press, 2010), 57.

116. René Girard and James G. Williams, eds., *The Girard Reader* (New York: The Crossroad Publishing Company, 1996), 9–19.

117. Michael Esfeld, "Quantum Entanglement and a Metaphysics of Relations" (April 2004), 7, http://philsci-archive.pitt.edu/1735/ (accessed 2 February 2012).

118. Clausewitz, *On War*, 90–99, 579.

119. Clausewitz, *On War*, 388–389.

120. Clausewitz, *On War*, 486–487.

121. Girard, *Battling to the End,* 186–187.

122. Girard, *Battling to the End,* 183.

123. Paret, Clausewitz and the State, 341–342.

124. Harald Atmanspacher, "Quantum Approaches to Consciousness," in *The Stanford Encyclopedia of Philosophy,* ed. Edward N. Zalta, Summer 2011, under "Mind and Matter as Dual Aspects" http://plato.stanford.edu/archives/sum2011/entries/qt-consciousness/ (accessed 2 February 2012).

125. Alan Beyerchen, "Clausewitz, Nonlinearity, and the Unpredictability of War," *International Security* 17, (1 December 1992): 59–90.

126. David Bohm, Wholeness and the Implicate Order, reissue (New York: Routledge, 2002), 186.

127. Roger L. Martin, *The Opposable Mind: How Successful Leaders Win Through Integrative Thinking,* 1st ed. (Boston: Harvard Business School Press, 2007), 65.

128. Daniel Kahneman, *Thinking, Fast and Slow,* 1st ed. (New York: Farrar, Straus and Giroux, 2011), 12–13.

129. Philip E. Tetlock, *Expert Political Judgment* (Princeton, NJ: Princeton University Press, 2005), 214.

130. Thomas Barfield, *Afghanistan: A Cultural and Political History* (Princeton, NJ: Princeton University Press, 2010), 1–16.

131. "Remarks by the President in Address to the Nation on Libya," http://www.whitehouse.gov/the-press-office/2011/03/28/remarks-president-address-nation-libya (accessed 3 February 2012).

132. BBC, "Mali: Tuareg Rebellion Sparks Angry Protests in Bamako," BBC News Africa Web site (London), http://www.bbc.co.uk/news/world-africa-16853692 (accessed 2 February 2012).

133. Peter Coleman, *The Five Percent: Finding Solutions to Seemingly Impossible Conflicts,* 1st ed. (New York: PublicAffairs, 2011), 138.

134. Thomas Schelling, *The Strategy of Conflict* (Cambridge, MA: Harvard University Press, 1980), 119–161.

135. Clausewitz, *On War*, 604.

Chapter 3
Exploring Outside the Tropics of Clausewitz: Our Slavish Anchoring to an Archaic Metaphor
by Christopher R. Paprone and William J. Davis, Jr.

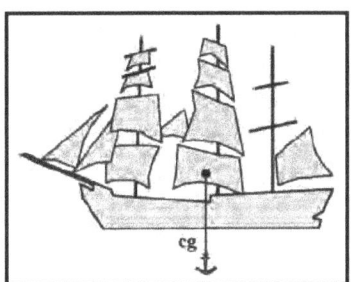

Figure 1. COG Schooner.

We employ neo-institutional theory to investigate how Carl von Clausewitz's physics metaphor "center of gravity" (from his book On War*) has not only become a constraint to the individual and collective thinking and acting of the United States military as an organization; but, because of slavish adherence to using it as a central construct in the theoretical approach to operational warfare, it also has become detrimental to the further development of innovative concepts. We particularly subscribe to Walter W. Powell's and Paul J. DiMaggio's "iron cage" explanation of institutional isomorphism: how coercive, mimetic, and normative social pressures serve the* **Anglo-American analytic paradigm**, *reifying ways of theorizing about warfare. We conclude that: (1) Clausewitz's* CENTER OF GRAVITY *metaphor has received too much attention inside the self-referencing, spiraling circle of military analysts who are determined to find or create operational definitions by displacing this dead metaphor;(2) Professional Military Education (PME) schools should design curricula more toward multi-perspective frames of reference, with accompanying seminar-facilitated critical inquiry, dialogue, spurred by multi-disciplinary readings; and, (3) PME should embrace the arguments and educational philosophy of "institutional reflexivity."*

In the works of Donald A. Schön

When Carl von Clausewitz spoke to Center of Gravity he was using a metaphor available from the natural science of his day – namely physics. He used a wide array of other tropes throughout his text: friction, resistance, walking through water, suspended magnets, field of wheat, pruning trees, spheres, tributary streams and rivers, forces, boxing, levers, culmination, ends, means, to name a few. In his text, he was not attempting to scientificize his argument; rather, he was attempting to be imaginative in employing familiar terms to analogously describe otherwise inexplicable phenomena of war. Indeed, in Book Two, Chapter Two of *On War*, Clausewitz devoted a lot of attention to criticizing the idea of a positive science (a.k.a. doctrine) and he took pains to equivocate the meaning of war-in-theory itself, resorting to Hegelian ideal types rather than to an objectivist epistemology and to the experimental methods of the physical sciences emerging in his day. Based in his obvious aversion to making war theory a Jominian mathematical science, his selection of the Center of Gravity metaphor seems not of isolatable value to the gestalt of his treatise. Using Center of Gravity, as with his many other metaphors, was a matter of his humanistic writing style and the literary imagery available to him in the contextual wake of the Napoleonic wars, not a precise use of terminology to prescribe an "objectively" definable phenomenon.

Many of today's interpretations of Clausewitz's figurative language in *On War* are biased by doctrinaires' upbringing in (and subsequent predisposition to) a Western-style, modernist worldview that includes methods of targeteering, weaponeering, disambiguation, priorities of intelligence collection, and logics tied to assumptions of positive determinations of linear causality among clearly defined "operationalized" variables. Cognitive linguists George Lakoff and Mark Johnson, refer to this underlying paradigm as the "Anglo-American analytic philosophy."[1] Contrary to our interpretation of Clausewitz's literary intent, modernist doctrinaires have attempted to define Center of Gravity as an Jominian variable (e.g., the enemy's Center of Gravity to be kinetically- and psychologically- targeted and one's own to be protected).[2] In modernist military doctrine, the meaning of Center of Gravity has morphed to become the process of analyzing and operationalizing wartime objectives – one of the first analytic steps in synoptic planning.[3] This concept morphology is indicative that today's normative military science is anchored to positivistic philosophy and ignores potentially valuable alternative frames of reference.[4] The growth and dominance of operations research, systems engineering sciences, and their scientific-management offspring, particularly in the tradition of British and US militaries, are primarily responsible for this unbridled, analytic approach to all aspects of military interventions.[5]

The Extensions, Displacements, and Limits of Metaphor

Lakoff and Johnson, as do others, contend that most human conceptualizations (i.e. theories for action), are "metaphorically structured:"[6]

> We see metaphor as essential to human understanding and as a mechanism for creating new meaning and new realities in our lives. This puts us at odds with most of the Western philosophical tradition, which has seen metaphor as an agent of subjectivism and, therefore, as subversive of the quest for absolute truth.[7]

In other words, the concepts in our military knowledge community are rooted in borrowed meaning and those meanings are extended to better describe the otherwise perplexing phenomena at hand. This social-linguistic process may be referred to as *concept extension and displacement* – over time, how words, morph away from original meaning and are elaborated into new meaning(s).[8] There is generally a residual of analogical meaning between the old and extended meanings that may go unrecognized.

Unless one becomes attuned to this morphological process, words can eventually become extended to the point the original meaning becomes removed from any connection to the now dead metaphor. Extensions continue, new constructions spin-off into other knowledge disciplines, and, all the while, those who share in extending these meanings may not recognize that the concept displacement process (that may take generations) is underway.

Concept displacement theory demands that investigators trace meanings to root metaphors.[9] Assuming the translators' accuracy, it is apparent that Carl von Clausewitz, in *On War*, derived his root metaphor from the physics of his day.[10] To understand the root meaning, let us take a critical look at these physics models of Center of Gravity prepared by NASA, Figure 2:

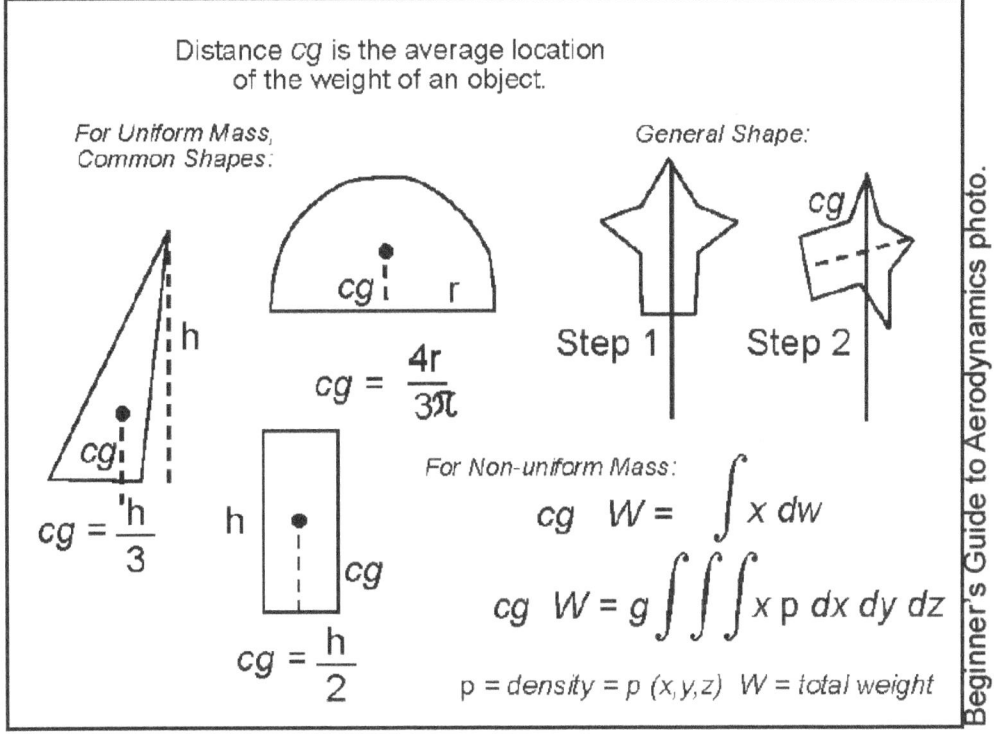

Figure 2. Various Computations of COG.

These models reflect the important qualities as we explore what we refer to as the root meanings associated with Newtonian physics: (1) Center of Gravity is computed differently as we test the theory from uniform shapes to non-uniform shapes; (2) Center of Gravity involves measureable factors (location, mass, height, weight, radius, etc.) for analysis, uniquely characteristic to the object under consideration; (3) Specifically predicted by the calculus of force, mass, and acceleration, Center of Gravity implies objects can be made to tip over (i.e. there is a literal, single point of failure for an otherwise stable object). We imagine these qualities made the use of the physics metaphor very attractive to Clausewitz. In its correlation of meaning to Clausewitz's intent (what we refer to as the *true zone of analogy* in Figure 2), the Center of Gravity metaphor likewise helped him to convey the concepts of: (1) accounting for different kinds (shapes) of war; (2) incorporating analytic

67

factors to deduce where the Center of Gravity is; and, (3) deducing that the strategy of war involves targeting the opponent's Center of Gravity, for example, to topple its army, capitol, (indirect method) or regime (direct method).

As we attempt today to make sense of the meaning he extended from the root metaphor, we can easily fall into what we call a *displaced zone of analogy* through contemplating Clausewitz's extended meanings (e.g., place of decisiveness, point of victory, possibility of having more than one, e.g., political with respect to military, Centers of Gravity) without expressly recognizing he was communicating figuratively, not scientifically.[11] Today, discussions of the original meanings, tied to the Newtonian root metaphor, have seemed to all but disappear from the texts of the military community of theorists; Figure 3.

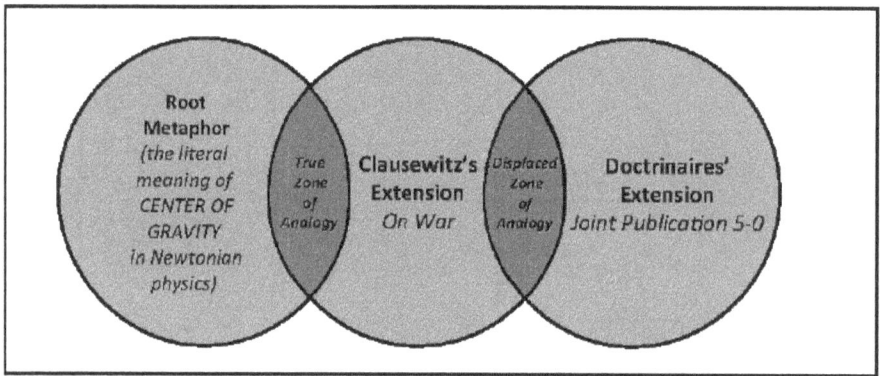

Figure 3. Without Reflection - Metaphoric Displacement of Meanings.

We find little evidence in recent mainstream institutional dialogue that recognizes Clausewitz's true zone of analogy; hence, we are now faced with an unending morass of further meaning displacement. In the arguments among institutional theorists, there is unawareness that Center of Gravity is a dead metaphor.

Institutional Reflexivity

For those who remain unreflexive, displaced physics metaphors may leave the impression that one can create an objective view of reality in war – in the present case, the belief that Center of Gravity analysis is a tangible variable in war. However, recognizing that the displaced concepts become objectified by the institution, they may be better studied as reifications.[12] As we seek to resurrect the origins of meaning and the ensuing morphology, this exposure and exploration of root meanings can help emancipate theorists away from habituated linguistic constraints; hence, leading to more reflexive research questions, such as: [13]

1. Lack of Interdisciplinary Awareness. If this is an effective analytic tool, why haven't other disciplines, such as civilian public- and business- administration fields mimicked the term center of gravity as a "benchmark" or "best practice" (as they did strategy)?

2. Operationalizing Jargon. Why did doctrinaires attempt to more deeply institutionalize the concept of center of gravity as a systems analysis tool in recent (2011) edition of Joint Publication 5-0, Joint Operation Planning, when the term was hardly a central concept in past and present capstone publications, such as the 2011 version of Joint Publication 3-0, Joint Operations?

3. Locus of Attention. Why was the root physics metaphor, center of gravity, selected from Clausewitz's text as the principal trope for this book when there are hundreds of others?

4. Institutional Disenthrallment. What alternative sources of metaphor (other than the traditional physical sciences) may extend into new, imaginative theories of war?

5. We remain speculative as we address these.

Lack of Interdisciplinary Awareness. Institutional theorists postulate that there are at least three ways isomorphism unfolds in- and across- disciplines of study (please pause to note that "isomorphism" is a metaphor borrowed from the science of biological mimicry in ecosystems!).[14] The first kind is normative isomorphism (how institutions become insular and spirally self-referential), for example, as the Army profession sought to re-legitimize their post-Vietnam War societal position by advocating "active defense" doctrine.[15] The second, coercive isomorphism occurs when those at the top of a hierarchical organization decide and direct to adopt what they perceive to be legitimate theories for practice (often called "benchmarking" or searches for "best practices" in pop management literature). For example, when General Martin E. Dempsey commanded US Army Training and Doctrine Command, he reportedly became enamored with the teleology portrayed in book The Starfish and the Spider (note the use of metaphors!) that was then a popular seller. He directed its theories be adopted doctrinally by the US Army (e.g., the concept of "mission command"). Now, from his authoritative position as Chairman of the Joint Chiefs of Staff, General Dempsey is directing the adoption of the book's extended logics-for-action into joint doctrine and futures concepts.[16]

The third type is *mimetic isomorphism* which attempts to account for institutional members who begin to search outside their otherwise normative paradigm for alterative frames of reference, especially when there is a perceived crisis of insider knowledge.[17] In the case of the Center of Gravity, we queried the number of "hits" in Boolean searches using the online data base, EBSCO.[18] Since 1994 this phrase was present in texts from of: *Harvard Business Review* (HBR, 21 hits), *Administrative Science Quarterly* (ASQ, 3 hits) and *California Management Review* (CMR, 6), and *Military Review* (MR, 132 hits). We can compare these data with number of hits from the same journals that contained the key word STRATEGY in the text (HBR – 2,891 hits; ASQ – 637 hits; CMR – 546 hits; and MR – 1,371 hits).

From eyeballing these data, Center of Gravity appears to have experienced relatively weak mimetic isomorphism insofar as other disciplines find little value in the concept; albeit, evidently it has become a shibboleth for military analysts. We speculate insider attribution to its importance to be more a mixture of the coercive- and normative-types of institutional isomorphism.[19] The writings and professional debates reflect both compliance with an "authoritative" signing of the concept into official US joint doctrine and an institutionally-normalized affinity for positivist doctrine. In contrast, business- and public- administration disciplines have for decades extended the metaphor of the otherwise military proprietary meaning of STRATEGY and we now have interdisciplinary mimicry associated with top-management teams in a variety of organizational settings employing their versions of *strategic management*.[20] One of the present authors attempted to explain in a previous study:

> ...the idea of "STRATEGY" began with a literal meaning – reflecting the rather romantic image of an ancient Greek general standing on a hill overlooking the field of battle, able to see and send orders to the sub-*strata* below in order to maneuver his forces to a positional advantage. Over the centuries, the physical idea has been extended and displaced conceptually to the point STRATEGY has become, in an elaborated rationalist abstraction, a *general theory of relative advantage* to achieve a desired end. Indeed, the idea migrated across many nonmilitary realms, to include sports (ends: winning the season), management (ends: best use of resources), business (ends: high profits), leadership (ends: influenced behavior), politics (ends: winning power through elections and re-elections), and so forth.[21]

The concept of STRATEGY has been elaborated into an apparent full-fledged theory of social action as those in the other fields perceive it to be worth mimicking in their own extensions. One conclusion is that STRATEGY has romantic appeal to others who are enamored with the stories of heroic generalship that can be mimicked by CEOs, professional football coaches, etc.[22] Center of Gravity, apparently, has not enough "sex appeal" or is perhaps to flawed a concept to attract such mimetic processes; in other words, Center of Gravity remains stilted, unidisciplinary, and relationally unattractive to the extra-disciplines of social science.

Operationalizing Jargon. So why does the institution attempt to operationalize what is arguably a dead metaphor? Again, institutional theorists postulate this also occurs through normative processes of isomorphism. The more ambiguous and uncertain the environment seems to the profession of arms, the more likely that the institution will succumb to social-psychological pressures to prove their societal worth with revised esoteric knowledge or new goals, theories, technologies, doctrines, and so forth. The perceived failures of applied knowledge by a community of military theorists, for example, as those applied experiences in the wake of the US involvements in Vietnam and more recently in the weak results in Iraq and Afghanistan-Pakistan, lead to existential searches for technically reliable and externally valid logics-for-action that serve as social-psychological justification for institutional existence. Ultimately, the community is motivated by the prospect of renewed trust and autonomy and respect given by their service to a modern society that continues to perceive a "professional" institution apply its technical knowledge-in-action. Donald A. Schön interprets this as a tenacious although fallacious dedication to "technical rationality" which he characterizes as a "crisis of professions" and the loss of an often-undervalued aspect to professions—artistry.[23]

We speculate that Center of Gravity theorists have been motivated to pursue more definitional vigor in the ideological tradition of the Anglo-American analytic paradigm. This philosophy was particularly personified by Air Force planner, Colonel Jack Ward (mentioned in Kurt VanderSteen's chapter of this book), and the highly-vaunted "successes" of the air campaigns of operations Desert Storm (against Iraq) and Allied Force (against Serbia). Also contributing may be the interest in "effects-based operations" (EBO) in the US Air Force community of targeteers, epitomized by authors such as Edward C. Mann, Gary Endersby, and Thomas R. Searle.[24] Here, Ludwig von Bertalanffy's General Systems Theory (GST is an offspring of the early twentieth century logical-positivist movement) serves as a key frame of reference.[25] Similar GST frameworks for military operations have also sprung such theories as Operations Research and Systems Analysis (ORSA) and Systemic Operational Design (SOD), the latter developed more recently by Shimon Naveh and others.[26] GST, ORSA, and SOD are Western cultural manifestations of the Anglo-American analytic paradigm.[27]

Locus of Attention. One explanation for why the other contributors to this book (and their forerunners indicated by all of the citations brought to bear) spend so much time extending the Clausewitzian trope is that they arguably reflect a culture that is biased toward the ontology of objectivism, the epistemology of progressivism, and the methods compliant with logical positivism.[28] In other words, the compulsion for a viable, esoteric body of knowledge is an example of *normative isomorphism*, manifested as the ideology of Anglo-American analyses (i.e. that war can be broken down into analyzable variables or components).

In a similar social constructionist argument, science historian Thomas S. Kuhn characterizes this normative process as evidence of a "paradigm," which he describes as "the entire constellation of beliefs, values, techniques, and so on shared by members of a given community."[29] Kuhn furthermore characterizes objectivism as a mythology in that "theories [are] simply man-made interpretations of given data...."[30] In other words, as we rely on language and other forms of human-created symbols, there can be no neutrality in their meanings; hence, ideology (arguably the lowest form of philosophy) is at work. Kuhn criticizes progressivism as "a persistent tendency to make history of science look linear and cumulative, a tendency that even affects scientists looking back at their own research."[31] In other words, a community (in some cases referred to as an institution or profession) becomes unreflexive or self-referencing. Insofar as positivistic methods of finding causal relationships, Kuhn argues there is no "external standard" of being positive in our methods as we are all limited by the distortions of human perception and technologically-extended sensors.

We argue there can be measures of insularity, indicating a community of theorists can be stuck in a paradigm. We note that out of almost 600 citations in the other six chapters of this book, more than half were insular to the community of military theorists – field manuals, joint publications, or military papers (articles from military review, Defense Department-published monographs, etc). Another fifth of the citations were attributable to various interpretations of Clausewitz's metaphoric extensions by others in the Defense community (such as studies by the RAND Corporation). An indeterminable number of others were written in political science and international relations communities by retired officers or those employed by national security think tanks. What these data suggest is that the community of military theorists sees Center of Gravity as an important locus of attention, yet the displacement goes unrecognized, suggesting blinkeredness and a lack of institutional reflexivity.

Institutional Disenthrallment. Institutional reflexivity demands a wider attention to the richer availability (such as through today's electronic media) and variety (multidisciplinary studies) of metaphors today, as compared to the early 1800s when Clausewitz wrote his treatise. Military theorists should not be anchored to Center of Gravity – a concept that should seem as archaic to today's security environment professionals as Newton's assertion of the law of gravity might be to physicists who subscribe to theories of quantum physics.[32] Disenthrallment requires admission of the subjectivity of extending and displacing outdated metaphors as habituated grounds for theory. The military community should capitalize on the emancipatory prospects of employing multiple frames on war.[33] In his seminal work, social-philosopher Karl Mannheim puts it this way:

> …it is precisely the multiplicity of the conceptions of reality which produces the multiplicity of our modes of thought, and that every ontological judgment that we make leads inevitably to far-reaching consequences…. [W]e begin to suspect that each group seems to move in a separate and distinct world of ideas and that these different systems of thought, which are often in conflict with one another, may in the last analysis be reduced to different modes of experiencing the 'same' reality.[34]

Mannheim later demonstrates the value of metaphoric imagery in his "moving staircase" metaphor to describe the unreliability and invalidity of single points of view:

> To use a simple analogy, what happens is that in our empirical investigations to become aware of the fact that we are observing the world from a moving staircase, from a dynamic platform, and, therefore, the image of the world changes with the changing frames of reference which various cultures create. On the other hand, [traditional] epistemology still only knows a static platform where one doesn't become aware of the possibility of various perspectives and, from this angle, it tries to deny the existence and the right of such dynamic thinking…. Instead of perspectivism, the out of date epistemology must set up a veto against the emerging new insights, according to which man can only see the world in perspective, and there is no view which is absolute in the sense that it represents the thing in itself beyond perspective.[35]

For example, the "new sciences" of *chaoplexity*[36] (chaos theory and complexity science) may provide a plethora of new root metaphors associated with more promising qualities, ripe for imaginative extensions into military frames of reference:

1. Self-organizing networks/complex adaptive systems;
2. Spontaneous emergence/swarm theory;
3. Bifurcations/Butterfly effects; and,
4. Fractals/novel patterns.[37]

Antoine Bousquet projects how the chaoplexity metaphor is already affecting military theorists and concept writers who are not anchored to Newtonian metaphors such as Center of Gravity:

> Drawing further from the writings of complexity theorists and deploying biological metaphors, military theorists appeal to the 'swarm', the networks of distributed intelligence that enable bees, ants and termites to evolve complex forms of collective behavior on the basis of the simple rules of interaction of their individual members. Of particular interest are the resilience and flexibility of these swarms as amorphous ensembles whose continued existence and successful operation is not critically dependent on any single individual. Military swarms promise not only more adaptable and survivable forces but also new offensive and defensive tactics better suited to the contemporary battlespace.[38]

Other sources of sensemaking about war and other sorts of military intervention may emanate from the humanities and fine arts including: dance, painting, sculpting, literature, poetry, theatrical comedy, science fiction movies, sports casting, war stories (to include the plethora war historiographies, novels and movies), and music. For example, the ORCHESTRA metaphor may be used to describe the military leader's role as conductor of military operations where his subordinates play from the "same sheets of music" (the operations plan). One could compare this "theory of leadership" to one that describes it more as improvisational jazz, where each member may lead in-the-flow (suggesting an *Auftragstaktik* image where who takes initiative depends on the situation).[39] There is also evidence of the appearance of postmodern influence in theories of the related discipline of international relations (IR), originating from the roots of critical- and interpretive- arts. For example, the following is an extract from an IR theorist who employs the postmodern logic of social construction theory:

> Take first the [European Community] EC, in which the process of unbundling territoriality has gone further than anywhere else. Neorealism ascribes its origins to strategic bipolarity; microeconomic institutionalism examines how the national interests and policy preferences of the major European states are reflected in patterns of EC collaboration; and neofunctionalism anticipated the emergence of a supranational statism. Each contains a partial truth. From the vantage of the present analysis, however, a very different attribute of the EC comes into view: it may constitute the first "multiperspectival polity" to emerge since the advent of the modern era. That is to say, it is increasingly difficult to visualize the conduct of international politics among community members, and to a considerable

measure even domestic politics, as though it took place from a starting point of twelve separate, single, fixed viewpoints. Nor can models of strategic interaction do justice to this particular feature of the EC, since the collectivity of members as a singularity, in addition to the central institutional apparatus of the EC, has become party to the strategic interaction game. To put it differently, the constitutive processes whereby each of the twelve defines its own identity-and identities are logically prior to preferences-increasingly endogenize the existence of the other eleven.[40]

Note the author does not reject other paradigms, but critiques them for their limitations and suggests a multiple perspective approach (as we have tried to advocate for the military science community in this chapter).

Conclusion – How Would Clausewitz Write Today?

It is our position that Clausewitz's Center of Gravity metaphor has received too much attention inside the self-referencing, spiraling circle of military analysts who are determined to find or create operational definitions by displacing this dead metaphor. GST-wedded doctrinaires have become unreflective about institutional assumptions of objectivism, progressivism, and positivism that reflect the Anglo-American analytic models of warfare (that include ORSA, EBO and SOD). As a community of military theorists, it is time to disenthrall the institution from such singular and overextended metaphors and stay opportunistically tuned to alternative heuristics available, develop a multitude of theories for action from more than a single paradigm, and practice reflexively.

This prospect should give us pause to consider the social-psychological entrapments that the analytic paradigm may entail and give rise to Professional Military Education (PME) to reorient on more liberating and artistic opportunities for theory development, to include: meta-paradigmatic philosophy;[41] the sociology of knowledge and social construction theory;[42] the Trivium of the liberal arts;[43] linguistics and the study of tropes;[44] postmodernism;[45] and, interpretive inquiry,[46] among others. PME schools should also design curricula away from doctrinal manuals tied strictly to the rational-analytic models and more toward multi-perspective frames of reference, with accompanying seminar-facilitated critical inquiry, dialogue, spurred by multi-disciplinary readings.[47]

Finally, to navigate away from the pursuit of technical rationality, PME institutions should embrace the arguments and educational philosophy of institutional reflexivity based in the works of Donald A. Schön. Schön calls for refocusing professional education toward artistry and a more open philosophical ideal of "reflective practice" – unmoored from institutional dogma or objectified knowledge structures. The community of military theoreticians should raise anchors and permit dead metaphors, such as Center of Gravity, to sink, while setting sail for the explorations ahead.

Notes

1. Lakoff and Mark Johnson, *Metaphors We Live By* (Chicago: University of Chicago Press, 1980), 196.

2. Clausewitz warned us that there can be no *positive* doctrine of war (like that pursued in the natural sciences), recognizing the paradoxes (e.g., once you think you find a rule, the "genius" breaks it and wins). He does surmise that a positive doctrine may be possible in tactics. Carl von Clausewitz, *On War*, edited and translated by Michael Howard and Peter Paret (Princeton NJ: Princeton University Press, 1984), 140 and 152, respectively.

3. Another name for the Anglo-American analytic philosophy is the "Rational Actor Model," explained as making "optimal choices in narrowly constrained, neatly defined situations" – one of three frames for exploring alternative meanings for US actions during the Cuban Missile Crisis. Graham Allison and Philip Zelikow, *Essence of Decision: Explaining the Cuban Missile Crisis* (2d ed.) (New York: Longman, 1999), 17. See Nancy Roberts, "The Synoptic Model of Strategic Planning and the GPRA: Lacking a Good Fit with the Political Context," *Public Productivity and Management Review* 23, No. 3 (2000): 297-311. Synoptic planning is described by Roberts as "integrated comprehensiveness ...a conscious effort launched by top management to integrate decisions that compose the overall strategy to ensure that plans are consciously developed, mutually reinforcing, and integrated into a whole" (299).

4. Gibson Burrell and Gareth Morgan, *Sociological Paradigms and Organisational Analysis: Element of the Sociology of Corporate Life* (Portsmouth: Heinemann, 1979). Also known as logical positivism, the latter a term coined by a multidisciplinary conference of scientists convened in the 1920s, nicknamed the Vienna Circle. Positivists "seek to explain and predict what happens in the social world by searching for regularities and causal relationships between its constituent elements. Positivist epistemology is in essence based upon the traditional approaches which dominate the natural sciences" (5). This worldview spawned theories of operationalism, microeconomics, and behaviorism that dominate military science today.

5. It is interesting to examine the history of operations research and systems analysis and its institutionalization in the US Army. For example, see Charles R. Shrader, *The History of Operations Research in the United States Army*, Volume I: 1942-62; Volume II: 1961-1973; Volume III: 1973-1995 (Washington DC: Office of the Deputy Undersecretary of the Army for Operations Research, 2006, 2008, 2009). For a critique on the use of analytical models in conducting the US-Vietnam War, see Julian J. Ewell and Ira A. Hunt, *Sharpening the Combat Edge: The Use of Analysis to Reinforce Military Judgment*, (Washington DC: US Army Center for Military History, 1974). An artifact of Anglo-American analytic paradigm is modern military training – based in a geared to replication and mass production of standardized operant behaviors wherein the determination and approval of meanings for action (e.g., the pre-engineered tasks and standards for training) are to be left to those positioned in the upper-tiers of the bureaucracy (e.g., those occupying offices authorized sign official documents of doctrine, policy, or rules of departmental administration).

6. Lakoff and Johnson, *Metaphors We Live By*, 56. The list of others who have stressed the study of metaphor and concepts/theories is long. Here are a just few: Hayden White, *Tropics of Discourse: Essays in Cultural Criticism* (Baltimore: Johns Hopkins, 1978); Gareth Morgan, *Images of Organization* (updated edition) (Thousand Oaks: Sage,

2006); and, Antoine Bousquet, *The Scientific Way of Warfare: Order and Chaos on the Battlefields of Modernity* (New York: Columbia University, 2009).

7. Lakoff and Johnson, *Metaphors We Live By*, 196.

8. This is the thesis of Donald A. Schön, *Displacement of Concepts* (London: Butler & Tanner, 1963).

9. Donald A. Schön and Martin Rein, *Frame Reflection: Toward the Resolution of Intractable Policy Controversie*s (New York: Basic Books, 1994).

10. The original term in German is *Schwerpunkt*, literally "heavy point." However, we yield to the more expert interpretation and translation of Clausewitz's *On War* by Michael Howard and Peter Paret.

11. Examples of extended meanings are found on pages 487, 596, 617 of Clausewitz, *On War*.

12. In the social sciences, there are several concepts and theories for this objectification-of-meaning process: reification, institutionalization, worldview, habituation, sedimentation, hypostatization, concretization, self-fulfilling prophecy, competency trap, enculturation, indoctrination, single-loop learning, ideology, and so forth. Rationality involves objectifying reality – we even call our goals "objectives!" See Peter L. Berger and Thomas Luckmann, *The Social Construction of Reality: A Treatise in the Sociology of Knowledge* (New York: Anchor, 1967).

13. Mary Douglas, *How Institutions Think* (New York: Syracuse University, 1986), 3.

14. Paul J. DiMaggio and Walter W. Powell, "The Iron cage Revisited, Institutional Isomorphism and Collective Rationality in Organizational Fields," pp. 41-62, in Paul J. DiMaggio and Walter W. Powell (Eds.), *The New Institutionalism in Organizational Analysis* (Chicago: University of Chicago, 1991), 67.

15. John L. Romjue, *From Active Defense to AirLand Battle: The Development of Army Doctrine 1973-1982* (Fort Monroe: TRADOC, 1984). Outsiders, such as Colin S. Gray and US Senator Gary Hart, took notice, 13.

16. Ori Brafman and Rod A. Beckstrom, *The Starfish and the Spider: The Unstoppable Power of Leaderless Organizations* (New York: Penguin Group, 2006). See Jena McGregor, "What Gen. Martin Dempsey, Joint Chiefs of Staff Chairman, Thinks about Leadership," *Washington Post Blog* (21 Oct 11) accessed 27 Apr 12 at http://www.washingtonpost.com/blogs/post-leadership/post/what-gen-martin-dempsey-joint-chiefs-of-staff-chairman-thinks-about-leadership/2011/04/01/gIQAFYyt3L_blog.html.

17. DiMaggio and Powell, "The Iron Cage Revisited," 67. Normative- and mimetic-type isomorphic processes arguably occurred after the United States pulled out of South Vietnam. For a historic case in the US Army, see Romjue, *From Active Defense to AirLand Battle* where he speaks to the search for new ideas began with the Israeli Defense Force successful practices in their 1973 war, 3.

18. EBSCO is an acronym from the founder of the Company, Elton B. Stephens. We chose these as exemplars of conceptual-based bodies of peer-reviewed literature that have been published consistently over a reasonably long period (HBR data were available from 1922-present; ASQ data were available from 1956-present; CMR data were available from 1958-present; MR data were available from 1994-present. Therefore, all data calls were from 1994-present).

19. We also searched The Journal of Military History where data were available since its inception in 1937. In more than 70 years, we found center of gravity in 46 hits in the EBSCO data base. Compare this to 4,293 hits for strategy. This may indicate COG is more of a "buzzword," that is, and we speculate here, the rise in interest associated with "center of gravity" is influenced

by when it became more of a coercive, doctrinal process of "joint preparation of the operational environment" – a process reminiscent of the Jack Warden-inspired systems analysis for targeting in Operation Desert Storm. It could well be that with the phrase center of gravity, the normative source of jargon (a.k.a. "groupthink," "catchall" or the "bandwagon effect") is at work in the military community. See C. Marlene Fiol and Edward J. O'Connor, "Waking up! Mindfulness in the Face of Bandwagons," The Academy of Management Review, 28, No. 1 (2003), 54-70, where these authors conclude "that mindfulness [of the bandwagon effect] leads to expanded scanning, which, in turn, leads to more context-relevant interpretations and more discriminating decision behavior. The resulting success [of staying on the bandwagon], if left unchecked, will tend to lead to overconfidence and less subsequent mindfulness," 68.

20. A business example would include H. Igor Ansoff, *Corporate Strategy* (New York: McGraw-Hill, 1965) and a public administration correlate would be John M. Bryson, *Strategic Planning for Public and Nonprofit Organizations* (San Francisco, Jossey-Bass, 1988), now in its fourth edition.

21. Chris Paparone, *The Sociology of STRATEGY: Romancing the Image.* Unpublished study, Feb 12, part of a "Consortium Research Fellows Program (CRFP) as part of work package 405 (Strategic Thinking for Command) in support of the Fort Leavenworth Research Unit of the U.S. Army Research Institute for the Behavioral and Social Sciences (ARI).

22. The number of popular business books on best seller lists that call upon heroic stories of military strategy and leadership are numerous.

23. See his two part treatise: Donald A. Schön, *The Reflective Practitioner: How Professionals Think in Action* (New York: BasicBooks, 1983); and, *Educating the Reflective Practitioner* (San Francisco: Jossey-Bass, 1987).

24. Edward C. Mann, Gary Endersby, and Thomas R. Searle, *Thinking Effects-Based Methodology for Joint Operations* (Maxwell Air Force Base: Air University, 2002).

25. Ludwig von Bertalanffy, *General Systems Theory: Foundations, Development, and Applications* (New York: Braziller, 1968).

26. For example, Shimon Naveh, "Operational Art, Operational Command, Systemic Operational Design: Transforming the Triad, Extending the Potential." slide presentation January 2007, Fort Leavenworth, Kansas: School of Advanced Military Studies.

27. This overarch in paradigm has also been referred to as functionalism in Burrell and Morgan, *Sociological Paradigms and Organisational Analysis*.

28. In philosophy, critical examination of *ontology* would question the assumptions of "human being" and "being human," along a subjective ßà objective continuum and is associated with the question *what is real* or *appears to be real*? Critiques of *epistemology* would question truth-of-knowledge coherency (e.g., simplified ßà complexified) associated with *grounds* for communicating it to be real or appear to be real. Critical aspects of *methodology* would include deconstruction of research traditions and associated processes of investigation and assimilation that are assumed to legitimize knowledge as positive (nomothetic) ßà interpretable (humanistic).

29. Thomas S. Kuhn, *The Structure of Scientific Revolutions* (3rd ed.) (Chicago: University of Chicago, 1996), 175.

30. Kuhn, 126.

31. Kuhn, 139.

32. One of the present authors developed a framework to evaluate the many sources of metaphor in a previous essay: Christopher R. Paparone, "Reflections on Metaphors We are Led By," *Military Review* (Nov-Dec 2008): 55-64. The three categorical sources of

metaphor presented are: the humanities and fine arts; the Newtonian sciences (mentioned sufficiently above as the source of "COG"), and post-Newtonian sciences. The "mixing bowl" of imaginative theory-building, then, comes from the improvisational extension of meanings from all three of the sources ("sensemaking").

33. This is the principal thesis of Morgan's *Images of Organization* and the postmodern resurgence of "design philosophy."

34. Karl Mannheim, *Ideology and Utopia: An Introduction the Sociology of Knowledge*, translated by Louis Wirth and Edward Shils (New York: Harcourt Brace Jovanovich, 1936), 99.

35. Karl Mannheim in his April 15, 1946 personal correspondence with Kurt H. Wolff published in an edited work: Wolff, Kurt H. (1959). "The Sociology of Knowledge and Sociological Theory" (pp. 567 – 602) in Llewellyn Gross (Ed.), *Symposium on Sociological Theory*. New York: Harper and Row, 1959).

36. A neologism and portmanteau suggested by John Horgan, *The End of Science: Facing The Limits Of Knowledge In The Twilight Of The Scientific Age* (Reading: Addison-Wesley, 1996), 191.

37. As mentioned in Bousquet, *The Scientific Way of Warfare*, 163-183.

38. Antoine Bousquet, "Chaoplexic Warfare or the Future of Military Organization," *International Affairs* 84, No. 5 (2008), 928.

39. We got this idea from Karl E. Weick, "Improvisation as a Mindset for Organizational Analysis." *Organization Science* 9 (1998): 543-555.

40. John G. Ruggie, Territoriality and Beyond: "Problemetizing Modernity in International Relations," *International Organization* 47, No. 1 (1993): 139-174.

41. For examples, see Nicholas Rescher, *Philosophical Reasoning: A Study in the Methodology of Philosophizing* (Malden: Blackwell, 2001) and Stephen C. Pepper, *World Hypotheses: Prolegomena to Systematic Philosophy and a Complete Survey of Metaphysics* (Berkeley: University of California, 1966) (original published in 1942). In the latter, Pepper calls this idea "multiplicative collaboration" (p. 320) or "postrational eclecticism," 333.

42. Mannheim, *Ideology and Utopia;* Kuhn, *The Structure of Scientific Revolutions;* Berger and Luckmann, *The Social Construction of Reality*; and so forth.

43. For example, Miriam Joseph, *The Trivium: The Liberal Arts of Logic, Grammar, and Rhetoric* (Philadelphia: Paul Dry, 1937).

44. Hayden White, *Tropics of Discourse: Essays in Cultural Criticism* (Baltimore: Johns Hopkins, 1978); Herbert Blumer, *Symbolic Interactionism: Perspective and Method* (Berkeley: University of California, 1969); and so forth.

45. Jean-François Lyotard, *The Postmodern Condition: A Report on Knowledge*, Translated by Geoff Bennington and Brian Massumi (Minneapolis: University of Minnesota, 1984); and so forth.

46. Such as Paul Ricœur, *Interpretation Theory: Discourse and the Surplus of Meaning* (Fort Worth: Texas Christian University, 1976).

47. There are many authors that provide multiple frames for practice, for examples: Keith Grint, (Ed.), *Leadership: Classical, Contemporary, and Critical Approaches* (Oxford: Oxford Press, 1997); Mary Jo Hatch, *Organization Theory: Modern, Symbolic, and Postmodern Perspectives* (Oxford: Oxford University, 1997); Henry Mintzberg, *Mintzberg on Management: Inside Our Strange World of Organizations* (New York: Free Press, 1989); and so forth.

Figure 2. "Center of Gravity - cg," Beginner's Guide to Aerodynamics, Benson, Tom; http://www.grc.nasa.gov/WWW/k-12/airplane/cg.html, CGSC Copyright Registration Number: 12-1072 C/E.

Chapter 4
Center of Gravity Analysis—the Black Hole of Army Doctrine
by Stephen L. Melton

Twenty five years after the 1986 version of FM 100-5, Operations, introduced the term "center of gravity" into official Army parlance and made the concept the premier consideration in Army operational doctrine, debates still rage among commanders, staffs, doctrine writers, and military school faculty and students regarding the term's meaning and practical significance. No other modern doctrinal concept has cramped as many brains, unleashed as many rivers of ink, knotted as many tongues, and evoked as many thousand-yard stares as has the "center of gravity." Complicating the conversation is the ever shifting definitions and explanations of center of gravity (COG) promulgated in the Army's ever changing, yet authoritative, doctrinal manuals. Worse, as Antulio J. Echevarria II noted in 2002, our doctrinal definition of COG as the "source" of power is based on Howard and Peret's 1976 mistranslation of the German word *"Schwerpunkt"* in Clausewitz' original text, making it awkward for modern American military practitioners to accurately link the doctrinal expression back to any philosophical basis or historical usage.[1,2] But in this short chapter I will not argue that we should abandon the COG concept merely to put an end to a quarter century of confusion. Rather, I will attempt to demonstrate that COG should be demoted from its current perch atop the doctrinal hierarchy and be made just one of many elective considerations in operational design—sometimes useful, but sometimes not. COG is a reductionist tool that simply cannot be used to accurately summarize all belligerent systems; nor is COG always a powerful construct for envisioning the ways and means of modern military contests. As a concept, COG becomes less relevant the further warfare evolves away from the monarchical warfare system that Clausewitz analyzed. Furthermore, COG is unlikely to be helpful in the military contests that will attend the geopolitical struggles of the 21st Century.

In terms of organization, this essay will first explore the Clausewitzian world of monarchical warfare and why the Prussians, given their position in that system, solved their military problem by advocating decisive battles between COGs. Next we will discuss why our military leaders of the 1980s embraced Clausewitz' long-forgotten COG hypothesis as the solution to their defensive conundrum in Europe's Central Front and discuss the mutations of the COG concept in post-Cold War Army doctrine. We will then explore the validity of the Clausewitzian COG hypothesis in American military's historical experience, to test how the reality conforms, or mainly fails to conform, with Clausewitz' predictions. Then I will offer a systems description of warfare large enough to accommodate asymmetric struggle—something outside of Clausewitz' relevant framework—and provide a list of considerations that could be more useful for assessing and planning modern struggles with military components. Penultimately, we will delve into Chinese perceptions of 21st Century warfare to determine whether COG is in any way a relevant consideration in our likely military contests with this emerging geopolitical rival. Finally, I will conclude with recommendations to improve joint and Army COG doctrine.

Clausewitz' COG-Theory and Practice

Clausewitz was fairly clear as he wrote about the COG (*Schwerpunkt* in the original German, literally "heavy point," also commonly translated as "main point" or "focal point."). Clausewitz consistently envisioned the COG in an astronomical sense, as the heaviest or weightiest part of a combatant force, through which the strength of the combatant force was connected and balanced gravitationally. Take away the COG and the enemy constellation of forces loses its cohesion and flies apart. (Indeed, Clausewitz developed his theory after listening to a series of physics lectures at the University of Berlin)[3] To determine the true COG, Clausewitz advises that the "first principle is: To trace the full **weight** (*Gewicht*) of the enemy's **force** (*Macht*) to as **few centers of gravity** [*Schwerpunkte*] as possible, when feasible, to one…"[4] Nor was Clausewitz shy in describing where the COG could be found throughout the gamut of geopolitical situations;

> Alexander the Great, Gustavus Adolphus and Charles XII of Sweden, and Frederick the Great each had their centers of gravity in their respective armies. Had their armies been destroyed, these men would have been remembered as failures. In states with many factions vying for power, the center of gravity lies mainly in the capital; in small states supported by a more powerful one, it lies in the army of the stronger state; in alliances, it lies in the unity formed by common interests; in popular uprisings, it lies in the persons of the principal leaders and in public opinion.[5]

King, army, capital, alliance—these are the hubs and spokes of the theory. Not given to analytical disaggregation, Clausewitz declares that, the "center of gravity of France lies in the armed forces and in Paris" and offers no further explanation, apparently feeling the conclusion to be trivial and self evident.[6] Divining the COG was seemingly a formulaic, almost linear problem; defeating the enemy COG was the only true act of genius;

Clausewitz advocated attacking the enemy COG with all available force at the earliest possible moment, seeking decision in the largest single battle or campaign that could be operationally arranged;

> Just as the [physical] center of gravity is always found where the mass is most concentrated, and just as every blow directed against the body's center of gravity yields the greatest effect, and—more to the point—the strongest blow is the one delivered by the center of gravity, the same is true in war."[7] The Clausewitzian ideal is to attack the enemy COG directly with one's own COG as soon as practicable.

> The attack on these [enemy] sources [Schwerpunkte—COGs-- in the original German text] must be compressed into the fewest possible actions—again, ideally, into one. Finally all minor actions must be subordinated as much as possible. In short, the first principle is; act with utmost concentration. The second principle is: act with the utmost speed. No halt or detour must be permitted without good cause.[8]

Clausewitz strongly believed that only major battles were worth fighting. "Our conviction that only a great battle can produce a major decision is founded not on an abstract theory of warfare alone, but also on experience. Since time began, only great victories have paved the way for great results; certainly for the attacking side, and to some degree for the defense."[9] Clausewitz further notes that "the decision that is brought about by a battle partly depends on the battle itself—its scale, and the size of the forces involved—and partly on the magnitude of success."[10]

The centerpiece of Clausewitz' theoretical construct, as the previous paragraph suggests, is not the COG, but the decision; battles between COGs are mere instruments through which militaries deliver decisions, the sought after political outcome, to their heads of state. However, in Clausewitz' universe of monarchical warfare, however violent the climactic battle of the military COGs might become, the range of decisive outcomes their political masters would seek was generally be very limited indeed. The monarchs of Europe were, after all, intermarried, mutually supporting, and largely agreeable to playing the same game by the same rules. They understood that all warfare would seek only limited objectives—the capture of a border province, the restructuring of an alliance, the sanctioning or disapproval of a proposed royal marriage, or the seizure of colonies or spheres of influence. The monarchical geopolitical landscape that characterized Clausewitz' time disallowed any thought that any of the royal houses would exterminate one of the others or that any of the major powers would militarily dismantle one of the other great powers. War, if brutal, was not yet total. The term "unconditional surrender" was not yet part of the human lexicon; monarchs would offer each other acceptable terms that would allow their continued reigns. In this context of monarchs seeking advantage, not finality, Clausewitz wrote his famous dictum:

> War is simply a continuation of political intercourse, with the addition of other means. We deliberately use the phrase 'with the addition of other means' because we also want to make clear that the war itself does not suspend political intercourse or change it into something entirely different. In essentials (sic) that intercourse continues, irrespective of the means it employs. The main lines along which military events progress, and to which they are restricted, are political lines that continue throughout the war into the subsequent peace. How could it be otherwise? Do political relations between peoples and their governments stop when diplomatic notes are no longer exchanged?[11]

Further, Clausewitz assumed that, "in war the result is never final."[12] The defeated king would often agree to terms only as a "transitory evil" and find means to redress his losses by forming new alliances and raising new armies, preparing for yet another round in a never ending political and military contest among brother monarchs.

Though Clausewitz claimed his theory, derived as it was from scientific principles, applied to all the European wars he studied, his synthesis—offensive war, COG attacking COG, quick decision—was a uniquely Prussian formulation that, Clausewitz believed, solved his county's military-strategic problem. Prussia was, after all, a small and ambitious country, an aspiring and developing power surrounded by the far larger established powers of Western, Central, and Eastern Europe, namely Britain, France, Austria, and Russia. Prussia could not expand to achieve its imperial dreams of German unification on the defensive; offensive expansion was the only route forward. Neither could Prussia afford protracted wars nor attrition wars with her neighbors, all of which, given the fullness of time, could mobilize far more numerous and powerful armies than could Prussia, thereby bending the calculus of war to their favor. Moreover, Prussia's central position worked to her disadvantage in long wars, since concentrating all strength against one foe on one frontier would only invite the adventures of the other great powers against her exposed and indefensible other fronts. Consequently, Prussian statecraft consisted mainly of preventing alliances between the surrounding great powers. Decisive offensive wars, quickly fought in single battles or short campaigns against the surrounding powers, one by one, were the best way that Prussia could capitalize on its operational excellence and superior reserve system to impose the political outcomes needed to achieve her expansionary strategic aims.

In practice Clausewitz' theory survived his death in 1831 and proved remarkably effective in unifying Germany under Prussian domination and temporarily settling scores with France. In the seven week Austro-Prussian War of 1866, the Prussian armies marched against the Austrian army assembled at Koniggratz and drove them from the field with severe losses in men and materiel. Koniggratz, the largest battle ever fought in Europe up to that time, served as the decisive battle of the war, a shock from which Austria could not recover. It must be noted that Moltke, the Prussian commander, chose not to pursue and destroy the Austrian army for political reasons; Germany would have future need for a Central European ally and therefore had to limit the bitter feelings that greater bloodshed would engender. Nevertheless, Habsburg Austria had no option after Koniggratz but to concede that Berlin, not Vienna, would be the nucleus of the growing Germanic federation, reversing the power relationship of the prior six decades. Four years later, the Prussian-led North German Confederation attacked into France in 1870 and in a spectacular six-week campaign trapped and destroyed the main French army at Sedan, inflicting stunning losses on the French defenders and capturing the French emperor, Napoleon III. Having won the decisive battle and capturing the monarch, the Prussians assumed that they could dictate suitable cease-fire terms to the French and were stunned when the French, instead, abandoned the monarchy, formed a republic, and raised new armies to stop the German invasion. Ultimately, Prussia would have to lay siege to and occupy Paris to secure the 1871 treaty that would deliver her immediate war aims-- the Alsace-Lorraine and indemnities. But now the tide of history was flowing in directions Clausewitz had not imagined, undermining the logic of his theory. The age of monarchical warfare was crumbling under the democratic influences emanating from the west. And Prussia, having won dominance in Germanic Central Europe and having embarrassed highly regarded great powers in doing so, became the threat against which all the rest of Europe would unite. The Clausewitzian age of short and decisive monarchical wars was fading away, replaced by the mass mobilizations and attrition warfare of the new democratic industrial age. The Germans, slow on the uptake, nevertheless continued to seek the climactic battles that Clausewitz prescribed during the two world wars, and often operationally achieved spectacular initial successes, only to find themselves drawn into their worst strategic nightmare—protracted attrition warfare-- against the more powerful allied nations encircling them.

COG and the US Army

For 150 years, until the late 1970's, Clausewitz's writing was virtually unknown in the United States. English translations were poor. And "On War's" ponderous and obscure dialectical style, so characteristic of early 19th century German philosophy, was sure to bore any but the most academic American reader to tears. The US Army, steeped in American pragmatism and enjoying the tremendous success of its own military traditions, had neither the inclination nor the need to contemplate Clausewitz's deeper meanings. The appearance of a better English translation of "On War" in 1976, while America was struggling to understand its agonizing defeat in Vietnam, was the coincidence of events that propelled Clausewitz, against all odds, into the center of American military thought. The Michael Howard and Peter Paret translation of "On War" may have died an obscure death, like so many scholastic volumes gathering dust in so many libraries, had it been published at another time. The new Clausewitz translation was not an overnight bestseller. The library at the US Army Command and General Staff College (CGSC) at Fort Leavenworth, Kansas bought just two copies, and set them on the shelf alongside their two copies of the 1950 Infantry Journal Press translation and their four copies of the 1911 Graham translation.

The Army's Clausewitz infatuation did not spread from within, but came to us from our joint brethren in the Navy and Air Force. The Howard and Paret translation became a primary textbook at the Naval War College in the year it was published and was similarly adopted by the Air War College in 1978. Only in 1981 did it become mandatory reading at the US Army War College in Carlisle, Pennsylvania.[13] It was there that Colonel Harry Summers, at that time on the faculty, melded Clausewitz's ideas with his reflections on his own experience in Vietnam, and wrote his bestselling book, "On Strategy: a Critical Analysis of the Vietnam War," published in 1982.[14] Clausewitz is the featured star of this acclaimed work, quoted dozens of times, almost on every page, much like a preacher would cite scripture. The analysis, in summary, is that the North Vietnamese Army, not the Viet Cong, was the enemy COG, against which the US military should have focused its strength. South Vietnam could have survived if only we had concentrated our effort against North Vietnam, perhaps, Summers suggests, by cordoning Indochina along the Demilitarized Zone.[15] More than any other individual, Summers made Clausewitz, and especially COG analysis, the new craze in American military thought. Suddenly, everyone in the military science community was wading through "On War" and arguing about what, if anything, it meant. Overnight, Clausewitz became mandatory reading for the faculty and students at Fort Leavenworth's CGSC and the War College. In 1984, the Princeton University Press had to reprint the Howard/Paret translation to meet the demand and the CGSC library upped its holdings to almost 200 volumes. CGSC recently bought over a thousand new volumes of the new 1989 edition, now having nearly as many copies of Clausewitz as it has students to read them.

Clausewitz simultaneously invaded the US Army's capstone doctrinal publications. There is not a hint of Clausewitz in the 1968 or 1973 versions of Field Manual 100-5, Army Operations, or in earlier editions dating back to World War II. All of these field manuals preached the heavy firepower doctrines suitable for America's industrialized attrition warfare. The 1982 edition of FM 100-5, the first of the Airland Battle series, was the first to quote Clausewitz, though only once. However "On War" did merit a featured mention in the manual's brief bibliography. The 1986 version of Field Manual 100-5, however, gushed Clausewitzian theories, quoting him four times. (Only General Patton merited more quotations: five.) Here the US Army learned for the first time in its proud 211 year history that there is an "operational art" and that identifying the enemy COG is its "essence."[16] Appendix B, Key Concepts of Operational Design, paraphrases Clausewitz in its explanations of COGs, lines of operation, and culminating points. In a mere ten years--150 years after his death--Clausewitz emerged from the dustbin of history and hit the big time as the new philosophical guru of the most powerful military in the history of mankind.

Perhaps we can understand the neo-Clauswitzian COG craze that began around 1980 by considering the central problem the US Army in Europe, the strategic focus of American land power, faced in the closing decade or so of the Cold War. Similar to the predicament Clausewitz's Prussians faced a century and a half before, the Army judged itself to be operationally excellent and well equipped, but facing a foe in the Red Army capable of launching and winning an attrition war of unprecedented scale if fully mobilized. Rather than accept war on those terms, the Army sought some method to disrupt the flow of Soviet forces from the Russian heartland and achieve a favorable political decision before the weight of the Russian hordes could overwhelm NATO's thin veneer of high-tech, professional troops. Placing the weight of the American military effort against the Soviet follow-on echelons, the alleged enemy COG, would be crucial in bringing rapid and decisive victory. Along with winning the battle against the Russian's initially-committed forces with NATO divisions already in place, interdicting the Soviet second echelon with deep strikes would, we believed, cause the Soviet offensive to collapse without resorting to prolonged or escalating warfare. Never tested against its envisioned enemy, mercifully, the AirLand Battle concept drove the Army and Air Force modernization programs that, after the collapse of the Warsaw Pact, proved so effective against the hapless Iraqis and Serbians in the 1990s. Despite the implosion of the Soviet menace, the momentum that the neo-Clausewitzian COG gained in American doctrinal literature in the 1980s continued into the new millennium. The 2001 version of Operations, now renumbered Field Manual 3-0 and the first of the Full Spectrum Operations series, included COG discussions in fourteen different paragraphs.

The 2011 Field Manual 3-0, written with the Army's failure to quickly win the wars in Afghanistan and Iraq squarely in mind, features a tortuous discussion of COG, which, despite these humbling experiences, remained the central idea in Army operational art and design. Rather than abandon the COG as unworkable in practice, the Army expanded its definition and challenged its staffs to try harder to discern it.

7-30. A *center of gravity* is the source of power that provides moral or physical strength, freedom of action, or will to act (JP 3-0). This definition states in modern terms the classic description offered by Clausewitz: "the hub of all power and movement, on which everything depends." The loss of a center of gravity ultimately results in defeat. The center of gravity is a vital analytical tool for planning operations. It provides a focal point, identifying sources of strength and weakness.

7-31. Understanding the center of gravity has evolved beyond the term's preindustrial definition. Centers of gravity are now part of a more complex perspective of the operational environment. Today they are not limited to military forces and can be either physical or moral. Physical centers of gravity, such as a capital city or military force, are typically easier to identify, assess, and target. They can often be influenced solely by military means. In contrast, moral centers of gravity are intangible and complex. Dynamic and related to human factors, they can include a charismatic leader, powerful ruling elite, religious tradition, tribal influence, or strong-willed populace. Military means alone usually prove ineffective when targeting moral centers of gravity. Eliminating them requires the collective, integrated efforts of all instruments of national power.

7-32. Center of gravity analysis is thorough and detailed. Faulty conclusions drawn from hasty or abbreviated analyses can adversely affect operations, waste critical resources, and incur undue risk. Thoroughly understanding the operational environment helps commanders identify and target enemy centers of gravity. This understanding encompasses how enemies organize, fight, and make decisions. It also includes their physical and moral strengths and weaknesses. In addition, commanders should understand how military forces interact with other government and civilian agencies. This understanding helps planners identify centers of gravity, their associated decisive points, and the best approach for achieving the desired end state.[17]

The latest Army doctrinal manuals allow all echelons of command to employ the operational art, thereby implying that different COGs can exist at strategic, operational, and tactical levels of war.[18] Though COG analysis is not a specified step of the Army's military decision making process nor COG enumeration a required paragraph in the Army operations order format, Joint Publication 5-0, Joint Operation Planning, dictates that friendly and enemy COGs at both the strategic and operational level will be specified in joint orders.[19] Remarkably, all of the US military COG definitions continue Howard and Paret's mistranslation of Clausewitz' *Schwerpunkt* as "source of strength." The definitional clarity Clausewitz sought has been sacrificed to the point that the COG can be anything the commander might designate it to be. Gone, too, is any discussion regarding how the COG is linked to political "decision." "Decision" is, after all, the goal; the COG battle was merely Clausewitz' preferred instrumentality for achieving a political decision and, should the victory in battle be won, ending a war on favorable terms.

Unfortunately for the doctrine writers, the American experience in war does not support an assertion that defeating singular or multiple COGs is the path to decision. Indeed, the evidence suggests that COG-centric warfare is more a chimera than a reality, as this brief summary of American warfare demonstrates:

1. Revolutionary War: British forces could find no COG, even though they occupied all the principle cities in America at one time or another. Washington's Fabian defensive strategy denied England a decisive battle. The Patriot's protracted struggle drained the English treasury

and, with no prospect for victory, the British abandoned the struggle and ceded American independence.

2. War of 1812: Mainly indecisive battles with the British, though not against the Indians. After Napoleon's defeat, the British government declined the opportunity to deploy additional land armies to America, believing that they would experience the same frustrations as bedeviled their efforts in the Revolutionary War.

3. Indian Wars: Attacking and destroying Indian villages was the preferred Army and/or militia solution to either forcing the Indians to move further west or agree to resettle onto reservations. The village was the basic--often the only--political and economic institution of Indian society, and its destruction ended all hopes of Indian opposition. Though the village was not a COG in the Clausewitzian sense, attacking the village and its people, rather than chasing down and defeating Indian war parties, served to simplify the Army's task.

4. Mexican War: America's most Clausewitzian war. Scott's march to Mexico City, defeating the main Mexican army en route, is a textbook example of Clausewitz' COG concept. The Mexican government had no option but to concede its northern border states to American sovereignty. The generals who fought the war, which began in 1846, were well schooled in Napoleon's campaigns and fought the war accordingly.

5. Civil War: Attrition war won by the side with the greater population and industry. No decisive battles. The Union targeted and destroyed the Southern economy over the course of the war. Both sides viewed their capitals as COGs, but Richmond fell only after the Confederate armies had been reduced to ineffectiveness by years of heavy casualties.

6. Spanish-American War: Won when the US Navy sank the bulk of the Spanish navy and severed lines of communication between Spain and her colonies. No decisive land battles. Capital cities not involved.

7. Philippine Insurrection: Three year war without a COG or decisive battle. After the capture of Aguinaldo, the war becoming mostly a rural insurgency. Various measures—attraction, concentration, counter-guerilla operations—eventually exhausted the insurgents and ended armed resistance to American rule.

8. World War I: Attempt by Germany to repeat her 1870 victory over France on a larger scale. Her initial offensive campaign did not bring

decisive victory and the war became an attrition struggle, both militarily and economically, which Germany eventually lost. The German monarchy collapsed as a result. Similar results led to the collapse other major European monarchies.

9. World War II, Europe: German attempt to reverse her World War I loss with better tactical means and operational execution. Despite spectacular initial victories, the war once again became an attrition struggle that Germany lost. Despite the near total Allied destruction of the German economy, Berlin fell only after the German army collapsed from years of casualties. Forced into unconditional surrender in a total war, Germany suffered a defeat of staggering dimensions and, in the war's aftermath, abandoned militarism as an instrument of policy.

10. World War II, Pacific: Japan's hopes for decisive battles faded after 1942 as the United States locked her in a merciless attrition campaign in the Pacific and China. Facing crushing material, food, and manpower shortages in 1945, Japan nevertheless held out hopes of "victory" until the United States detonated its new atomic bombs over Japanese cities. Surrendering unconditionally, Japan abandoned militarism as an instrument of policy.

11. Korea: No decisive battles. The war eventually became an attrition struggle between the United States and Communist China. General Macarthur was relieved of command for suggesting that the war effort be extended into China, which he believed to be the COG in the China-North Korea alliance. The war was ended when Stalin died and Mao elected not to sustain continued heavy casualties.

12. Vietnam: Rural insurgency that pitted US doctrine of attrition warfare against Vietnamese doctrine of protracted struggle and exhaustion. No decisive battles. Despite inflicting horrendous casualties on the Communists, both France and the United States decided to forsake our efforts in Vietnam rather than endure the financial costs and military losses needed to continue the struggle.

13. Cold War (post-Vietnam): Having abandoned attrition warfare in the wake of Vietnam, the Army sought non-nuclear ways to avoid an attrition fight with the Soviet Union in Europe, should the Kremlin go on the offensive. The result was AirLand Battle doctrine, based on the notion that destroying the Red Army's COG would bring NATO defensive victory with reasonable casualties and rapidity. The Army's neo-Clauswitzian philosophies emerge at this time. The Cold War struggle, however, was decided by peacetime competition, and Russia, bankrupted by its economic inefficiencies and exorbitant military

expenditures, retreated inward, jettisoning its empire and union in the early 1990s.

14. Iraq: Destroying the bulk of the Iraqi military in Desert Storm (1991), including the spectacular 100 hour ground campaign, did not bring about all the desired political outcomes. In OIF (2003), the US military again destroyed the Iraqi military, occupied Baghdad and the remainder of the country, and deposed the Ba'athist regime, only to unleash anarchy and sectarian civil warfare. The Surge (2007) was largely designed to stabilize Baghdad, the Iraqi GOG, and buy time for favorable political decisions. No doubt, the Surge succeeded in its mission of reducing Iraqi-on-Iraqi violence and sidelining extremist elements. However, the political outcome of the long American war in Iraq is still being decided at the time of this writing. Meanwhile, the American public has grown tired of the effort and its expense.

15. Afghanistan: A largely rural insurgency with strong religious and ethnic components aided by out-of-country supporters and sanctuaries. No identifiable COG or decisive battles. This war is now in its eleventh year, the longest in American history. As in Iraq, the American public has grown tired of the effort and its expense.

16. War on Terror: No identifiable COG in this Islamist attack on American global hegemony. Adopting a cellular structure and basing their operations in a host of developing countries and ungoverned spaces. The terrorists continue to recruit and plot. The United States conducts a global campaign against the terrorist leadership—using predator drone attacks, Special Forces raids, and other measures—to keep the terrorist cells off balance. Evidence suggests that the Islamic terrorist networks view their Islamic identity and anti-Western attitude as their COGs, but no evidence exists that the terrorists have a cogent formulation of American strategic and operational COGs.

The fullness of the American military experience suggests that the COG is much more an ideal than a concrete reality, an intellectual hypothesis not borne out by the evidence. War outcomes are decided far more often by attrition or exhaustion than they are by lightning strikes against COGs. Indeed, little in the record demonstrates that nations can reliably employ stratagems that would help them avoid paying the fullest price in the wars they contemplate. Rare is the victory that is bought as cheaply as the generals, quoting their doctrines, might suggest. Only by exception do we find a war that is "on schedule" and "under budget." Rather than try to divine a COG in the enemy's system that can be profitably attacked to produce a quick decision, in more cases than not we would be better advised to prepare for long and costly wars that will continue until one side or the other-- hopefully the other—loses the means or the will to continue the fight. Even our wars with minor powers or even tribes end up in frustrating and interminable wars. Why is this so?

A Systems View of War

War is a competition between two or more open systems in a given common environment. The outcome of the competition will be largely determined by which side acts more powerfully within that environment and against the opposing force. The following figure describes the essential elements of the two warring systems.[20] (All complex systems are actually hierarchies or networks of smaller systems, however the simplified model works at the macro- or micro-level for all systems.) Each system receives messages from its environment and the enemy system through its sensory receptors. The receptors send the messages on to the control apparatus—a brain, headquarters, or government—that filters the messages through its world view—internalized notions of identity, official truths, values, purposes, and goals--finally deciding what, if anything, to do. Once the control apparatus decides on an action it wishes to take, it sends a message to an effector—think of it as an instrument of power—to act on the environment and/or the enemy system, as it is designed and trained to do. The effector's influence on the environment and the enemy may be immediate or delayed, but in either case the environmental and enemy change, if any, will be sensed by a receptor, providing feedback to the control apparatus. In this manner, effector outputs of one system will likely be sensor inputs to the other. Powerful effector outputs usually provide powerful sensor inputs to the opposing system and also create significant environmental change; weak outputs may have little effect on either the opponent or the environment and may be difficult for the other system to sense. It must be noted that in complex, adaptive systems, the array of receptors and effectors the system deploys are based on the world view and goals of the control apparatus. Systems do not waste energy creating receptors to gather information they believe is unimportant, nor do they expend resources building and deploying effectors they believe would be irrelevant in influencing their given environments and opponents. Because control apparatus are not omniscient, they will generally have gaping holes in their understanding of the realities of their environment and enemies, causing them to be unaware of important matters which affect their performance and survival. Because of the "unknown unknowns," systems may employ receptors and effectors that are less effective than they would desire. The entire design and functioning of the system is world view and goal dependant. Consequently, understanding the world view and goals of the adversary is the single most important aspect of war planning and operational design.

A systems view of war goes far to explain why strategic designs and operational approaches that succeed against one type of opponent may prove ineffective against another. The strategy, operations, and tactics a system employs are reflections of its world view and goals; only in the rarest of circumstances will each side mirror the other. In Clausewitz' world of monarchic warfare, all the players were from the same culture, fought with agreed upon rules, and shared similar geopolitical understandings. Unsurprisingly, given the symmetry of the opponents and the homogeneity of the environment, the kings of Europe's major powers were willing to fight decisive COG battles to settle their differences. But away from Europe, in the much different cultures of the other continents, against opponents playing by different rules, the COG formula loses much of its power to force decision. In these asymmetric struggles, where the rules each side plays by are as different as their cultures and political goals, formulaic victory is elusive. So the United States, having largely defeated its major power (i.e., symmetric) adversaries during World War II with surprising ease, was nevertheless frustrated in its post-war conflicts with minor Third World nations for precisely this reason. The major powers competed in agreed fashions; the emerging nations, seeking liberation from the major power colonialism, did not. Indeed, our very notion of regular and irregular warfare is an anachronism. Regular warfare along European cultural lines is now part of an historical past that ended with the epochal American victories in World War II and the Cold War. For the foreseeable future, all the wars we will fight will be with populations in non-European cultures and, therefore, will be irregular and asymmetric, Figure 4.

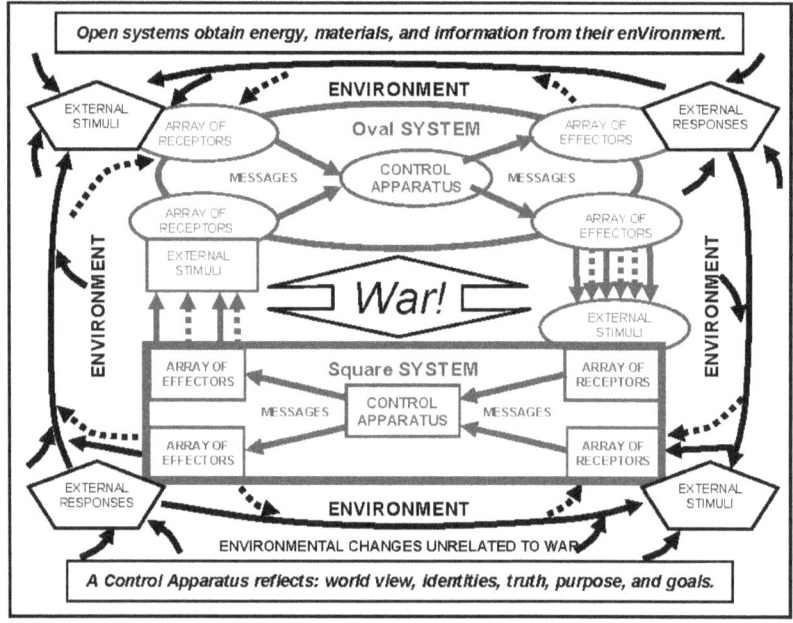

Figure 4. Center of Gravity Systems Slide.

Consider the following list of war strategies:

1. Single decisive battle of annihilation (ala Clausewitz)
2. Attrition (US preference through Vietnam)
3. Exhaustion
4. Fabian defense
5. Attacking the civilian population
6. Deterrence
7. Ethnic cleansing

8. Terrorism
9. Leader focused-warfare—assassination or cooption
10. Insurgency
11. Population-centric counterinsurgency
12. Punitive raids
13. Divide and conquer
14. Proxy war
15. Hybrid war
16. Unrestricted warfare (in the modern Chinese sense)
17. High tech local war
18. Assassin's mace (breakthrough technology that changes the game)

These strategies are vastly different from each other with respect to ends, ways, and means. Each has been used, is being used, or will be used again as an approach to solving a system's competitive problem with another system. The selection of strategy is a reflection of the system's situation, values, goals, and capabilities. Strategies that we might reject as inappropriate given our geopolitical position and world view might be appealing to others given their quite different circumstances and culture-based perceptions. While we might deem some of these strategies illegal or repugnant, the competitive games that matter are never fair or without consequence. Any strategy that confers advantage over adversaries in a given competitive environment will be (and, many would argue, should be) employed.

Further, the systems view accounts for the ever evolving environment in which wars are fought, for combatant systems do not compete in a static arena, but rather in a dynamic setting in which the very sources of systemic power—most importantly energy, materials, and information—are ever changing. In this systems world, understanding one's environment—its limitations and possibilities—is as important as understanding one's opponent. Clausewitz could not have foretold how the exploitation of fossil fuels, industrialization, and democratization would forever change the nature of European warfare and make the United States and, for a time, Russia the world's preeminent powers, all to Germany's detriment. Nor did mid-Twentieth Century Europeans appreciate that their Third World colonies would soon become the emerging great powers of the 21st Century while they themselves would fall into geopolitical decline. The ever quickening pace of globalized technological progress confers no permanent advantage to any national system or cultural grouping. Indeed, as the global environment changes—economically, technologically, politically, culturally, and in many other ways—so must we rethink the way we define victory and the means with which we seek it. The strategies that worked in one age are not necessarily those that will be productive in the next. Even if the decisive COG on COG land battle worked in the Clausewitzian era, the subsequent advent of vast nations on nearly continental scales, protracted industrialized warfare, weapons of mass destruction, precision weaponry, and persistent space-based intelligence—to name only a few evolutions in the environment of war—make the Clausewitzian formula often maladapted to the new realities. Consider how completely nuclear weapons changed the nature of major power warfare, making it too lethal and risky to contemplate for rational actors.

Further, because human systems are adaptive rather than brittle, wars tend to be protracted and costly, ending either when the defender can no longer withstand the attrition, and in some manner surrenders, or until an attacker, exhausted by the cost and effort of imposing his will, quits the war. Human systems often display tremendous resourcefulness and resilience, especially when forced to defend themselves. Rather than having a single source of strength, warring entities can draw on many. Defeating one adversary advantage generally causes him to switch strategy, operational approach, or tactical pattern to achieve a new advantage. Destroying one enemy asset more often than not leads to the creation of another, especially in asymmetric fights. The adaptive nature of combatants increases the cost of war for all involved. Rather than finding a single Clausewitzian COG in the enemy that, if targeted correctly, will cause the entirety of his force to lose balance, connectivity, and strength, we find instead that opposing forces at war heal, find work-arounds and alternative methods, or simply do without as they carry on the struggle. This holistic flexibility was true of all our major opponents in war—the Indians, the Confederacy, the Filipinos, Germany, Japan, the North Koreans and Red Chinese, and the Communist Vietnamese—and continues to be true of the anti-coalition Iraqis, the Taliban, and the Islamic terrorists today. Generally speaking, a combatant who realizes he must adapt to win seeks to prolong the struggle and postpone decision, thereby lengthening the war and increasing its cost to its adversary. A war of exhaustion is often the result.

Lastly, human systems will generally resist change forced by an attacker. The greater the change the attacker seeks, the greater will be the resistance. Most systems espouse world views that can accommodate the occasional humiliations and setbacks required by their necessary interactions with other systems. Generally, small concessions to opponents' ambitions are possible without threatening a system's world view, identity, values, and major goals. But as an attacker's political aims escalate, often to the point of forcing systemic change upon the defender, the defender will escalate his resistance. If the demands of the attacker cannot be met within the prevailing world view and political structure of the defending system, total and unconditional war will often result. The American experience from the Indian Wars, the Civil War, and World War II suggests that imposing transformational system change on a defender requires victory through attrition—meaning inflicting severe casualties and crippling economic destruction—so ardently will the defender resist fundamental changes to his accustomed system and way of life. Only the hardest of wars can predispose a society to fundamentally changing their world view, making them willing to trade in their old ways for the new ways of the attacker they can no longer avoid.

Chinese Notions of War

By all accounts, America's principle geopolitical adversary in this new century will be China. Economists are unanimous in their forecasts that China's skyrocketing economy will surpass the American in terms of gross domestic product within the next twenty years and come the dominate global commerce by mid-century. Her increases in military expenditures and capability match her growing economic clout. Geopolitical realists predict that armed struggle of some sort—whether minor clashes, regional wars, global warfare, some long term virtual or deterrence contest, or some other form of warfare—must accompany the transition from a US-centric to a Sino-centric world. Consequently, the true test of COG doctrine is not how well it may or may not describe past wars, but rather how useful the construct is likely to be in preparing for and executing the crucial wars we may fight with China in the strategic near-future. Raised in a far different cultural tradition than we, and considering their possibilities in a new strategic environment, the Chinese are developing appropriate doctrinal solutions of their own, which, I will argue, demote COG to relative unimportance. We, too, should consider whether our joint doctrinal mandate to identify strategic and operational COGs, then designing our operational approaches based on those determinations, is the most powerful way we can parry the Chinese military challenge.

At the level of strategy, the Chinese are disinclined to see view military struggles in terms of GOGs. Rather, they see their geopolitical struggles with other world powers in terms of holistic Comprehensive National Power (CNP), of which military power and military actions are a minor, albeit important, component. While the debate rages within China regarding how to qualitatively and quantitatively compute relative CNP, Chinese writers on the subject generally agree that CNP is some function of economic performance, military power, scientific and technological advancement, social progress and cohesion, population and territorial size, natural resources, and diplomatic strength. The Chinese have invested tremendous effort developing their concepts of CNP and believe it is useful in determining: "the status hierarchy in world politics, the power of potential rivals and potential partners, which countries will best exploit the ongoing revolution in military affairs, and which side will win a war."[21] The current Chinese concern with measuring and comparing CNP sprang to life during the early 1980s, when Deng Xiaoping reversed Chairman Mao's military doctrine that "world war was unavoidable," by instead predicting that "world war probably can be avoided."[22] Deng and his successors, realizing that war with the United States would abort China's necessary opening to the world and rapid economic development, and cognizant of the likely suicidal outcome of war between nuclear armed states, decided to pursue Chinese interests through a "peaceful rise" in a globalizing world. Lacking the CNP to directly challenge America at the time, the Chinese felt they had little choice but to continue their internal development in a unipolar world dominated by the United States. In the Chinese view of the world, all nations must defer to the strongest, as determined by CNP. Now is America's time of ascendancy. With continued development coupled with American decline, China's time will come and the nations of the world will have no option but to conform their actions to her interests.

But if CNP doctrine deemphasizes the role of Chinese military action in the near term, the concept also allows for a continuation, even an escalation, of the geopolitical struggle with the United States through other means. The breakthrough idea became popularized as "Unrestricted Warfare," the title two People's Liberation Army colonels, Qiao Liang and Wang Xiangsui, selected for their 1999 book on the changing nature of war.[23] The principle thesis in the book is that the age of deciding political issues through military means alone is over. In a globalizing world of complex and varied relationships, all the elements of CNP can be transformed into weapons in the larger geopolitical struggle. The authors lampoon the American military's fixations on purely technological means and decisive GOG battles, noting that, in the new environment, great power struggles play out on a far vaster canvas--in space, time, and method.[24] Envisioned as a "cocktail mixture," the 21st Century war is a combination of military, trans-military, and non-military means. The military means include all the usual suspects, like atomic and conventional warfare, but notably also include terrorist and ecological warfare. The trans-military category includes eight forms of warfare: diplomatic, network, intelligence, psychological, tactical (sic), smuggling, drug, and virtual (deterrence). Non-military means include: financial, trade, resources, economic aid, regulatory, sanction, media, and ideological.[25] The authors claim that, "there is nothing in the world today that cannot become a weapon."[26] The very purpose of war changes from the Clausewitzian formula of "using armed forces to compel the enemy to submit to one's will" to "using all means, including armed-force, military and non-military, and lethal and non-lethal means to compel the enemy to accept one's interests."[27] (Of course, China's position is that she has interests which are not adequately recognized in the America- led world.) The primary battlefield in the struggle may not be military.[28] Any form of struggle that increases China's CNP and reduces America's creates a world more conducive to Chinese interests.

As the Chinese envision military struggles in the upcoming decades, the emergent school of thought known as "High-Tech Local War" seems to describe best the operational level contribution armed conflict will likely make in China's on-going strategic struggle with the United States;

> War has always demanded that the military object conform to the political object. The particular content of this demand on high-tech local war is that the limitation of the political object has a more decisive bearing on the limitation of military objects...first, peace and development, the theme of this era, have laid the political foundation for the further restriction s on the object of war. Secondly, the competition of comprehensive national power based on economy and led by science and technology is becoming more and more intense. The economic globalization is moving faster. The interdependence and mutual restraints among countries are also deepening...Thirdly, high-tech weapons and equipment provide low-risk and high-efficiency tools to accomplish limited political objects, and the skyrocketing war consumption [of contemporary military operations] reduces the sinews of a nation to afford the [long or widespred] war, so the necessity and possibility of war control are increasing simultaneously. Fourth and finally, modern information technology makes war more transparent, which helps public opinion impose more influence on war.[29]

Conforming to previous doctrinal developments, only very limited wars--clashes really—are seen as beneficial in the current environment. But even given the limited nature of combat, the authors recommend further limiting the bloodshed by targeting the key integrating mechanisms of the opponent force, not attacking it head on;

> If we have paralyzed the enemy's information system, its whole system loses the brain and nerve; if we have destroyed the enemy's supply system, his other systems will lose material base and energy sources. Therefore, the future operational center of gravity should not be placed on the direct confrontation with the enemy's assault system. We should persist in taking the information system and support system as the targets of first choice throughout. [30]

Reflecting the yin and yang of Chinese thinking, the authors view America's superiority in information and logistics systems as critical American advantages and, therefore, vulnerabilities, should China find a means to attack those capabilities.

The main direction of "High-Tech Local War" is to limit the scope of engagements and their casualties to an absolute minimum. Their only goal is to get Chinese interests recognized at the lowest risk adjusted cost imaginable, not to invite a larger, more destructive war with America. In this vein, the Chinese are likely to resort to a trans-military means, "virtual warfare," a demonstration of capabilities short of war or actual offensive employment against living targets, to get their way. Given the assumptions behind CNP, the Chinese may believe that merely displaying their ability to disrupt American mission command, disrupt intelligence and information systems, destroy forward bases, or sink American ships in mid-Pacific with anti-ship ballistic missiles, among other means, could cause the United States over time to rethink its military commitments in the Far East and, consequently, accede to Chinese demands for regional hegemony. China may even arrange for proxies to operationally demonstrate the effectiveness of some of its weapons, innocently exported of course, against American targets. Notably, the Chinese believe that time is on their side and are in no hurry to press for immediate decisions that may lead to unwanted wars, as their policy toward Taiwan so clearly indicates. In the fullness of time, the Chinese believe, will have little choice but to bow to Chinese power.

Modern Chinese notions of struggle represent a philosophical polar opposite from Clausewitz' COG-centric formulations. Where Clausewitz sought to reduce the essence of his strategic foe to a single point of effort, the COG, the Chinese see their adversaries as organic holistic systems best thought of in terms of CNP. (Just as the Chinese would be hard pressed to condense America's manifold power to a single COG, so to would we be simplistic in describing China's multifaceted strengths in such an abbreviated manner.) Where Clausewitz sought the largest possible battle to impose a Prussian monarch's will, the Chinese seek the smallest possible battle to demonstrate interest and resolve. Where Clausewitz sought rapid decision, the Chinese are patient. While Clausewitz would declare, "We are not interested in generals who win victories without bloodshed," modern Chinese authors are given to quoting Sun Tzu's famous dictum, "The highest excellence is to subdue the enemy's army without fighting at all."[31] The difference in method between these two rising powers, separated by nearly two centuries, could hardly be greater. But, from a systems perspective, one could hardly expect that the two countries, operating in vastly different environments against different foes, imbued with different world views and cultural traditions, would arrive at anything other than disparate conclusions.

Recommendations for US Doctrine

Over the past two years, several of my students at the Command and General Staff College have insisted that in our current wars "the people" are the COG, repeating the statements they have heard from their commanders overseas. Apparently unable to use the COG concept to reduce the enemy to one (or a few) key points, the Army in current practice is expanding the COG concept to include the entire human system in the conflict environment. Rather than provide clear focus and orientation, as Clausewitz intended, COG in its current incarnation has become increasingly expansive, and accordingly less powerful as an analytic tool. Were COG a generally useful concept around which we could design military operations, we could forgive the doctrinal sleight of hand. However, the paragraphs above provide ample historical evidence that deducing an enemy COG rarely produces the payoff the war planners desire. Nor is COG likely to be a powerful analytic tool in our current geopolitical struggles.

What to do?

First, joint and Army doctrine must determine a single definition for COG. Clausewitz' definition is the best, "the main concentration of enemy strength or power." In practice, this concentration is often the enemy capital city and its defenses, as Clausewitz noted. US doctrine should abandon the notion that a COG is a "source" of power. Not only is it a mistranslation of Clausewitz, but, as the previous discussions of systems theory and Chinese CNP suggest, competitive and combatant systems have manifold sources of strength and have proven resourceful in adapting to the trials of war. Identifying a single "source of power" or even several "sources of power" often forces a conclusion that poorly reflects the reality. Ambiguous, intangible, or cultural extensions of the COG definition,--e.g., will of the people, religious beliefs, tribal political structures, etc--should be stricken from the Army's COG definition. Though these are important considerations commanders must understand and address, they need to be discussed on their own merit, not be subsumed into a catchall COG definition, a formula so diffuse that it creates more confusion than clarity. The discussion of COG must include the statement that an enemy COG may not exist (Wellington's conclusion regarding the United States during the War of 1812.) or may not be immediately assailable by friendly forces. Looking for a COG that isn't there is a fruitless endeavor. Our doctrine must acknowledge that there may be no rapid path to favorable decision. More wars are won through attrition and exhaustion than by assaults on declared COGs, and our operational design doctrine should overtly recognize this overarching reality.

Secondly, joint and Army operations orders at the strategic and operational level should adopt a systems view of enemy forces. Rather than start the Paragraph 1 discussion of the adversary with an enumeration of adversary COGs, we would be far better served by explaining the adversary's world view, the political decisions he seeks, and the courses of action he may employ to achieve his desired outcomes. In offensive wars or operations, we should be similarly clear about the decisions we seek to impose on our enemy and the means he might take to avoid those decisions. "Critical capabilities" should be described from the enemy perspective, i.e., the system effectors the adversary wishes to use to change the environment or friendly activities in ways contrary to our interests. The adversary's receptor network could additionally be highlighted as a critical capability, if the shoe fits. The "critical vulnerabilities" paragraph should explain weaknesses and single points of failure in the adversary's system that are targetable. Often these vulnerabilities stem from a lack of robustness in the way the enemy system gathers its necessary energy or materials from the environment, e.g., Japan's complete dependence on imported oil during World War II. Other vulnerabilities are internal to the architecture of the enemy system, e.g., the Chinese believe that the US over-relies on digitized command and control systems and considers those systems a targetable US vulnerability. As both Clausewitz and current Army COG doctrine notes, a system's control by key and unique leaders may make those individuals targetable systemic vulnerabilities. Presumably, successfully targeting enemy systemic vulnerabilities will reduce the enemy's holistic efficiency and force a quicker or more favorable political decision. At worst, successful targeting of vulnerabilities will shift the tactical attrition and political exhaustion calculus more in our favor.

Conclusion

COG need not be the black hole from which no illumination comes. Getting our doctrinal definition of GOG succinct enough for normally intelligent officers to comprehend will be a giant step forward. Similarly, making our COG doctrine conform to the reality of warfare, rather than forcing our perceptions of war into an ill-conceived COG construct, will provide salutary results. However, COG cannot be reformed in place, as the centerpiece of Army and joint doctrine, rather it must be demoted to a secondary and optional consideration in operational design. Rather than reduce the enemy to a few key points by straining him through the COG filter, we should instead describe the enemy as the holistic system he actually is. Rather than focus on an instrument designed to force decision in a long-gone monarchical environment, we should instead consider how our current adversaries actually seek or avoid decision in the current environment. Only a systems view of warfare allows sufficient precision and clarity. Consequently, the upper echelon joint and Army planning processes, operational design doctrine, and orders formats must be restructured, in part, to focus on the critical questions: who is the enemy?, what is his world view?, what political decision does he wish to seek or avoid in this conflict?, how does he intend to achieve those political goals?, what are his systemic strengths and weaknesses?, and, finally, how do we force a decision favorable to our interests? The answers to these questions will be as dissimilar as the adversaries we will face and the environments in which the conflicts will occur.

Notes

1. Echevarria, Antulio J. II, "Clausewitz's Center Of Gravity: Changing Our Warfighting Doctrine—Again!," Strategic Studies Institute, 2002.

2. Clausewitz, Carl von, *On War,* edited and translated by Michael Howard and Peter Paret, (Princeton, NJ, Princeton University Press, 1976).

3. Echevarria, Antulio J. II, "Clausewitz's Center Of Gravity: It's Not What We Thought," *Naval War College Review* (Winter 2003): 110.

4. Echevarria, "Clausewitz's Center Of Gravity: Changing Our Warfighting Doctrine—Again!," 7.

5. Echevarria, Clausewitz's Center Of Gravity: 114. Echevarria's translation from Clausewitz' original German text.

6. Clausewitz, 633.

7. Echevarria, Antulio J. II, "Clausewitz's Center Of Gravity: Changing Our Warfighting Doctrine—Again!," 11.

8. Clausewitz, p 617. Original German from Echevarria, Antulio J. II, "Clausewitz's Center Of Gravity: Changing Our Warfighting Doctrine—Again!," 121.

9. Clausewitz, 260.

10. Clausewitz, 261.

11. Clausewitz, 605.

12. Clausewitz, 80.

13. Stuart Kinross, *Clausewitz and America: Strategic Thought and Practice from Vietnam to Iraq*, (New York, Routledge, 2008) 75-6.

14. Harry Summers, *On Strategy: a Critical Analysis of the Vietnam War*, (Novato, CA: Presidio Press, 1982). In the bibliography Summers calls the Howard/Paret translation "masterful... the language more readable...an understandable and usable guide to modern strategy." 216.

15. Summers, 122-4.

16. FM 100-5, (Washington DC: Department of the Army, 1986) 10.

17. FM *3-0, Operations*, (Washington DC: Department of the Army, 2011) 7-6.

18. ADP *3-0, Unified Land Operations*, (Washington DC: Department of the Army, 2011) 9-10.

19. Joint Publication 5-0, *Joint Operation Planning*, (Washington DC: Department of Defense, 2011, A-3.

20. Portions of this figure from von Bertalanffy, Ludwig, *General System Theory: Foundations, Development, Applications,* Revised Edition, (George Braziller, Washington, DC, 1968) 43.

21. Pillsbury, Michael, *China Debates the Future Security Environment*, (National Defense University Press, 2000) 203-4.

22. Pillsbury, 210.

23. Qiao Liang and Wang Xiangsui, *Unrestricted Warfare*, (Pan American Publishers, 20020.

24. Qiao Liang, 105, 168.

25. Qiao Liang, 123.

26. Qiao Liang, 16.

27. Qiao Liang, pxxii.

28. Qiao Liang, 163.

29. *Science of Military Strategy*, edited by Peng Guangquin and Yao Youzhi, Military Science Publishing House, Beijing, 2005, 423.

30. Guangquin, 464-5

31. Clausewitz, 260. Sun-Tzu, *The Art of Warfare*, Roger T. Ames, (New York, Ballantine, 1993) 111.

Chapter 5
Thoughts on Clausewitz, Strategy, and Centers of Gravity: When Jargon Meets Reductionism
by John T. Kuehn

Again, unfortunately, we are dealing with jargon, which, as usual, bears only a faint resemblance to well defined, specific concepts.
—Carl von Clausewitz [1]

Introduction

Carl von Clausewitz's concept of the center of gravity has been the focus of much discussion in both military and academic circles of late. Most of the discussion centers on how current United States military and joint doctrine uses, misuses, or misrepresents the concept of center of gravity. It is not the purpose of this paper to critique or to examine the semantics and logic of the various arguments in these communities about a proper definition of center of gravity.[2] Rather, this paper examines Clausewitz's own use of the term within the context of his written work, principally in *On War*.[3] It argues that use of the concept became convoluted for two primary reasons: confusion over Clausewitz's use of the term *strategy* and his own different usages of the term "center of gravity" in the different books that comprise *On War*—especially "Book Six Defense" and "Book Eight War Plans" from *On War*. This paper further argues that the concept was used differently in the two books. However, in the sense that he meant center of gravity to be used as a planning tool at all, and there is some doubt about this, the evidence reviewed here suggests that at best he intended it be *used as a metaphor or illustration useful in planning in or at the operational level of war*. In other words, its use at the highest levels of strategy and grand strategy is inappropriate.[4] This essay offers something of a case study on how sloppy usage of military terminology and jargon can lead to confusion—something that war is already well supplied with.

"Strategical" Confusion

Before dealing with the confusion about center of gravity, the contextual issue of confusion over the concept of strategy—including how Clausewitz used the term—must be addressed.[5] This is because center of gravity is often used within the context of Clausewitz's use of the term strategy. Therefore, it is imperative that we understand his use of this word first. Sloppy [imprecise? Negligent?] use of terminology and jargon, long recognized but still tormenting us today, has often had to do with misusing the word *strategy* to describe actions at the operational level of war. After World War I, for example, General Hugo von Freytag-Loringhoven captured the essence of the problem succinctly:

> All that pertains to operations as such takes place, on the whole, independently of actual combat, whereas in the term 'strategisch' (strategical) things become easily confused, as has been proved by the example of our enemies who are wont to speak of strategical conditions when it is merely

a question of purely local matters. At any rate, the term 'strategy' ought to be confined to the most important measures of high command.[6]

Freytag-Loringhoven refers here to "enemies," and one presumes among these adversaries he meant the Americans as well as the British and the French. In any case, as we shall see, Clausewitz, too, acknowledges? that this topic area presents difficulties.

The problem today further traces to use of definitions and then how we link those definitions to their use in the past—again the problem of context. Let's first look at how Clausewitz used the term. In Clausewitz's day only two levels of war existed for the professional officer, the tactical and the strategic, although he does acknowledge, in his book on defense, another higher level: "At the next stage, the war as a whole replaces the campaign, and the whole country the theater of operations."[7] This level he consigned to policy, or in his day the leader of the state, often a prince. In our own day, and at least since the early 1980s as far as US doctrine is concerned, there are three levels of war—tactical, operational, and strategic.[8]

Readers of *On War* as translated by Michael Howard and Peter Paret first collide with Clausewitz's use of the term strategy in Peter Paret's translation of Clausewitz's unfinished note at the beginning of the book: "The theory of major operations (strategy, as it is called)... ."[9] Clearly strategy here correlates to the operational level of war as defined in the 1982 version of FM 100-5 *Operations*: "The operational level of war uses available military resources to attain strategic goals within a theater of. Most simply, it is the theory of larger unit operations. It also involves planning and conducting campaigns."[10] Clausewitz, continuing in his note, broaches the topic of the difficulty of use of the term because it "... presents extraordinary difficulties and it is fair to say that very few people have clear ideas about its details—that is, ideas which logically derive from basic necessities." Clausewitz himself is cautioning future readers about the topic and its tendency to cause problems.

The issue is further muddied by conflict about when this particular note was written, if it indeed was written in 1830, that is within a year of Clausewitz's own death. The note earlier claims that Clausewitz only considered Book One "On the Nature of War" as finished. If the major books dealing with strategy and war planning are unfinished, how can *On War* be trusted for its definitions of strategy, tactics and center of gravity that are in them? Doesn't using them present "extraordinary difficulties"? Fortunately this conundrum about the date of the note casting doubt on the maturity of Clausewitz's concepts can be resolved if one accepts that it was most probably written at an earlier date (prior to 1827) as persuasively claimed by Jon T. Sumida.[11]

Even if Sumida is incorrect we need only examine the definitions for consistency to see if we can trust them. In the case of strategy our approach yields happy results, both as to the definition and its residing in a modern sense at the operational level of war. In *On War* Clausewitz devotes the entirety of Book Three to a discussion of strategy and first defines it as:

> Strategy is the use of the engagement for the purpose of the war. The strategist must therefore define an aim for the entire operational side of the war that will be in accordance with its purpose. ...he will draft the plan of the

war, and the aim of the war will determine the series of actions intended to achieve it: he will, in fact, shape the individual campaigns and, within these, decide on the individual engagements.[12] [emphasis mine]

Compare this with the Army definition found in FM 3.0:

The strategic level of war is the level of war at which a nation, often as one of a group of nations, determines national or multinational (alliance or coalition) strategic security objectives and guidance and develops and uses national resources to achieve these objectives. ...Strategy is a prudent idea or set of ideas for employing the instruments of national power in a synchronized and integrated fashion to achieve theater, national, and/or multinational objectives (JP 3-0). The President translates national interest and policy into a national strategic end state.[13] [emphases original]

Clearly Clausewitz's definition is at a lower level of war when compared to this definition. In particular, the current definition focuses especially on the national and international level and resources, not just military. Here, too, the context of Clausewitz's times, the Napoleonic Wars, is betrayed by where he locates the strategist in the activity of war—not back in the capital but, "...it follows that the strategist must go on campaign himself." [14] The strategist is a campaigner in the early 19th Century, but not so in the 20th and 21st. As one proceeds through the book on strategy one finds just how congruent Clausewitz's view of strategy in action was with that of his contemporary Baron Antoine Jomini. In fact, the chapters in Book Three sound like a Jominian recitation—"Surprise... Cunning, Economy of Force...The Geometrical Factor."[15] Clausewitz's book on strategy is clearly about what we in the 21st Century refer to as the operational level of war—although he does cloud the issue slightly in linking war aims to the campaign (which really is a function of strategy).

Center of Gravity as Analogy

Clausewitz's use of the term strategy, as shown above, frames how modern readers should interpret his usage in *On War*. If he normally uses "strategy" to refer to the operational level, then when he discusses strategy in concert with the term center of gravity, we should regard the latter term also as an operational concept. However, viewing his usage of center of gravity is not the only tool one must use to understand how he used this term.

Center of Gravity first appears in a rather odd place, Book Six on defense. In fact, Book Six is the longest of the books in *On War* at 166 pages and this too should suggest how the term, as first used, should be treated by the modern student of Clausewitz. Jon Sumida's *Decoding Clausewitz* brings proper attention to the book on defense's primacy of place among *On War*'s eight books due to length and persuasively argues that Clausewitz's claim that "defense is the stronger form of war" constitutes one of the few universal principles in *On War*. [16] In other words, the book on defense is a key to understanding what Clausewitz thought most important in his treatise on war. As one might expect, center of gravity makes its first appearance in this most important book. As mentioned earlier, and again as one would expect, Clausewitz clearly defines what he means by strategy on the second page of the very first chapter of Defense—"At the strategic level the campaign replaces the engagement and theater operations takes the place of the position." This makes perfect sense since he defines his usage consistently so the reader will be clear as to the level of war he is at—the operational in modern usage.

Clausewitz's initial goal for Book Six involves a lengthy treatment of the nature, ease, and strength of defense. However, after almost 80 pages during an operational discussion, in the chapter "Defense of a Theater of Operations," the reader first comes across the text, almost in passing, that mentions center of gravity. The discussion reads very much like a physical science discussion about the influence of the "scale of a victory" and how it depends on the size or mass of the "defeated force." Alan Beyerchen, a historian of science, has demonstrated that Clausewitz used scientific language in *On War* as a means to demonstrate his complex concepts using the latest cutting edge scientific concepts like magnetism and friction and to emphasize war's complex and non-linear nature.[17] The wording preceding the usage is extremely important because Clausewitz then clearly tells his reader that:

> ...the larger the force with which the blow is struck, the surer its effect will be [against the greatest concentration of enemy troops]. This rather obvious sequence leads us to an *analogy* that will illustrate it more clearly—that is, the nature and effect of a center of gravity. [emphasis mine][18]

First, the discussion is clearly operational and involves numbers of troops attacking at an operational or even tactical level. Second, Clausewitz clearly states he is using an analogy to "illustrate" more clearly what he is talking about. He follows his introduction of the analogy with even less compromising language about center of gravity's usage in this instance: "A center of gravity is always found [in nature] where the mass is concentrated most densely. It presents the most effective target for a blow; furthermore, the heaviest blow is that struck by the center of gravity."

However, he follows the analogy with a problematic linkage: "The same holds true in war. The fighting forces of each belligerent—whether a single state or an alliance of states—have a certain unity and therefore some cohesion. Where there is cohesion the analogy of the center of gravity can be applied."[19] This illustration of alliances opens the door for the misuse of his more general use of the analogy for operational purposes to that of the higher strategic and political levels of war and has led to unending confusion ever since by cherry-picking thinkers and doctrine writers. The analogy of center of gravity helps to illustrate the principle that cohesion of mass, in whatever level of war, offers opportunity, but the discussion that gave rise to this idea was clearly operational. This may seem like semantics, however, the principle that Clausewitz really wishes to expose here is the one of cohesion—and it is clear from this short discussion or a re-reading of the passage that he clearly allows for situations without cohesion and therefore without a center of gravity.

In the same chapter, when Clausewitz again returns to the usage he is clearly at the operational level or lower again with the utility of the analogy within the context of the defense. Clearly Clausewitz refers here to the operational level of war:

> Our reflections are intended to demonstrate the general reasons for dividing ones forces. Basically, there are two fighting forces; one the possession of the country [or countryside], tends to disperse the fighting forces; the other, a stroke at the center of gravity of the enemy's forces, tends, in some degree, to keep them concentrated. [new paragraph] This is how operational theaters, or individual armies' zones of operations are created.[20] [emphasis mine]

In summary, center of gravity, when first used in the all-important Book Six, is an operational term borrowed from science as an analogy to illustrate the handling of military forces in a theater of operations.

War Planning as Opposed to the Conduct of War

The most famous of Clausewitz's discourses on center of gravity, and the one often used to illustrate the concept for war college students, does not come from the book on defense, but rather from Clausewitz's eighth and final book entitled War Plans. Before examining the key passages in chapter 4 of Book Eight we would do well to return to arguments about the structure of *On War*. Returning to Jon Sumida, this author aligns with his proposals in *Decoding Clausewitz* that sees Book Eight on war plans as fundamentally different than the other seven books. In war plans Clausewitz is not looking at war as it *is*, but rather as how one plans for its conduct—one moves from the present tense to the future tense. Because of this, Sumida argues, many inconsistencies in the book can be resolved. In fact, use of center of gravity in *On War* is one of the inconsistencies that Sumida resolves, there is evidence to suggest that using this approach can help clarify problems with how Clausewitz used center of gravity in Book Six versus a different usage and emphasis in Book Eight.[21]

Historians Beatrice Heuser and Jon Sumida are agreed that Clausewitz used the term center of gravity in two senses, a narrow (operational) sense as well as in a more intangible and conceptual way in Book Eight.[22] The following passage from *On War*--which follows an operational and strategic (modern usage) discussion of the factors one must consider for "The Defeat of the Enemy"--applies to their discussions:

> What the theorist has to say here is this: one must keep the dominant characteristics of both belligerents in mind. Out of these characteristics a certain center of gravity develops, the hub of all power and movement, on which everything depends. That is the point against which all our energies should be directed.[23]

This discussion can certainly apply to just about any level of war, certainly the operational and even tactical levels—indeed both Sumida and Heuser think it does. Then Clausewitz discusses directing one's force, principally against the enemy's force—he uses the singular—again we are essentially at the lower operational level. However, he continues and identifies "acts we consider most important for the defeat of the enemy…Destruction of his army…Seizure of his capital…Delivery of an effective blow against his principal ally… ."[24] Clearly these are strategic (modern sense) objectives—especially the last two.

Although the term "center of gravity" is not used specifically for these three uses, he uses it again shortly thereafter and leaves no doubt that these uses are examples of centers of gravity: "There are very few cases where this conception is not applicable—where it would not be realistic to *reduce several centers of gravity to one*. Where this is not so, there is admittedly no alternative *but to act as if there were two wars or even more, each with its own object*."[25][emphasis mine]

Even Clausewitz's intangible usage of the term in these passages brings him back to what I will call its "normal"("narrow") usage. He emphasizes a reductionist approach that admits one must *reduce* and simplify to make the term helpful, which accords with Sumida's claims that Book Eight is the only consistently reductionist book in *On War*. In fact, Sumida resolves the issue by claiming that Clausewitz's discussions of" guerilla" or "insurrectionary" war forced him to acknowledge the "intangible" form of center of gravity as "the personalities of leaders and public opinion."[26]

It is interesting to note that these characterizations appear? prior to Clausewitz's reductionist discussion mentioned above where he recommends that one identify multiple centers of gravity should circumstances dictate. This makes even more sense when one considers that Clausewitz had real experience of just both these factor in what he probably regarded as the most important two campaigns that he participated in—the 1812 Russian campaign and the 1813 campaign in Germany. In the first Clausewitz saw most clearly, as an officer in the service of the Tsar, the importance of both the popular feeling of the Russians against the invading French as well as the key intransigence of the Russian Tsar himself to Napoleon's operations. In the second case it was less a case of personalities as of unity in the alliance and the popular feeling of revolt against the Napoleonic system by the various German states.[27] In some sense Clausewitz was accounting for the failure of Napoleon's identification of normal, that is operational level, centers of gravity in these campaigns by coming up with an explanation at the higher levels of war.

As we can see from this review, Clausewitz was not as careful as he might have been in how he used the concept, relying on context to help his readers understand his usage. Or maybe he underestimated how lazy his military readership was or might become. In summation, the discussion suggest that, as far as Book Eight is concerned, there are two types of center of gravity—one that is a reductionist planning concept for operations, and another that is more intangible and seems to be associated with complicated and messy wars, peoples' wars or insurgencies. It has been suggested, and implied by Sumida, that in fact for these wars the term "center of gravity" has little utility at the operational level beyond identifying the difficulty of operationalizing a defeat mechanism. Finally, because war planning lends itself to reductionism, the result of planning, of center of gravity analysis as military professionals call it today, must always be held to some sort of skepticism. Once the plan collides with reality (and the enemy) a different process of calculation and re-calculation using the initial framework must take place. The mass no longer is stationary but shifts or even disperses so as to make identification of key points or centers of gravity themselves difficult (and thus the need for genius) or even counterproductive and useless.

Two Letters on Strategy—A case of missing evidence?

Clausewitz's "Two letters on strategy" seem to be a case of missing evidence. These letters were translated during the renaissance in the United States Army following Vietnam that included great interest in the writing and work of Clausewitz. The letters themselves, written in 1827 as noted above, were in response to specific war planning problems generated by the German General Staff, whose chief at the time was Lieutenant General von Müffling. Müffling and Clausewitz had both been students and planners under General Gerhard von Scharnhorst. These problems involved a defense of Prussia on the southern or central front (presumably against the Austrians). Clausewitz was one of five officers who held other assignments but attached to the General Staff for consultation.[28] Given that the letters involved strategy (operations) and war planning one would expect to find some sort of center of gravity (COG) analysis taking place. However, the term is mentioned nowhere in the back and forth of these letters, neither in the communications from Major von Roeder (who offered one solution), from 'M' (presumably Müffling), nor by Clausewitz in his lengthy responses.

One explanation may be that these two letters preceded Clausewitz's use of the term in books Six and Eight. This is highly unlikely; if Sumida and Paret agree on anything it is that Clausewitz had completed major elements of these books by 1827, although revision had not yet occurred. Even if we go with the Paret's interpretation that *On War* was unfinished except for Book One, the first of the letters on strategy comes *after* his 27 July 1827 note that discusses the essential soundness of the ideas in the first six books as well as in Book Eight. That is to say, it is highly unlikely that Clausewitz came up with the term in 1828 or after since both books where center of gravity appear already existed.[29]

A second explanation offers itself. In his letters Clausewitz's first words put to paper castigate the authors of the solutions for removing the political context from these problems, thus limiting their utility as war planning exercises. In his first response to Roeder he writes:

> War is not an independent phenomenon, but the continuation of politics by different means. Consequently, the main lines of every major strategic plan are largely political in nature, and their political character increases the more the plan encompasses the entire war and the entire state. …How then is it possible to plan a campaign, whether for one theater of war or several, without indicating the political condition of the belligerents, and the politics of their relationship to each other?[30]

Then, in his response to 'M' he writes about the issue of terminology exacerbating the lack of political context:

> I hate the sort of technical language that leads us to believe we can reduce the individual case to a universal, to the inevitable. Strategists manipulate these terminologies as if they were algebraic formulae, whose accuracy has long been established…that may be used as substitutes for the original reality. But these phrases do not even represent clear and definite principles.[31]

Ouch. Perhaps it is not an accident that we find center of gravity nowhere in these two letters. What we do find, in Clausewitz's initial outburst to Roeder, something that approaches what we often call center of gravity, or a center of gravity type discussion in very clear language: "The political purpose and the means available to achieve it give rise to the military objective."[32] This is COG analysis without the COG. In fact, the course of the discussion that follows the quotation above reminds one of the similar discussion that in *On War* gave rise to the allusion to a center of gravity in the first place. But "center of gravity" itself is not used—should this surprise anyone given his outburst above, especially to 'M'?

Perhaps the explanation for the missing COG has more to do with the relationship of political purpose to the operational level of war. Without political objectives and context stated clearly then the identification of operational objectives that he might label centers of gravity cannot exist. This seems as reasonable as his firm intent to avoid any inappropriate usage (i.e. center of gravity) that might confuse things further absent political context. In other words, absent political considerations center of gravity has no place in operational war planning.

Concluding Thoughts

This author is not convinced that Clausewitz intended center of gravity for use in any other than a primarily operational sense and *perhaps* tactical sense. Tactical refers to the "narrow" sense as discussed by both Sumida and Heuser and of *schwerpunkt* as used by several generations of German officers and discussed by them in a contextually correct tactical manner.[33] Certainly it has value as an allusion or as a metaphor for higher strategic level discussion, but that value is limited and must employ clear language that matches ends, ways, and means in a coherent, reality-based manner. Students wishing to practice this sort of method might better refer to Arthur Lykke's key essay for the Army War College on strategy or employ the clear definitions promulgated by Professor Joe Strange. These are preferable than to try and freelance based on an incomplete reading of Clausewitz.[34] Operational usage has most value as emphasized in *On War* for the future, for campaign planning. Use of the term in any sort of way for the development of grand strategy or strategy in a reductionist way seems inconsistent with what Clausewitz intended and how he used the term most often in his own writing—when he used it at all.[35] Again, it has utility in the present for tactical operations and for the future as a campaign planning concept. It seems his intent was not for it to become something other than a military concept for the use at the operational level of war (campaigns) and possibly lower.

Finally, much of this confusion results from ignorance of *On War* or due to an incomplete reading (few war college students ever read the whole book); a lack of familiarity with the modern definitions of the levels of war; an American inattention to the concept of grand strategy by military and civilian leaders; and, finally, a failure to enforce consistent usage in modern doctrine. Perhaps we must simply accept the reality that "center of gravity" has become precisely the sort of term that irritated Clausewitz most. Military professionals would be better off thinking about war aims, objectives, and ways to defeat the enemy, thinking about what really goes on in the minds of the adversaries' leaders or the people, rather than wasting time puzzling over a physics analogy. Maybe Clausewitz's comment captures best the problem with trying to be too reductionist:

> "Again, unfortunately, we are dealing with jargon, which, as usual, bears only a faint resemblance to well defined, specific concepts."[36]

Notes

1. Carl Von Clausewitz, *Two Letters on Strategy*, edited and translated by Peter Paret and Daniel Moran (Fort Leavenworth, KS: Combat Studies Institute Press, 1984), 37.

2. Perhaps the best place to start for those interested in the debate is Dale C. Eikmeier, "Center of Gravity Analysis," in *Military Review* (July-August 2004): 2-5; for another perspective see Antulio J. Echevarria II, "Clausewitz's Center of Gravity: Changing Our Warfighting Doctrine—Again!" (Carlisle, PA: Strategic Studies Institute, 2002).

3. For this essay all citations and reference involving *On War* come from Carl von Clausewitz, *On War*, trans. by Michael Howard and Peter Paret (Princeton, NJ: Princeton University Press, 1984).

4. For a discussion of the issue of grand strategy versus strategy and the definitional problems related to it see John T. Kuehn, "Talking Grand Strategy" in *Military Review* (September-October 2010): 74-75.

5. See again the discussion in Kuehn, for the current definitional problems regarding strategy and grand strategy.

6. Cited in the introduction to Carl Von Clausewitz, *Two Letters on Strategy*, by Wallace P. Franz, xiii, n2.

7. Clausewitz, *On War*, 358.

8. Field Manual (FM) 100-5, *Operations* (Washington, DC: Department of the Army, 1982), 2-3, defines the three levels of war.

9. Clausewitz, *On War*, 70.

10. FM 100-5, 2-3.

11. Jon T. Sumida, *Decoding Clausewitz: A New Approach to On War* (Lawrence, KS: University of Kansas Press, 2008), xiii-xv. Sumida follows the arguments of Azar Gat about the actual date of the undated note being earlier and additionally uses the information in the first dated note of 1927 to argue persuasively that the first six books were essentially complete enough for an intelligent reader to "discover" his "basic" ideas about war.

12. Clausewitz, *On War*, 177.

13. FM 3-0, *Operations* (Washington, DC: Department of the Army, February 2008), 7-2.

14. Clausewitz, *On War*, 177.

15. Clausewitz, *On War*, vi.

16. Sumida, 2: see also *On War*, 358-359.

17. See Alan Beyerchen, "Clausewitz, Non-Linearity, and the Unpredictability of War," http://www.clausewitz.com/readings/Beyerchen/CWZandNonlinearity.htm (accessed 01/15/2012). Center of gravity is one of the scientific terms Beyerchen spends considerable time on.

18. Clausewitz, *On War*, 485; the German word here is *Schwerpunkt*.

19. Clausewitz, *On War*, 485-486.

20. Clausewitz, *On War*.

21. Sumida writes in the new preface to the second edition of *Decoding Clausewitz*,

"Clausewitz admits the prescriptive use of general propositions with respect the consideration of the yet undetermined future, but denies their prescriptive utility when considering the actual events of the past." 2-4. This pagination comes from a copy of the preface provided in an email from Professor Sumida to the author (hereafter Sumida Preface).

22. Sumida Preface,1-2: Beatrice Heuser "Clausewitz's Ideas of Strategy," in *Clausewitz in the Twenty First Century, eds.* Hew Strachan and Andreas Herberg-Rothe (Oxford, UK: Oxford University Press, 2007), 148-150.

23. Clausewitz, *On War*, 595-596.

24. Clausewitz, *On War*, 596.

25. Clausewitz, *On War*, 597.

26. Sumida Preface, 1-2; Clausewitz, *On War*, 596.

27. For a full discussion of these two campaigns see the author's, "The Reasons for the Success of the Sixth Coalition Against Napoleon in 1813" (MMAS Thesis, US Army Command and General Staff College, 1997), chapters 3 (which deals with Russia in 1812), 4 and 5 passim.

28. Clausewitz, "Two Letters on Strategy," 1-2.

29. Clausewitz, *On War*, 69-70; see also Clausewitz "Two Letters," 2-4.

30. "Two Letters," 21-22.

31. "Two Letters," 38.

32. Two Letters, 24.

33. For example see F.W. von Mellenthin, *Panzer Battles,* trans. H. Betzler (New York: Ballantine Books, 1956), 280.

34. Arthur F. Lykke, "Toward and Understanding of Military Strategy," in *Military Strategy: Theory and Application* (Carlisle Barracks, PA: U.S. Government Printing Office, 1989): for Dr. Strange's method using his own definitions for centers of gravity at tactical, operational and strategic levels using critical capabilities and vulnerabilities see Joe Strange, *Perspectives on Warfighting: Centers of Gravity & Critical Vulnerabilities, Building on the Clausewitzian Foundation So That We Can All Speak the Same Language* 2nd ed.(Quantico, VA: Marine Corps University Foundation, 1996).

35. Here it may be helpful to employ Beyerchen's discussion and posit that Clausewitz was simply searching for a cutting edge term from physics to make his point, rather than creating another concept for an enduring taxonomy, at least for the way the term was first referenced in Book 6.

36. "Two Letters," 37.

Chapter 6
Center of Gravity: Right Idea, Wrong Direction
by Phillip G. Pattee

"For every human problem there is a solution that is simple, neat and wrong."
s -- H.L. Mencken[1]

Many have written with the purpose of aiding would-be students of military strategy in their understanding of Clausewitz's ideas, in fact so many that one wonders if there is anything left to say on the topic. But because there remains a strong debate over the applicability and usefulness of Clausewitz's definitions and ideas, I have undertaken the writing of yet one more paper discussing the Center of Gravity (COG). Just as Clausewitz observed that "wars can have all degrees of importance and intensity, ranging from a war of extermination down to simple armed observation," discussions of controversial topics from his work, such as the COG, can have all forms of utility ranging from brilliantly useful to mystic twaddle.[2] In a recent article, columnist Virginia Postrel argued that education did not have to be for a specific field to be economically useful. Within the article she quotes one of her friend's reflections on his college education. He remembered that his "professors stressed that they weren't there to teach us a soon-to-be obsolete skill or two… but rather the foundations of the field."[3] Similarly, Clausewitz wrote with the idea of educating future commanders, intending to provide them with a guide for their self-education.[4] He sought the durable over the perishable. My goal here is like that, to impart something to a military officer's education for the long term rather than specific training in a rapidly obsolete skill. If I stick to my goal, my hope is that this article will rise above mystic twaddle. The subsequent paragraphs begin with a critique of COG as it is used in the critical factor method currently favored by joint doctrine. By forcing the COG concept to fit the vagaries of ever-changing joint doctrine, the concept has been reduced to an unnecessary adjunct in planning. The article then discusses the role of theory in campaign planning and how COG fits at the strategic level. The COG concept retains its value as an idea that should guide strategic assessment and decision-making in an ambiguous and uncertain environment.

A way to begin is to sort out doctrine from theory. Theory is not a recipe for action; it is a model for understanding. This article addresses theory later. Here is what doctrine says about itself. "Doctrine provides a military organization with a common philosophy, a common language, a common purpose, and a unity of effort."[5] "Joint Doctrine presents fundamental principles that guide the employment of US military forces in coordinated and integrated action toward a common objective. It promotes a common perspective from which to plan, train, and conduct military operations. It represents what is taught, believed, and advocated as what is right (i.e., what works best)."[6]

Joint doctrine standardizes terminology, training, relationships, responsibilities and processes among all US forces to free Joint Force Commanders and their staffs to focus efforts on solving the strategic, operational and tactical problems confronting them.[7] To accomplish this, doctrine writers naturally break the processes they describe into component parts: definitions, steps, functions, etc. By doing so, doctrine presents ideas

113

and tasks in a manner straightforward enough that others can use it to train personnel in a variety of military tasks. The analytical reductionist approach is particularly useful for planning and plans production. It is, however, not without its shortcomings as well. As this article looks at the COG concept, its defects will begin to show. What follows is how COG is currently used in doctrine, and how other analysts have attempted to both modify or clarify its function in doctrine to surmount problems each has encountered in planning,

Currently, joint doctrine defines the COG as "the source of power that provides moral or physical strength, freedom of action, or will to act."[8] This working definition stems from one of Clausewitz's passages on the topic, "One must keep the dominant characteristics of both belligerents in mind. Out of these characteristics a certain center of gravity develops, the hub of all power and movement, on which everything depends. That is the point against which all our energies should be directed."[9] Doctrine pulls from this passage to attribute several characteristics to COGs: that they are linked to objectives, and that they proceed from an adversarial relationship (the relationship between friend and adversary is important, COG is context dependent, and COGs exist for both friend and adversary). A problem presents itself here in that a more literal reading of Clausewitz implies a unitary COG that emerges from the characteristics of both belligerents whereas doctrine stipulates a minimum of two, one friendly and one enemy. Doctrine also claims that COGs exist at each level of war; and because COGs are linked to objectives, a COG may be transitory. When objectives change—as they do with phases of a campaign, and because of actions taken by friend and enemy alike over the course of a campaign—COGs will change as well. Because of all the above, in the end, planners following doctrine must deal with more than two COGs within a single campaign or major operation.

The definition joint doctrine uses today has been greatly influenced by previous critiques of COG and how it was treated by doctrine. The issues that various analysts had with doctrine tended to align with confusion over the abstract nature of COG as a concept and the debate that ensued because of that confusion. The article "Center of Gravity; What Clausewitz Really Meant," by Dr. Joseph L. Strange and Colonel Richard Iron, British Army, has arguably had the most influence on current doctrine. This article takes COG from an abstract idea to something concrete that planners can easily use. This article also introduced *critical factor* analysis by defining terms and a method to arrive at critical capabilities (CC), critical requirements (CR), and critical vulnerabilities (CV), all related to the COG.

Strange and Iron argued that the NATO definition was confusing and that the definition was the root of disagreement on centers of gravity. Because of this confusion, planners wasted hours in "fruitless argument that could be better spent on planning."[10] At the time doctrine postulated that a COG could be an enemy vulnerability, lines of communications and a host of other physical or abstract things. Their reading of Clausewitz left no doubt that COG meant the main strength of an enemy.[11]

Another important point made by the pair was the importance of the COG's adversarial nature. Using J.J. Graham's previous translation of *On War,* Strange and Iron stated, "Clausewitz described centers emerging from the 'overruling relations (Verhaeltnisse) of both parties'; that is, a center of gravity is relevant only in relation to an enemy. It is not an isolated concept."[12] When one compares that to Howard and Paret's more recent, "One must keep the dominant characteristics of both belligerents in mind," Strange and Iron conclude that the adversarial element in the concept of COG is largely missing from the newer translation. The term dominant characteristic, introduced by Paret and Howard, is the origin of the confusion originally present in the NATO definition. Dominant characteristic "implies that a COG can exist in its own right and is a function of 'nation, alliance, military force, or other grouping' taken in isolation. This assumption," contend Strange and Iron, "is obviously wrong. Nothing in war is vital except in the context of the balance between combatants."[13]

The adversarial nature of COG is appealing, but as Strange and Iron use the COG concept it also does not appear to be essential. If one insists that a COG is a strength, which they do, how is it that this is only relative to another party? Is it possible that a COG only need to be capable, or strong enough, to accomplish its objective? In a conflict, the issues and the enemy create a context that one uses to decide on objectives, but there are contexts for military operations in which one might be unopposed. Strange and Iron are correct, context absolutely matters. Would Strange and Iron argue that COG does not apply to humanitarian assistance? Maybe so, but their ideas about CC, CR certainly do apply. When they elaborated on this idea, they said, "A center of gravity exists because of its effect on an enemy or situation (for instance, striking a heavy blow), not because of its inherent capabilities. A center needs certain capabilities as well as characteristics and locations to achieve the effect, but that effect is the starting point, not the capability."[14] Here we see the necessary modification to adversarial relationship introduced: the enemy *or situation.* Are situations adversarial? A military response following a hurricane is a situation. The unit's CCs do matter, as do the CRs. The authors also use this idea for a transition to their discussion of moral centers of gravity. Someone has to will the application of a capability, and for a reason. But this creates another problem too. Do moral COGs have capabilities? Does a moral center produce an effect on an enemy or situation? It seems to me that Strange, Iron, and we will see later other authors, Eikmeier, Rueschhoff, and Dunne acknowledge what Clausewitz had to say about moral COG, but choose to treat moral aspects as a requirement for a COG rather than a potential COG outright.

This quote from Strange and Iron highlights their difficulty discussing moral COG: "A strong-willed population is a source of moral strength and, conversely, a weak-willed one is a critical vulnerability."[15] Now, we know that they are adamant that COGs are strengths, not vulnerabilities and that their opinion was that COGs were adversarial. Yet as they discuss moral COG here, the public will appears that it could be both the strength (i.e. a COG) and a CV depending on the issues. But keep in mind will is a source of strength, it is not the strength. It is probably better to think of will as a CR which may or may not be vulnerable. But it isn't clear that this is how Strange and Iron think of will. At one point, the COG is, as Strange and Iron put it, the one, or ones, with the will—which is a person or the people, i.e. "Saddam Hussein, a strategic moral center, remained undefeated."[16] Later the authors said, "The information operation undermined popular will (another potential strategic center) to fight on his behalf."[17] And again, "How does one identify moral centers of gravity? The process begins and ends with people, for only they can create and sustain moral resistance."[18] Is the COG the people, or popular will? What are the CC and CR of this COG? The moral COG remains a bit murky. To sum up the Strange and Iron position, they state:

> By appealing to the original concept of centers of gravity, one can determine that they are dynamic, positive, active agents (people in formations and groups or individuals), obvious (more for physical than moral centers, depending on the quality of intelligence gathered on an enemy), and powerful and strike effective blows. Physical centers of gravity can be visualized more easily as armies or units, those things that resist an enemy. By contrast, moral centers of gravity are less obvious. Yet it is essential to understand them since they are likely to be more important on the strategic level.[19]

So in the end, Strange and Iron recognize the greater importance of strategic center of gravity, but offer no obvious shortcut to identifying them. How do we avoid useless debate then? They concede that "there is no alternative, short cut, or analytical model to make up for inaccurate assessment of the enemy when deciding on centers of gravity."[20] This is why, in my assessment, that Strange and Iron avoid the strategic level of war to focus on operations. They want to plan and need someone else to accept the risk of identifying the context, central issues, and the grand strategic objectives.

What Strange and Iron propose is a model of nested COGs, something like a zipper. Once you grasp the pull and tug, it comes apart. "The decisive operation, the act that causes the culmination of the enemy, is normally that which brings about the defeat of an enemy's operational or tactical center of gravity in a given campaign or military operation.[21] To bring about a nation's defeat, these lower level, i.e. tactical and operational, COGs must link to other higher operational and strategic COGs. This is not a surprising assertion, planners and strategists have believed in such a causal chain for a long time, the question is what to attack that will bring this about. Their answer is the COG, but identifying the COG became the problem. Strange and Iron postulated that errors in identifying COG came from poor and confusing definitions. They proposed that Clausewitz really meant that a COG was a strength—one must think of it this way to properly weed out other potential targets that would not ultimately effect the COG:

> Whether the defeat of a given center of gravity leads to the quick or inevitable culmination of national resistance depends on the existence of remaining centers of gravity and the potential emergence or creation of new ones—physical or moral. More often, the culmination of national resistance occurs only after the cumulative physical and moral effect produced by defeating or neutralizing a series of physical or moral centers of gravity in multiple campaigns at various levels of wars.
>
> Centers of gravity can exist at all levels of war—tactical, operational, and strategic. But it is misleading to think of a single center of gravity existing at a particular level of war, as if each level is a discrete component rather than a continuum from small unit actions up to grand strategy. Indeed a

center of gravity—both friendly and enemy—will exist for every level of command that's got a combat mission, regardless of whereabouts within the levels of warfare that unit and mission sit.[22]

This sounds reasonable, but similar to the Aleph-null (the smallest infinite cardinal set) this thinking eliminates a host of possibilities only to leave the planner with an impossibly large set of COGs—multiple exist for every level of command. A better mental picture of what they propose might look something like a mountain in the distance. As one gets closer, rock formations are discernible. Closer still the picture becomes increasingly granular and one can make out what looks like boulders, still closer one begins to see that it is actually piles of gravel. The only way to move it is to start shoveling. It no longer matters where one begins. One location is as good as any other.

The idea that a confusing or inadequate definition is the key issue involving the COG has fascinated military thinkers for some years. COL (Ret) Dale Eikmeier has engaged in this debate from as early as 1998 when he wrote, "The Center of Gravity Debate Resolved."[23] In that monograph, he argued that because;

> the debate is the result of a misunderstanding of the concepts, military graduate schools can provide the solution. ... The schools also need to separate the modern definition of center of gravity from Clausewitz. While Clausewitz deserves credit for originating the concept, instruction should stress the current systems-based definition, not Clausewitz's obsolete linear concept. The best way to do this is to change the name of the concept from center of gravity to essential systems. This would create a clean break from Clausewitz's obsolete concept and establish the concept in systems theory. Therefore people looking for understanding of the concept would correctly look to systems theory and not be confused or [misled] by Clausewitz's nineteenth century concept.[24]

Eikmeier's analysis led him to conclude that debate existed because some military intellectuals viewed the center of gravity and systems theory as incompatible. He concluded that incompatibility appeared valid when one used Clausewitz's definition of COG, but by using a modern definition the two concepts, COG and systems theory, were entirely compatible.[25] With the problem pin-pointed as an outdated linear-based definition by a long dead Prussian military thinker, the solution naturally followed; stop using his concept in campaign design, replace it with a modern systems-based concept, debate will cease.[26]

Six years later, the Eikmeier's conception of the problem had morphed somewhat. Joint doctrine still contained the COG concept; it had not been dropped for an analysis of essential systems. Military students apparently used their own experience-based definitions of COG, and like blind men describing an elephant, they consistently arrived at the wrong answer: the will of the people. Eikmeier lamented that "the center of gravity is too important a concept to guess at." To rectify this intolerable problem, students needed a method, which was something that could be created by a simple definition and framework. Eikmeier's advice, "Ignore the joint definition; it only leads to confusion and debate," the ideas of Strange and Iron provided a framework suitable for determining COG[27].

Strange and Iron defined a COG as the "primary sources of moral or physical strength, power, and resistance." A COG is the source of power that creates a force or a critical capability that allows an entity to act or accomplish a task or purpose.[28]

Eikmeier reminded his readers what the Prussian strategist Carl von Clausewitz had to say about the concept and noted that army and joint doctrine diverged from the original intent. He also argued that the definition must be simplified. Among his recommendations was to combine several redundant and confusing terms, such as freedom of action, physical strength, and will to fight—because the latter are prerequisites for freedom of action. He correctly notes that "without 'will' or 'strength,' one cannot act, and the ability to act is a definition of power." Eikmeier's simplified definition of COG then became a "system's source of power to act."[29] This definition therefore included both physical and moral aspects in the COG but obscured this distinction as well. This act was deliberate because his method attacks only capabilities. Moreover, in Eikmeier's 2008 article, "Center of Gravity Analysis," the author argued that there are only two forms of power at the strategic level: military and economic.[30] In a subsequent conversation with Eikmeier, he indicated that he would delete the modification limiting this discussion of power to the strategic level, and he holds that his statement is true at all levels of planning and operations.[31] He went on to say, "We must not be misled by the other so-called elements of power: diplomacy and information (the oft-cited 'will of the people')."[32] He argued that information, by itself, is simply information therefore it is not power. Moreover, his argument equates diplomacy with foreign policy.[33] This essay deals with each of these points next.

Eikmeier judged that diplomacy and information are not elements of power. We know that he believes information has capacity to change behavior because he wrote articles that attempted to persuade the joint force to think and act differently. Do articles provide incentive for behaviors via punishments and rewards? People and nations have reasons for choosing their objectives and methods based on interests and values. Debate is intended to inform. Informed people make choices that differ from those made by misinformed or uniformed people. Eikmeier writes to persuade his readers that his ideas merit their consideration more than other ideas, and that if his methods are adopted efficiency will result. He does not wield the capability to coerce or entice. His capability resides in crafting and delivering an argument. It ends there. The argument, when delivered, allows the readers to modify their behavior to produce a result that both they and Eikmeier want. Eikmeier explains this by stating that the power lies with the individual making the choice, while the information in the article is a tool used to make a choice. Power, as defined by Eikmeier, is the "ability to get someone to behave in a way they otherwise would not do." He amplifies the definition with an example, "If someone freely accepts an idea after studying it, no power was involved. On the other hand, if someone complies with the idea under some incentive or threat, then power was involved."[34] From the foregoing, one can understand that Eikmeier's model uses diplomacy more as a capability and information as a requirement rather than considering diplomatic and informational power as soft power in the manner proposed by scholars such as Joseph Nye.[35]

Clausewitz writes that power of resistance "can be expressed as the product of two inseparable factors, viz. the total means at his disposal and the strength of his will;"[36] means and will—inseparable. In another passage, Clausewitz wrote, "Military activity is never directed against material force alone; it is always aimed simultaneously at the moral forces which give it life, and the two cannot be separated."[37] Or, put another way, material resources and will combine to create capabilities. One directs information more at the will than the resources. Soft power manifests itself by combining the wielder's will with a target's will and the targets resources. What is clear is that when Eikmeier chose to focus on capabilities (or capacity to act), he was concerned mainly with material resources and not will. He preferred hard power to the exclusion of soft power. He sees moral factors and will as at best a critical requirement for the COG. That is why he rejects a moral COG it. He attempted to explain this view with several examples:

> What about "will of the people" or great leaders? Why is Franklin D. Roosevelt, Winston Churchill, Joseph Stalin, or the will of the people not a center of gravity? The answer is simple if one recalls critical capability versus critical requirement. Although these leaders were requirements who enabled the center of gravity to be created or function, none by himself had the inherent ability to defeat Germany and Japan; therefore, none was a center of gravity.[38]

And:

> Consider Chinese resistance to Japanese occupation during WWII. Chinese will was against Japanese occupation. If will to resist was a center of gravity, *it should have had, by itself, the inherent ability* to drive out Japan, but it could not because it did not have that ability. It was not a center of gravity.[39]

Notice that while Eikmeier accepted aspects of the Strange and Iron definition, he simultaneously rejected their notion of what constituted a moral COG. His examples here were fair enough as far as they went: the will alone is not sufficient. When discussing war making capability, however, as Clausewitz observed, the will does not exist by itself. A capability is the will combined with resources; inseparable. An armed force is animate. It is part material and part moral. Both are necessary in some measure, neither by themselves suffices. Neither can resources by themselves have the inherent ability to achieve objectives. I agree with Eikmeier that a system is at work here—both physical and moral aspects of the system are in play. Eikmeier's aim here was to expunge the moral COG and maximize physical COG so he could make a case that to attack capabilities one goes after the physical resources.[40] I don't dispute that there is a strong case for attacking capabilities this way. The destruction of a capability by destroying critical resources temporarily prevents the enemy from acting to achieve a presumed objective, but he adapts, reconstitutes, etc. How do you get an enemy to concede, to change his mind, to bend to your will? In a short passage, Eikmeier argued that the Allies won during WWII because the alliance COG (economic/industrial capability) was too strong for the Axis and produced more stuff.[41] You don't win simply because you have more stuff. Will is what translates stuff into capability. The allies had more stuff before WWII started. So why would Germany and Japan attack? Is it because they misidentified the COG? Is it because they were math-impaired and couldn't assess all the stuff? Or is it perhaps that they misjudged the will of the allies? Will ebbs and wanes in war, its dynamic. This has to be considered.

A few years later, Eikmeier wrote another article addressing COGs. His issue this time was that the COG determination process lacked "clear rules and structure that might rationalize, discipline, and therefore improve campaign planning." Because of the inherent value of the COG as a conceptual tool, he determined this time to rectify the unfortunate situation with a "better process for determining a center of gravity than the current guess-and-debate method." Once again, he identified the definitions as a root of the problem. He proposed, "clear terminology, accepted definitions, and by linking COG analysis to the strategic framework," with these one could then" create rules and structure that permit the creation of art from chaos."[42] Instead of starting with the COG and using critical factor analysis as in the Strange and Iron process, Eikmeier proposed starting first with the ends, ways, and means analysis. Once these had been decided, only then could "critical capabilities (ways), critical requirements (means) be determined. It is the critical capability contained in the ways, and the means that the critical capability requires, that identify a center of gravity."[43] I concede that at the operational level and lower this can work, but at the strategic level there still needs to be debate to determine the ends, the COG identification helps determine the feasible and sound ends that become the basis for operational planning.[44] At the highest levels of strategy, I just do not agree that there is a way to back into the COG determination. Below the strategic level, as this article will later argue, it appears that the COG is not essential to the planning effort. One starts with ends-ways-means analysis and concludes with critical capabilities, critical requirements, and critical vulnerabilities. Why bother with COG determination after that?

Even more recently, Eikmeier proposed again the need to redefine the COG. He mused, "It does not matter what Carl von Clausewitz said about the Center of Gravity (COG) in the 19th century. What matters is how we want to use the COG concept in the 21st century."[45] He went on to state that joint doctrine was a problem because it relied on confusing and outdated definitions—doctrine needed to break from Clausewitz and develop new definitions that could be validated with clarity, logic, precision, and testability. He trashed the joint definition based on his criteria. Following that, he quite successfully tested his latest definition against his criteria. The definition he used is, "the center of gravity is the primary entity that possesses the inherent capability to achieve the objective."[46] I note that in 2004 his definition was, "a systems source of power to act."[47] He did not discuss a test of his old definition, one presumes he did and discarded it because it failed his criteria—hence the need for a new definition. Either that or the nature of war changes so quickly that concepts require new definitions after a few years rather than a century and an half. We also know that Eikmeier's goal has not changed, because the current joint doctrine definition of COG fails his testing criteria it must be replaced with one that does not. "Only then will the endless debate cease and will planners be able to focus on campaign planning assisted by the COG concept rather than being distracted by it."[48]

When discussing validating a COG using his criteria of logic, Eikmeier told the planner to ask, what is my objective? Rather than conducting a rigorous debate to determine suitable and feasible objectives, I suspect Eikmeier's method presumed that one simply looked the objectives up in commander's guidance or a higher authority's previously written order. This would be the case because his recurring theme was to devise a means of avoiding time-wasting debate. This is a recurring meme in all of these COG articles, not just his. If you had any doubt, Eikmeier says so one more time:

> What this method provides is a simple and clear process for the identification and selection of a COG and the ability to differentiate between a true COG and other candidates that are actually critical requirements. This method with its objective rationale contributes to the intent of JP 5-0 by avoiding wasteful and pointless debates.[49]

Sometimes it may be the case, especially at the operational level of war and below that a planner's objectives are clear and provided—once Eikmeier knows the objectives he can readily identify a COG. At the strategic level, where one grapples with the volatility, ambiguity, uncertainty, and complexity of the environment, objectives are not so easily discerned. Hard choices have to be made by leaders with incomplete, often erroneous information [Clausewitz has much to say about this under the topic friction]. Judgment and perspective are called for. Often one of the best ways to derive appropriate objectives is through hours, or days and weeks, of debate. Objectives are important. General George Marshall once said, "If you get the objectives right, a lieutenant can write the strategy."[50] George Marshall did not believe lieutenants needed help writing strategy; they needed help determining the right objectives. What we have in the ongoing debate over the definition of COG is Strange, Iron, and Eikmeier all engaged in providing lieutenants with a specific skill set.

Nevertheless planners still shy away from debate, looking for processes that yield not only the "right" answer, but also produce it quickly. Jan L. Rueschhoff and Jonathan P. Dunne took up this banner again noting that guidance provided by doctrine did not dictate a process whereby one could unambiguously decide on a COG. "Planning teams can take hours—if not days—arguing over what is and is not the enemy's COG. The contest of wills is often decided by whoever is the strongest personality on the planning team, not through any established analytical process."[51] They warn their readers that "without an objective approach to determine a COG, planners are vulnerable to faulty COG analysis." The question the Rueschhoff and Dunne started with then was what process planners should use to select the correct COG?[52]

Their discussion concocted a hypothetical case as the basis for highlighting the flaws with doctrine. At the time of their writing, joint doctrine stipulated that each level of war had only one COG. In the staff's attempt to determine the singular COG, The personnel identified ten CCs believed vital for the enemy to accomplish its mission. When they attempted to find a singular source of power for the CCs they were stymied. After determined analysis, their best candidate COG could only satisfy seven CCs, while another source provided the last three. They asked, "Are there therefore two COGs?"

They concluded, "The answer my very well be yes." Strange, Iron, Eikmeier, and even Carl von Clausewitz would likely agree. Clausewitz deals with just such a problem explicitly in *On War*.[53] The problem as they saw it was that service doctrine permitted multiple COGs while joint doctrine did not. They questioned whether planners should discard the three CCs that could not be linked to the proposed COG as were the remaining seven. The issue was not with the critical factor method, but with a doctrinal highlander clause—there can be only one.

The doctrinal need to identify a single COG only held up plans generation. Consider this, if these ten hypothetical CCs were truly critical, then the destruction of even one would then mean that the enemy could not achieve its objective. It the enemy could still achieve the objective then the capability in question was not actually critical. Their main point was this:

> The objective of COG analysis is not to provide a magic name of a COG by which the commander may speak and slay his foe. The objective is to identify weaknesses the commander may exploit that will uncover and eliminate the foe's ability to resist.[54]

Rueschhoff and Dunne argued that if the staff could identify critical factors leading to CVs, devise an operational plan to exploit them, which then denied an enemy its necessary CRs, thereby debilitating a CC, then the force still attacked an 'unspecified' COG. The time spent looking for the perfect description of an enemy COG was fruitless and better used on the critical factors.[55] What they have eloquently argued is that knowledge of the objectives will get you to CCs then CRs and CVs—one need not even identify a COG and it makes no difference in the planning effort.

Several times, these two authors point out Joint Doctrine's claim that attacking the right COG is the essence of operational art.[56] Based on their article and those previously discussed, however, the COG is not of great importance. Objectives are the key and the capabilities required to achieve those objects are important. From these one gets CC, CR, and CV—there is no need for the concept of COG to govern this process. "Regardless of whatever is named the COG—or even if one is specified at all—with the identified CC, the analyst may begin identifying CRs and CVs."[57]

Rueschhoff and Dunne, like Strange, Iron, and Eikmeier, had done considerable thinking about their topic, and struggled to avoid contradictions. They concluded that just because one might do away with the COG and rely on objectives for critical factor analysis that the need for continued planning and revision did not diminish. With an adversary defeated, as in the end of phase three operations, one could fall into the error of dismissing critical factor analysis in phase four. Nevertheless, as planners used phases to denote a change in objectives, they must keep in mind that a defeated adversary's objectives could also have changed. Moreover, other previously dormant groups might see that enemy's defeat as their time for action.[58] Here is the proverbial Alice-in-Wonderland rabbit hole, as the joint force's objectives changed, its COG potentially changed—by phase, by key operation, by level of war, etc. So the adversary's objectives could also change. And because objectives are often force oriented on an enemy, the COG could change again. In this critical factor method, not only are there COGs for every level of command, but there are also COGs for every objective at every level of command.

There is a meme that runs through each of these articles: If one could just get the definition of COG correct, then identifying the COG becomes simple, analysis becomes straightforward, and the actual "campaign should be a step-by-step process that directly or indirectly attacks these operational centers of gravity."[59] The flaw in this line of effort is that it is overly reductionist, treating war as a mathematical certainty. If one could only reliably identify *the correct* COG—based on a new definition that uses criteria of clarity, logic, precision, and testability—then one could also rapidly design a plan to attack that COG. Once a COG's critical capabilities are neutralized, the enemy must give up on his war aim and the war is nearly won. It works except when the war continues rather than ending. That is not a problem of the method. It is, however, attributable to the shifting nature of the COG. By allowing that the enemy will likely adapt to the new situation, this method avoids complete failure. As war progresses, objectives change, and therefore the COG will shift. Moreover, each author admits that there are COGs at every level of war. As a result, planners are put in a position of finding a correct enemy and friendly COG for possibly several temporary objectives. Moreover, this situation exists for planners at each level of war, thought of as a continuum from the individual foot soldier all the way up to grand strategy. Given that objectives change by campaign phase, friendly COGs will also change.

To summarize, these articles, taken as a whole, the authors agree on several points in what they tell us about COG and its importance to critical factor analysis. The authors also disagree on a few fundamental points. First, each author agrees that COG is important and key to planning. Therefore one must know how to identify what is a COG and determine what is not. Second, because of the systems and objectives involved, multiple COGs exist at every level of war, nested along a continuum. Third, COGs change with time because of changed objective and phasing. The various authors disagree, however, on the method for identifying the COG and its relationship to critical factor analysis.

Strange and Iron postulated that one begins with a mission, or task and uses that to determine a COG. With the COG identified, one analyzes the COG for its CC, then analyzes the CC for CR, and analyzes CR for possible CV. The logic trail looks like this: Mission/COG/CC/CR/CV. The method by which they identified the COG, however, is shrouded with haze. Strange and Iron defined the COG as the "primary components of physical or moral strength, power and resistance."[60] Yet, this definition is void of context. The mission and presumed enemy mission provide the context necessary to make a COG determination. One finds within the Strange and Iron definition of a CC that one determines the CCs by looking for "what the COG can do that puts fear (or concern) into your heart in the context of your mission and level of war."[61] Hence it appears that the key to identifying a COG is that one actually looks first at friendly and enemy missions and then capabilities to achieve, or thwart the given mission, i.e. looks to CC to identify a COG. This produces a true logic trail that flow Mission/CC/COG then back to CC/CR/CV. The COG identification happens in passing, and is unnecessary for the process of analyzing CR and CV.

Eikmeier recognized that Strange and Iron had produced a method of critical factor analysis that lacked a clear method of COG identification. To rectify the deficiency within the Strange and Iron critical factor methodology, Eikmeier proposed modifying the logic trail to Objective/CC/COG/CR/CV. Using the definitions for CC, CR, and CV originated by Strange and Iron, Eikmeier begins with the identified objective (or ends) then determines what ways are necessary to achieve the ends. The most elemental way becomes the CC. The next step is to "list the means required to enable and execute the way or critical capability."[62] This sounds like listing the CR, but Eikmeier does not use that term. The Strange and Iron definition of a CR used by Eikmeier is, "essential conditions, resources, and means for a critical capability to be fully operative."[63] The final step to COG identification is to "select the entity from the list of means that possesses the way or critical capability to achieve the end."[64] The process does in fact facilitate COG identification that is also clear, precise, logical and testable. My conclusion is that Eikmeier instructs going through critical factor analysis from objective/CC/CR then use the analysis that produced CC/CR to identify the COG. What remains for critical factor analysis is to return to the CR and decide upon potential CVs. Just as was the case with Strange and Iron, the COG becomes an unnecessary adjunct to critical factor analysis. This is precisely the point made by Rueschhoff and Dunne. The COG (as defined and conceived in doctrine) exists, but will become targeted simply by following the path objective/CC/CR/CV.

What this means is that the objectives matter most in determining CC, CR, and CV so the COG can remain indeterminate. The COG is nonessential to critical factor analysis. As a practical matter, the definition used for a center of gravity makes no difference because planners can safely skip identifying a COG to no ill effect in critical factor analysis—what the planner finds essential are the objectives, the capabilities, and the requirements (or the ends, ways, and the means). The COGs themselves are many, ranging from the great to the small, are unimportant, and ultimately non-essential. Of what value is the COG concept to operational art if planners identify a score or more (possibly infinite) COGs and even with omitting the step they could arrive at the same operational plan?

An objection to this conclusion is that it represents flawed reasoning. Planners, by omitting COG identification, could also arrive at a different plan. It's as if concluding that a shooter can still pull the trigger with his eyes shut and potentially hit the target, so why bother aiming.[65] The criticism implies that planning is aimless without the COG. This is not the case. A potentially correct plan does not become a random act by omitting COG identification from critical factor analysis. The objectives provide the aim point for the planners, just as they ultimately provide the context that determines COG. Moreover, planners will in many cases propose multiple and distinct plans (known as alternate courses of action) that are each capable of achieving the desired objectives. If the plans relied on different capabilities and resources, in all likelihood the distinct courses of action would involve different COGs.

We have Strange, Iron, Eikmeier, Rueschhofff and Dunne all postulating that planners waste time fruitlessly debating over a definition of COG and how to determine it when planners should be debating what is the COG within the specific context of the problem. That is why they have spent effort to define COG and develop methods to identify them.

They all propose the remedy in fixing the doctrinal definition of COG. Yet, they propose different definitions in their articles—even the same author in subsequent articles proposes a different definition. So, one can safely concluded that they aren't ending debate. By looking for COG at all levels of war, the planner is distracted by mucking about in the always changing, volatile and temporary aspects of planning at the operational and tactical levels instead of focusing on one big and more nearly constant thing. This emphasis on operations and tactical actions dilutes effort rather than provides focus needed to direct the campaign. COG is not necessary for operation and tactical levels of planning, it can be safely skipped to no adverse effect. That is not to say that any of these author's insights are without merit. The critical factor process works. I do, however, contend that a definition of center of gravity is not central to what they are attempting to address. They began with a premise that COG was central to planning and this article demonstrates that it is not. I say this in spite of the fact that their views can all be traced back to passages from *On War*. There is ample evidence in that tome to support their views. Clausewitz devotes book six, "Defense," and book seven, "Attack," to the operational level of war. Without doubt he has much to say about center of gravity in his book on defense. There is still a sense that COG is useful, so prematurely tossing the COG concept from doctrine is not the right approach. Instead, I propose that we look again at theory, as it applies to COG, and several other passages from *On* War—particularly those found in book eight, "War Plans"—to see what light they shed on the concept.

Milan Vego, a professor at the Naval War College and another frequent contributor to strategic discussions, observed that too often military officers are familiar with doctrine while ignorant of theory. He instructed that while sound military theory constituted a significant input to doctrine. "At the same time, a comprehensive knowledge and understanding of military theory should help an officer to appreciate strengths and weakness of military doctrine."[66] What I observe is that few military professionals question the validity of doctrine and instead use doctrine to interpret the validity of military theory, turning theory into a simple recipe for action rather than a basis for understanding. Clausewitz's idea was that "theory should be study, not doctrine."[67] Theory guides officers' education rather than accompany them to the field of battle. An educated mind is one that can see patterns in politics, war, and campaigns; one which views the phenomenon of war holistically. With that perspective, the idea of theory is to develop concepts and principles rather than definitions and processes.

First, let's start with the passage that seems central to doctrine's definitions of COG:

> *Es kommt darauf an, die vorherrschenden Verhältnisse beider Staaten im Auge zu haben. Aus ihnen wird sich ein gewisser Schwerpunkt, ein Zentrum der Kraft und Bewegung bilden, von welchem das Ganze abhängt, und auf diesen Schwerpunkt des Gegners muß der gesammelte Stoß aller Kräfte gerichtet sein.*[68]

How can one translate this? A kind of literal translation might look like this: It comes out of this, that one must have the prevailing conditions of both states in sight. From these emerge some heavy point, a center of strength and motion, on which the whole depends, and against this heavy point of the opponent must the collected shock of all forces be directed.

A translator exercises some latitude in the choice of words. Here is a list of some key German words with some possible English counterparts:

1. *Schwer:* difficult, hard, heavy, grave, serious
2. *Schweren:* heavy
3. *Punkt:* point, dot, spot, item, period, mark
4. *Punkte:* points, spots, items, etc.
5. Possibilities for *Schwerpunkt:* center of gravity, focal point, main focus, main emphasis, serious item
6. *Stoß:* push, shove, thrust, poke, punch, stab
7. *Zentrum:* center, heart, hub
8. *Staaten:* states, countries

So, Paret and Graham have given their translations, here is my option for a plain English translation: Therefore, one must consider the prevailing conditions of both States. From [consideration of] these [conditions], a main focus will emerge, a nexus of strength and motion, on which everything depends. The accumulated thrust of all our power must be directed against this, the opponent's focal point.

This translation deliberately avoided the term center of gravity simply to de-emphasize that as an issue. The main point (*Schwerpunkt* if you will allow), it that the focus is on the 'whatever it is' on which everything depends. Figuring this out will and should entail considerable debate. Another important point (*Schwerpunkt*) is that this consideration involves a strategic assessment; it is about the conditions that exist in and among states. In Paret's and Graham's translations of that passage from *On War,* each used the much more general terms belligerents and parties respectively for the German *Staaten.* The closest German words that I could find for the terms Paret and Graham selected were *Parteien* for parties, and *Kriegführenden* for belligerents. They dropped states from their translation. *Staaten* is a political entity, it translates to nation, state, perhaps province. Their choices for belligerent and parties are understandable when one is attempting to convey the gist of the idea. Nevertheless, this more generic translation—which, with Paret's "hub of power and movement" phrase, is the foundation for past and current doctrinal use of the term COG—has not been challenged. It has led to myriad discussion of COG at operational and tactical levels of war when the passage in dispute is actually dealing with a strategic question.

The goal of a strategic assessment is to determine which conditions prevail among the contending states. Analysis will yield understanding of their important issues, their relative strengths and weaknesses, and important relationships with other states. Others may object that such a process is too vague to guide planners, but I contend that the purpose is not to produce a doctrinal process that facilitates planning. Clausewitz pushed for education and honing a commanders judgment. Clausewitz observed, "Small things always depend on great ones, unimportant on important, accidents on essentials. This must guide our approach."⁶⁹ Within an environment beset with uncertainty and ambiguity, a strategist's search is for the great, the important, the essential. To that end, the Prussian theorist did provide some guidance:

> The first principle is that the ultimate substance of enemy strength must be traced back to the fewest possible sources, and ideally to one alone. The attack on these sources must be compressed into the fewest possible actions—again, ideally, into one. ... The task of reducing the sources of enemy strength to a single center of gravity will depend on....⁷⁰

This idea was important enough that Clausewitz reiterated it:

> The first task, then, in planning for a war is to identify the enemy's centers of gravity, and if possible trace them back to a single one. The second task is to ensure that the forces to be used against that point are concentrated for a main offensive.⁷¹

Note that there is nothing in these passages that contradict the idea the enemy strength is the substance of COG. Neither is there any phrase here that excludes the possibility of multiple COGs at levels below strategic. The emphasis of these passages is, however, to move past tactics and operations to get to the strategic issues. The well-known historian and thinker, Colin Gray articulates this well observing that by determining a COG "a candidate theory of victory in war is identified. Center of gravity is key to strategic thinking because its translation for a particular case...organizes the bridge between means and ends that truly is the realm of strategy."⁷² The point of such analysis is to understand the nature of the motives for war as well as the situations that give rise to them. The reason for this analysis is to enable the statesman and commander to exercise their judgment on their first and most comprehensive strategic question, namely the kind of war on which they are embarking.⁷³

If after having done some strategic analysis, the staff finds that it cannot trace the situation back to a single COG, it will still have bounded the problem set. The staff's next question is why is it that one cannot get to a single COG? Clausewitz anticipated this issue as well and provided some guidance:

> I would, therefore, state it as a principle that if you can vanquish all your enemies by defeating one of them, that defeat must be the main objective in the war. In this one enemy we strike at the center of gravity of the entire conflict.
>
> There are very few cases where this conception is not applicable—where it would not be realistic to reduce several centers of gravity to one. Where this is not so, there is admittedly no alternative but to act as if there were two wars or even more, each with its own object.⁷⁴

Choose a COG based on your dominant characteristics, the enemy's dominant characteristics, and the context in which you find yourself. This will admittedly sometimes imply a choice in the face of legitimate alternatives (ambiguity) where doubt and uncertainty will haunt your decision. Colin Grey stipulates that "application to particular cases is rarely easy, but this simple idea of a centre of gravity is essential, helping a defense community avoid the error of merely being active in war, rather than purposefully active."[75]

Nevertheless, when you have made your choice, you will have a "candidate theory of victory" from which to derive overarching objectives that subordinate planners will use. This outcome is what doctrine now generally conceives as the output of the design process, the conceptual source for guidance used by planners. An example from history is the Allies decision in WWII for Germany first. Defeat of Germany would lead to the defeat of all Axis powers on the European continent. It would not, however, lead to Japan's surrender. Similarly, the defeat of Japan would not produce a victory in Europe. This dilemma did present legitimate alternatives. America essentially treated the situation as if it were involved in two separate wars. The prevailing conditions within the Allied camp led to the decision to go on a strategic offensive against the German foe while remaining on a strategic defensive against Japan.[76]

Debate will help you determine a COG at the strategic level. This in turn is what helps define the objectives of your grand strategy and then the guidance that planners crave so they can get on with their business of filling out power point slides. The right place for the COG concept is at the strategic level. By keeping the COG concept at this level one can avoid the pitfalls associated with becoming overly reductionist, relegating theory to routine doctrinal planning process. If COG is to remain in doctrine, it belongs in design. The design process should ideally produce one [and only one] COG that then determines the overall aims of the conflict. One uses this to develop guidance for the campaign and subordinate objectives that will be met by major operations. Objectives change all the time and planners deal with this—why give them additional steps that have no value? Where the COG can truly help is at the most ambiguous, complex, and uncertain area of war—the strategic level. To the extent that this is possible, this COG remains fixed until the strategic situation is altered in some remarkable way, such as your enemy gaining a new, powerful ally. With the COG relatively inflexible, the ambiguity, complexity and uncertainty are reduced for subordinates and they can focus their efforts on dealing with the volatility that accompanies the operational and tactical aspects of the conflict.

Notes

1. H. L. Mencken, quoted in Donald Rumsfeld, "Rumsfeld's Rules," http://www.rumsfeldsrules.com, (accessed 24 January 2012).

2. Carl von Clausewitz, *On War*, edited and translated by Michael Howard and Peter Paret (Princeton: Princeton University Press, 1976), 81; "Center of Gravity Analysis" http://blog.usni.org/2009/01/09/center-of-gravity-analysis/ accessed 13 December 2010.

3. Virginia Postrel, "How Art History Majors Power the U.S. Economy," *Bloomberg* online at http://www.bloomberg.com/news/print/2012-01-06/postrel-how-art-history-major-power-the-u-s-.html accessed 6 January 2012.

4. Clausewitz, *On War*, 141.

5. Gen George H. Decker in, *Joint Publication 1* (JP 1), *Doctrine for the Armed Forces of the United States*, (Washington DC, The Joint Staff, 2 May 2007, Incorporating Change 1, 20 March 2009), I-1.

6. Joint Staff , *Joint Publication 1, Doctrine for the Armed Forces of the United States* (Washington DC, The Joint Staff, 2 May 2007, Incorporating Change 1 20 March 2009), I-1.

7. JP 1, A-1.

8. Joint Staff, *Joint Publication 5-0* (JP 5-0), *Joint Operation Planning* (Washington DC: Joint Staff, August 11, 2011), III-22.

9. The passage is from Clausewitz, *On War*, 595-96; the passage is explicitly referred to in JP 5-0, III-22.

10. Joseph L. Strange and Richard Iron, "Center of Gravity; What Clausewitz Really Meant," *Joint Forces Quarterly* (2004):24.

11. Strange, "What Clausewitz Really Meant," pg. 24.

12. Strange.

13. Strange, 25.

14. Strange.

15. Strange, 26.

16. Strange.

17. Strange.

18. Strange.

19. Strange, 27.

20. Strange.

21. Joseph L. Strange and Richard Iron, "Understanding Centers of Gravity and Critical Vulnerabilities; Part 2: The CG-CC-CR-CV Construct; A Useful Tool to Understand and Analyze the Relationship between Centers of Gravity and their Critical Vulnerabilities," 2, www.au.af.mil/au/awc/awcgate/usmc/COG2.pdf, (accessed 13 December 2011).

22. Strange, "The CG-CC-CR-CV Construct," 3.

23. Dale Eikmeier, "The Center of Gravity Debate Resolved," (Monograph, School of Advanced Military Studies, 16 December 1998), 40.

24. Eikmeier, "The Center of Gravity Debate Resolved," 40.

25. Eikmeier, 2.

26. Eikmeier, 3.

27. Dale Eikmeier, "Center of Gravity Analysis," *Military Review* (July-August 2004), 2.

28. Eikmeier, "Center of Gravity Analysis," 2.

29. Eikmeier.

30. Eikmeier, 4.

31. Dale Eikmeier to Phillip G. Pattee, conversation 2 May 2012.
32. Eikmeier, "Center of Gravity Analysis," 4.
33. Eikmeier.
34. Eikmeier to Pattee, 2 May 2012.
35. Joseph S. Nye, *Soft Power: The Means to Success in World Politics* (New York: Public Affairs, 2004), x.
36. Clausewitz, *On War,* 77.
37. Clausewitz, *On War,* 137.
38. Eikmeier, "Center of Gravity Analysis," 4.
39. Eikmeier.
40. Eikmeier to Pattee, 2 May 2012.
41. Eikmeier to Pattee.
42. Dale Eikmeier, "A Logical Method for Center-of-Gravity Analysis," *Military Review* (September-October 2007), 62.
43. Eikmeier, "A Logical Method for Center-of-Gravity Analysis," 66.
44. Clausewitz, *On War,* 597.
45. Dale Eikmeier, "Redefining the Center of Gravity," *Joint Forces Quarterly* 59 (2010): 156.
46. Eikmeier, "Redefining the Center of Gravity," 157.
47. Eikmeier, "Center of Gravity Analysis," 2.
48. Eikmeier, "Redefining the Center of Gravity," 157.
49. Eikmeier., 158.
50. George Marshall, quoted in Donald Rumsfeld, "Rumsfeld's Rules," http://www.rumsfeldsrules.com, (accessed January 24, 2012).
51. Jan L. Rueschhoff and Jonathan P. Dunne, "Centers of Gravity from the 'Inside Out,'" *Joint Forces Quarterly* 60 (1st qtr 2011): 120-121.
52. Rueschhoff, "Centers of Gravity from the 'Inside Out,'" 120-121.
53. Clausewitz, *On War,* 623.
54. Rueschhoff, "Centers of Gravity from the 'Inside Out,'" 122.
55. Rueschhoff, 122.
56. Rueschhoff, 122 and 124.
57. Rueschhoff, 122.
58. Rueschhoff, 123
59. Eikmeier, "Center of Gravity Analysis," 4.
60. Strange, "The CG-CC-CR-CV Construct," 7.
61. Strange.
62. Eikmeier, "A Logical Method for Center-of-Gravity Analysis," 64.
63. Eikmeier, 63.
64. Eikmeier, 64.
65. Eikmeier to Pattee, 2 May 2012.
66. Milan Vego, "On Military Theory," *Joint Forces Quarterly* 62 (3rd Qtr 2011): 61.
67. Clausewitz, *On War,* 141.
68. Carl von Clausewitz, *Vom Kriege* (Hamburg: Rowohlt Taschenbuch Verlag, 1963, 15th reprint 2006), 211.
69. Clausewitz, *On War,* 596.
70. Clausewitz, *On War,* 617.
71. Clausewitz, *On War,* 619.
72. Colin Gray, *Modern Strategy* (Oxford: Oxford University Press, 1999), 96.
73. Clausewitz, *On War,* 88-89.

74. Clausewitz, *On War*, 597.
75. Grey, *Modern Strategy*, 96.
76. Clausewitz offers a discussion along these lines for similar decisions taken during his day in *On War*, 597-98.

Chapter 7
Modernizing the Center of Gravity Concept—So It Works
by Colonel (Ret) Dale C. Eikmeier

"Ambiguity, artificial restrictions and contradictions regarding centers of gravity still exist, despite recent progress"
—Dr. Joe Strange and Col Richard Iron[1]

The center of gravity (COG) concept has failed to meet joint doctrine's intent. Much has been written about this failure and this monograph joins the lengthening critique. However, it also offers a practical solution to fix to the center of gravity's, "ambiguity, artificial restrictions and contradictions." The problem isn't the concept. It is doctrine's reliance on a 19th century Clausewitzian foundation which Dr. Alex Ryan, a former School of Advanced Military Studies instructor claims is, "so abstract to be meaningless."[2] This foundation is now crumbling under the weight of modern warfare and systems theory and no amount of scholarly repairs or patches can save it. Therefore it is time to discard Clausewitz's explanation and rebuild the center of gravity concept on a new foundation based on modern military and systems theories. This monograph proposes a modernization that recognizes the realities of 21st century warfare and makes the center of gravity the powerful analytical tool doctrine intends it to be. This paper will explain both the problem and solution in four parts.

Part one outlines the current and modernized center of gravity concepts. It includes a discussion of the current Clausewitzian based concept and its three main flaws: the issues contained in *On War* written by Carl Von Clausewitz,[3] doctrine's ever changing definitions that have not satisfied the military community, and the concept's lack of clarity, logic, precision and testability which renders it useless. The discussion continues with a proposed replacement—the modernized concept. This concept addresses and corrects the flaws by providing new definitions based on logic not metaphors. The discussion also includes an objective identification method and a validation test that makes the center of gravity the useful tool doctrine describes. The discussion concludes with a recommendation to adopt the modernized concept.

Part two answers questions about the modernized concept. These questions are often generated by the Clausewitzian concept; however, they are answered or solved using the modernized concept. Questions include: Is it useful? Does it exist at all levels of war? Is it compatible with modern systems theory? And can there be multiple centers of gravity? The answers will demonstrate the utility of the modernized concept.

Part three highlights the use of the modernized center of gravity and its key role in operational planning. It explains how the modernized concept fits into and compliments current doctrine on operational art and the operational planning process, including discussions on operational design, decisive points and lines of effort.

Part four compares the modernized methodology with center of gravity analysis and identification methods advocated by joint doctrine, and Drs. Strange, Vego, and Echevarria.

The comparison shows that, with the exception of Echevarria's three step method, the modernized method is compatible with joint doctrine, and is a logical extension of Drs Strange and Vego's methods.

Part One: The Current and Modernized Center of Gravity Concepts

Joint doctrine intends for the center of gravity concept to be a useful, "analytical tool to help JFCs [joint force commanders] and staffs analyze friendly and adversary sources of strength as well as weaknesses and vulnerabilities".[4] To achieve this intent, doctrine relied on ideas in Carl von Clausewitz's *On War*.[5] However, since the center of gravity's modern reincarnation in 1986 some military theorists attacked it as nonexistent, unworkable and a myth.[6] Some with justification claim, "The COG is theory and opinion, and it is under-theorized and insufficiently buttressed."[7] Their criticisms are valid and the most common solution proposed by the critics is to discard the center of gravity concept entirely. However, there is another option; modernize the concept so it not only meets doctrine's intent but is applicable in the 21st century.

The Intent of the Center of Gravity Concept

In simple terms the center of gravity concept is about efficiency and it suggests there is some entity that if attacked either directly or indirectly will bring down an adversary. The idea is to attack this 'center of gravity' and avoid wasteful peripheral efforts. It is all about focusing effort to increase the likelihood of success at reasonable cost. Military doctrine, specifically **Joint Publication 5-0** *Joint Operation Planning*, is clear on the concept's purpose and utility:

> One of the most important tasks confronting the JFC's [joint force commander] staff in the operational design process is the identification of friendly and adversary COGs. [centers of gravity].
>
> The COG construct is useful as an analytical tool to help JFCs and staffs analyze friendly and adversary sources of strength as well as weaknesses and vulnerabilities. This process cannot be taken lightly, since a faulty conclusion resulting from a poor or hasty analysis can have very serious consequences, such as the inability to achieve strategic and operational objectives at an acceptable cost.[8]

If doctrine is to meet this intent it must break with Clausewitz and modernize the center of gravity so that it is useful. Only then will the center of gravity become a cornerstone of operational art that doctrine intends.

The Clausewitzian Foundation

Doctrine writers recognizing the potential utility of the center of gravity concept understandably turned to the concept's originator Carl von Clausewitz to provide the intellectual and theoretical base. This established the Clausewitzian foundation. However, overtime shortcoming in this course of action became more apparent and reached the point where some advocated removing the concept from doctrine.[9] The Clausewitzian foundation's problem is that it contains three flaws, a reliance on 19th century military theory, definitions that do not satisfy, and the concept's lack of clarity, logic, precision and testability. Together these three 'strikes' argue for a break from Clausewitz and support the need for modernized concept.

Strike One: Clausewitz and the Center of Confusion

When a concept or theory doesn't work as it should, we often conclude that a flawed understanding or application is at fault. We believe if only we could be more diligent or sophisticated in our understanding and application of the concept, we could successfully apply it. The problem is many of us are so intimidated by the presumed wisdom Clausewitz that we dismiss our own misgivings as fantasies until others experts legitimizes them.[10]

The center of gravity has been the mainstay of the US military thought on "operational art" since 1986.[11] However it has never fully met doctrine's intent because of a reliance on 19th century military theory, weighed down by archaic German, flawed translations and imprecise metaphors.[12] But Clausewitz is not the problem, doctrine is the problem. Doctrine has treated Clausewitz's *On War* as if it was divinely inspired, handed down from Mt. Sinai and the definitive authority on the center of gravity concept. Some suggest the confusion surrounding the center of gravity results from an incorrect understanding of *On War* and the solution is more study. The fact is decades of study and countless articles on the subject have not produced better understanding. More study will only pass the confusion and debates to another generation of military planners. Doctrine needs to discontinue the reliance on Clausewitz's *On War* as the authority on the center of gravity for four reasons that collectively discredit any conclusion based on it.

First. Clausewitz did not write *On War*. His widow, assisted by military colleagues collected his notes and manuscripts after his death and compiled them. They eventually produced 10 volumes of which the first three became *On War*.[13] *On War* is not Clausewitz's magnum opus. It is a third party's interpretation of his notes, manuscripts, and incomplete drafts without the benefit of Clausewitz having reviewed or edited it. At best *On War* is an incomplete first draft forever waiting revision by the author.

Second. Prior to his death Clausewitz wrote a note saying his manuscripts were nothing more than, "a mass of conceptions not brought into form…open to endless misconceptions."[14] His note was a warning that his ideas and theories were incomplete and any attempt to comprehend or draw conclusions from them would be full of errors. It is clear he hadn't finished forming his theories and was not ready to stand behind them as authoritative. If Clausewitz was not willing to stand behind the work credited to him why should doctrine?

Third. Clausewitz was trying to explain 19th century European social-political theory and the phenomena of war –the ultimate social-political contest to military officers whose formal education was generally in engineering, not the social sciences. So he resorted to mechanical metaphors that successfully conveyed the social-political concepts to Prussian officers grounded in engineering.[15] The metaphors, while imperfect as all metaphors are, worked for 19th century military officers. The problem today is many military officers now have soft sciences backgrounds and mechanical metaphors confuse rather than clarify as they did in Clausewitz's time.[16] If a metaphor has to be explained then the use of a metaphor is inappropriate to begin with.

Another problem with the center of gravity metaphor is that Clausewitz never used the term "center of gravity", or in German, "Gravitationspunkt", he used the word schwerpunkt, which means weight of focus or point of effort which is different from center of gravity, hubs or sources of power.[17] But it is easy to understand how an engineer when picturing this point of effort could think of a center of gravity. Milan Vigo in Joint Operational Warfare Theory and Practice provides a detailed analysis of the evolution of schwerpunkt from focus of effort to center of gravity which is summarized below:[18]

1. Schwerpunkt – main weight or focus or one's efforts.

2. Mid 19th century, Schwerpunkt is associated with an enemy's capital as the point of focus. Germans and Austrians used the word Schwerpunktlinie to mean line of main weight or effort that links one's base of operations to the enemy's capital. This is the Schwerpunkt is 'the target' understanding.

3. Late 19th century it comes to mean a section of the front where the bulk of one's forces would be employed to reach a decision. Schwerpunkt is no longer the target is is the 'arrow'. This is a subtle shift from the point of focus at the target, to what is being focused, the arrow. This 'arrow' understanding is reflected in plans of Count Alfred von Schlieffen and the German military theory and practice up to WW II.

4. Schwerpunkt is mistranslated into English as "center of gravity" in Colonel J.J. Graham's 1874 English language translation of On War.[19]

5. Post World War I Schwerpunkt is progressively used to mean the focus of planning efforts. This is a natural evolution of the late 19th century hybrid of 'the arrow', and the 'target' understandings.

6. The Bundeswehr (German Army) now uses the English term "center of gravity" while the Austrian Army uses the German term "Gravitationspunkt" which translates to "center of gravity". Hence, Clausewitz's use of the term "Schwerpunkt" or focus of effort, 'the target', was mistranslated into center of gravity, 'the arrow' which became a source of power, but not focus of effort.

So the concept of the center of gravity or Schwerpunkt evolved from focus of effort which became the enemy's capital, to a location on the battle field where the forces were most concentrated, to a planning effort focus, to a hub or source of power. This continuing evolution is clear evidence of a 'conception not brought into form.' The fact that the concept has changed several times since the publication of On War and has been adapted to fit different environments is sufficient reason challenge On War's authority on the subject.

Fourth. Clauswitzian scholar Dr. Christopher Bassford describes the problems associated with any translation, especially those dealing with theoretical concepts:

> Any translation from one language to another necessarily involves interpretation not only of the language but of the conceptual content. Even the most honest and competent translation inevitably includes both technical errors and arguable or controversial—if not flatly wrong—conceptual interpretations. And not all translators are honest and/or competent. Further, even editors working in the original language have been known to take liberties with the writer's original words, sometimes because the writer (like most authors) genuinely needed editorial assistance. Other editorial interventions are prompted by political fear or ambition, conceptual confusion, or contrary conviction (of either a technical or ideological nature). Changes in the native version obviously can be reflected in translations. All of these factors have certainly had an impact on the translation of Clausewitz, so which edition you get can be important.[20]

To illustrate Dr. Bassford's point the phrase, "the hub of all power and movement" that is closely associated with the current definition is actually the invention of translators Michael Howard and Peter Paret, not Clausewitz.[21] There are many other instances in their translation *On War* where grievous errors were made and were never corrected, e.g. *Meldungen* are translated as intelligence instead of "reports"; *Kriegschauplatz* is translated as theater of operations (a term Clausewitz never used but Jomini did) instead the correct translation "theater of war."[22] Another example of how translations change context and meaning is when Colonel J.J. Graham's 1874 English translation is compared to Michael Howard and Peter Paret's 1976 translation. Graham says, "…this center generally lies in the capital." While Howard and Paret say, "the center of gravity is generally the capital.…" 'Lies in' and 'is generally the capital' have very different meanings.[23]

In addition to translating and editing problems there is the simple problem of correctly understanding 200 year old context and usage. Understanding Clausewitz's German is challenging even for modern native speaking German scholars such as Dennis Prange of the Munich Foundation who explained even correct literal translations contain errors in meaning and context.[24] For example early 19th century German officers would have understood Schwerpunkt as the target while early 20th century German officers saw it as the arrow because usage, not meaning, evolved over time.

Because of these factors the meaning of the center of gravity has become confused. If this were a trial there would be sufficient evidence to create reasonable doubt as to *On War*'s authority on the center of gravity concept. A jury would have to find *On War* not creditable, 'strike one'. So rather than continuing a 'holy grail' quest for understanding in *On War* we should build our own grail based on the imperatives of the 21st century warfare.

Strike Two: Changing COG Definitions

The US Army introduced the concept of the center of gravity in its 1986 version of FM 100-5 *Operations* which marked the rebirth of operational art. FM 100-5 stated,

"The center of gravity of an armed force refers to those sources of strength or balance. It is that characteristic, capability, or locality from which the force derives its freedom of action, physical strength, or will to fight. Clausewitz defined it as 'the hub of all power and movement, on which everything depends.'"[25]

Note that the definition assumes the adversary system is an armed force which is not the COG itself. However, the force's sources of strength or balance can be COGs. This source could be a characteristic, (adverb or adjective) a capability (verb), or a location (noun), but the definition does not explain what kind of characteristics. A reasonable conclusion is that anything an armed force requires is a potential source of strength. So planners could declare any requirement the center of gravity. The question then became which requirement or 'source' was the center of gravity. This question and the inability to distinguish a COG from other sources of power did nothing to focus planning efforts and contributed to lengthy discussions and debates. The only positive effect of this definition was to suggest attacking a force through its requirements or vulnerabilities.

In 1993 the Army revised the definition and declared, "The center of gravity is the hub of all power and movement upon which everything depends. It is that characteristic, capability, or location from which enemy and friendly forces derive their freedom of action, physical strength, or will to fight."[26] The definition's use of the phrase "hub of all power and movement upon which everything depends" closely links it to Howard-Paret's version of Clausewitz's *On War*. The change was significant; planners were no longer just looking for sources of strength. They were looking for the 'hub', usually single, upon which the force depended on. The COG was no longer just an important requirement or source of power, the COG was some central hub and critically important source on which everything depended. Planners would actually debate whether or not you could have multiple hubs which illustrate the danger in using metaphors. Planners were justly criticized for looking for "hubs" that in many cases did not exist due to dispersed networked systems. In later definitions the 'hub' metaphor was removed although it remained in expanded discussions.

In 1996, Dr. Joe Strange, of the US Marine War College offered his own definition. "Primary sources of moral or physical strength, power and resistance."[27] This shorter, simpler definition was a step in the right direction in that it addressed the two issues with the previous Army definitions. It limited the sources of strength to the 'primary', although the definition of primary was left open. Nevertheless it did constrain the COG candidate list which enabled greater focus. He also left out the 'hub' metaphor which system theorists argued overly constrained the list.[28]

When joint doctrine adopted the concept in 1994, JP 1-02 defined it as, "Those characteristics, capabilities, or localities from which a military force derives its freedom of action, physical strength, or will to fight."[29] A slight change in 2002, defined the COG as, "… those characteristics, capabilities, or sources of power from which a military force derives its freedom of action, physical strength, or will to fight.[30]" These definitions still limited the system to military forces, but using sound reasoning most planners were able to expand the definition to other entities. Since both definitions were based on the Army's 1986 definition they suffered the same flaws. Basically the COG could be anything as long as you deemed it important to 'freedom of action'. Planners would then pick their favored sources and proceed to argue why theirs was the better COG. It they could not agree on a single COG often they would list all the candidates as COGs which did little to focus efforts.

In 2006 joint doctrine changed the definition to, "The source of power that provides moral or physical strength, freedom of action, or will to act."[31] This definition was retained in 2011. The definition's 'source of power' implies one COG rather than multiple. It does recognize that systems other than military forces can have or be COGs which is an improvement. It leaves out hubs, characteristics, capabilities, and locations which simplifies the definition. But the definition does not significantly contribute to greater understanding or the ability to focus planning efforts.

NATO adopted the center of gravity concept and following US doctrine defined it in Allied Joint Doctrine AJP-01(D) as, "Characteristics, capabilities, or localities from which a nation, an alliance, a military force or other grouping derives its freedom of action, physical strength, or will to fight."[32]

The conclusion is that while joint doctrine is clear on the role of the COG in operational art and planning we just don't know exactly what it is or how to determine it. Fortunately we can fix this. Since we understand doctrine's intent and purpose, we can redesign and redefine the center of gravity so it becomes the useful analytical tool doctrine intended it to be.

Strike Three: A Lack of Clarity, Logic, Precision and Testability

While some question the existence or relevance of the center of gravity concept, the fact that it is a doctrinal mainstay in many militaries is sufficient evidence of acceptance and relevance of the concept's intent, if not the definition.[33] Therefore few people debate JP 5-0's description of the COG's value to operational art and planning processes, so the concept itself is not the issue. The issue is the definition. No other term in military circles generates so much debate.[34] This debate alone is sufficient evidence that doctrine puts planners in the position of not understanding a concept or how to use it, but agreeing that it is has tremendous value. Doctrine can remedy this situation by changing the definition of the center of gravity and its related critical factors.

Because the current COG definition lacks precision, it generates debate and confusion and leads some, such as Dr. Ryan to claim the COG concept is, "…so abstract to be meaningless".[35] This abstraction leads to unnecessary debates and distractions from critical planning tasks. A useful center of gravity definition must be clear, based on logic, precise, and lead to answers that can be objectively validated and does not rely on metaphors. Because the current definition lacks these qualities, doctrine should replace it. Otherwise the lack of clarity, precision, logic, and testability and a reliance on metaphors will continue to prevent the concept from meeting its intent.

The solution is a definition that meets the intent of JP 5-0 and not a slavish devotion to Clausewitz's *On War*. To fulfill doctrine's intent I propose that any revised definition should meet the following criteria:

1. Clarity – It explicitly states what the center of gravity is in simple terms.

2. Based on Logic – Contains rules that allow for a valid inference.

3. Precision – Is narrowly focused to exclude the extraneous.

4. Testable – It can be objectively tested using rules and logic.

Below is a test of the current JP 5-0 definition, ("The source of power that provides moral or physical strength, freedom of action, or will to act.") against the criteria of clarity, logic, precision and testability.[36]

Clarity. Does the definition tell us if the COG is only the source of power or is it the power? Is each source of power a center of gravity and if so can there be multiples? If there are multiples, which center of gravity should planners focus on? What characteristics distinguish a COG from any other source of strength? Does something with the will to act but not the freedom or strength have a center of gravity? If the definition raises questions rather than answering them it isn't clear. If you have to debate the answers the definition isn't clear. If you lack certainty as to what is and isn't a center of gravity, it is not clear. The joint definition fails the clarity test.

Logic. Definitional clarity is impossible to achieve without logic. A good definition provides principles and criteria on which a valid inference can be made. For example, a cat is a mammal because it meets the criteria in the definition of a mammal. Because the joint definition lacks logic and criteria it uses vague examples and a set of nebulous characteristics that obfuscate rather than clarify. For example, JP 5-0 lists 12 characteristics, but they are neither required nor exclusive characteristics. So these characteristics are suggestions rather than rules and therefore have marginal utility for making a logical inference. According to the definition a COG has the capability to provide morale or physical strength, freedom of action, or will to act. Must the COG provide all four? Are any of the four superior to the others? What is the difference between moral strength and will to act? Are they the same? Is freedom of action just an effect of morale and physical strength? There is simply no logic here, just words.

Precision. Clarity and logic allow for precision which is necessary for identifying a COG and turning it into the analytical tool doctrine intended. However, because there is no clarity or logic, precision is impossible to achieve. So in place of precision joint doctrine offers examples:

> At the strategic level, a COG could be a military force, an alliance, political or military leaders, a set of critical capabilities or functions, or national will. At the operational level a COG often is associated with the adversary's military capabilities—such as a powerful element of the armed forces—but could include other capabilities in the operational environment.[37]

These examples suggest the COG is a set of capabilities, which some argue are verbs, However, the definition says it's a source of power, which some argue would be a noun. So between the definition and the example there is potential for confusion. The example also suggests that the strategic level COG can be just about anything but the operational level COG is usually a military capability, but still could be anything which is not very precise. To achieve precision one must include and exclude things based on logical criteria. However, the joint definition attempts to achieve precision by providing examples to illustrate what is neither clear or logical. Not being able to logically exclude the extraneous, the examples attempt to cover all of the bases, just in case something might be left out. These examples even include the catch-all phrases such as, "…a set of critical capabilities or functions" and "…but could include other capabilities in the operational environment."[38] In other words just about anything can be a COG. This attempt to include rather than exclude obscures the COG and handicaps planners' ability to focus their plans. In lieu of criteria JP 5-0 lists the following 12 characteristics that can be associated with a COG:

Exists at each level of war.

    5. Mostly physical at operational and tactical levels.

    6. Is a source of leverage.

    7. Allows or enhances freedom of action.

    8. May be where the enemy's force is most densely concentrated.

    9. Can endanger one's own COGs.

    10. May be transitory in nature.

    11. Linked to the objective(s).

    12. Often intangible in limited contingency operations.

    13. Can shift over time or between Phases.

    14. Often depends on factors of time and space.

    15. Contains many intangible elements at strategic level.[39]

Notice the use of the qualifying words; may, can, often, and mostly. These are not definitive and leave latitude which contributes a lack of precision in the definition. This is not to say the 'art of war' requires precision, it does not. However, when dealing with terminology and definitions precision is desired.

Testable. Since the current definition lacks clarity, logic, and precision it is impossible to validate or test a COG selection. Doctrine says to test a COG selection by postulating that if a COG candidate is neutralized the adversary will have to change his course of action or objective.[40] This test only determines if something is critical, not if it is the COG. If everything that is critical can be validated as a COG, the concept loses meaning and its ability to focus planners. This is why planners eventually grow frustrated with what JP 5-0 says is a useful analytical tool.[41]

Since the current definition fails the clarity, logic, precision and testable criteria, military planners lack the necessary understanding needed to identify centers of gravity and meet doctrine's intent. Doctrine should replace the definition with one that does. Only then will planners be able to focus on operational planning assisted by the center of gravity concept rather than being distracted by it.

Proposed Modernization

By addressing the flaws in the Clausewitzian foundation the proposal modernizes the center of gravity concept making it relevant for 21st century conflict while meeting the doctrinal intent. The proposal has three parts. First is a new set of definitions that draw on systems theory rather than Clausewitz. The second is an easy to use center of gravity identification method based on objectivity and logic. Last is an identification validation method. This modernization, if adopted will finally make the center of gravity concept the useful analytical tool doctrine first envisioned it to be.

Redefining the Center of Gravity

Joint doctrine is clear on the concept's purpose and utility. What doctrine needs are new definitions of the center of gravity and its critical factors. The criteria of clarity, logic, precision and testability will guide the definitions. Additionally the definitions should not only stand up to modern military theory but be based on them. New definitions would then allow for improved center of gravity identification and validation methods based on logic and objectivity. The modernized definition is; *The Center of Gravity is the primary entity that inherently possesses the critical capabilities to achieve the objective.*[42]

Clarity. This definition is a simple declarative statement of what a COG is. It is the primary entity that achieves the objective. Unlike the joint definition, it is not a list of characteristics or descriptions separated by commas. The words used in the proposed definition have limited meaning, unlike the phrase "a source of power" which can have several meanings. Clarity is achieved which then allows for logic.

Logic. This definition has two criteria when met lead to a valid inference. First, the COG is the primary entity, the key word being *primary*. Secondly it has the capability to achieve the specified objective or purpose. The logic is: *A (primary entity) + B (capability to achieve the objective) = COG*. Using these simple criteria one can infer what is and what is not a COG. Note that the capability must be directly linked to attaining the objective. This linkage provides purpose to action and supports doctrine which correctly states that, "An objective is always linked to a COG."[43] The COG is the primary possessor of the capability that achieves the objective. It isn't a source of power; it is the possessor and wielder of that power.

The logic is further illustrated by asking three questions. What is the objective? How can it be achieved (the required capability)? What has the capability to do it? The answer to the last question is the center of gravity. This logic then excludes other contenders allowing for greater precision.

Precision. Clarity and logic provide precision. Use of the word "primary" excludes the secondary, supporting or extraneous. If something is secondary or supporting, even if essential, it is a requirement, not a COG. This distinction allows planners to focus on the COG and its relationships with other elements. The COG is the primary doer, it has the inherent capability required to achieve the objective. If an entity does not have that capability, it is not a COG and the system needs to find or create a COG with the requisite capability.

Testable. The logic in the definition provides for the Supported and Supporting validation test. The real COG is supported, it is the doer. Other candidates are supporting. The COG is inherently capable of achieving the purpose or objective and executes the primary action(s) that achieves it. It uses or consumes supporting resources to accomplish it. If something is used or consumed to execute the primary action it is a requirement. If it contributes to, but does not actually perform the action, it serves a supporting function and is a requirement. It is not a center of gravity.

In this definition there are no 'moral' COGs' only physical COGs. Removing moral COGs contributes to clarity by reducing abstractness. Intangibles, such as moral strength, public opinion, or a righteous cause are not COGs because they have no inherent capability for action. They can be requirements. A tangible physical agent must perform the action. This is an important distinction and highlights a key difference between the proposed and current definitions. The intent of the proposed definition is to limit COGs to tangible agents that have a physical existence. The reason is simple; we can more easily target things for defense or attack that physically exist. For example, an idea is intangible; however it resides in tangibles such as a mind, a book, or other type of physical media that is targetable. Morale resides in individuals and organizations; it does not exist in a targetable sense on its own. However, an individual or organization can be a target of attacks designed to affect morale. Here is another way of looking at this issue. Police do not target speeding, although they say they do, because speeding is intangible. They target speeders –people exceeding the speed limit. You may think you are promoting or attacking moral power but in reality you are targeting individuals or organizations motivated by that moral power. This brings us to critical factors.

So how are intangibles such as 'moral COGs' accounted for? They can be critical factors—targets for indirect attacks. Critical factors are critical capabilities, requirements and vulnerabilities of a COG.[44] An intangible such as popular support is at best a critical requirement for some physical entity such as a government or an army to perform some action that achieves a goal. However, like the COG definition, doctrine needs to revise the definitions of, critical capabilities, critical requirements and critical vulnerabilities associated with the center of gravity concept.

Manual JP 5-0 says that planners should analyze COGs within a framework of three critical factors –critical capabilities, critical requirements, and critical vulnerabilities.[45] In 1996 Dr Joe Strange created and defined the idea of critical factors:

1. "Critical Capability: Primary abilities which merits a Center of Gravity to be identified as such in the context of a given scenario, situation or mission.

2. Critical Requirements: Essential conditions, resources and means for a critical capability to be fully operative.

3. Critical Vulnerabilities: Critical requirements or components thereof which are deficient or vulnerable to neutralization, interdiction or attack in a manner achieving decisive results."[46]

These factors and their definitions were a tremendous step forward in COG analysis because they created a logical hierarchy that helped separate the true COG, the doer, from other contenders which may only be requirements. Critical factors also linked systems theory to the COG concept. The COG was no longer a single mass or point. It was part of a system with connections to capabilities and requirements. Additionally these factors provided planners insights on how to attack or defend a COG by showing what a COG does, what is needed and what is vulnerable. However, for reasons unknown, joint doctrine significantly changed Dr. Strange's definition of critical capability. Two versions of the joint definition of critical capabilities, from JP 5-0 Aug 2011:

1. "Critical Capability - a means that is considered a crucial enabler for a COG to function as such, and is essential to the accomplishment of the specified or assumed objective(s)."

2. "Critical Capabilities are those that are considered crucial enablers for a COG to function as such, and are essential to the accomplishment of the adversary's assumed objective." [47]

Dr. Strange, in his definition, refers to abilities which are verbs. The first joint definition refers to means and enablers which can be thought of as verbs or nouns. The second definition replaces "means" with "those" which refers back to capabilities which are generally expressed as verbs. This ambiguity between abilities or things confuses rather that clarifies. If one believes that means and enablers are things (nouns), then the first joint definition could be synonymous with Dr. Strange's definition of critical requirements. One solution is to accept Dr. Strange's wording for critical capability which emphasizes *Primary Abilities* which cannot be confused with nouns and returns the focus to actions that accomplish the objective. However, an advantage of the joint definition is the phrase, "essential to the accomplishment of the adversary's assumed objective." This clearly links the COG's purpose and capability to achieving the objective and supports the proposed center of gravity definition. If we combine elements from Dr. Strange and the joint definition clarity and logic can replace ambiguity and confusion. The proposed definition of critical capabilities is, "primary abilities essential to the accomplishment of the objective which merits a Center of Gravity to be identified as such." This revised definition of critical capabilities reinforces the idea that the COG is the primary agent or "doer" that possesses the ability to achieve the objective. It also links the critical capabilities to a purpose–achieving the objective. This contributes to logic and precision.

Both Dr. Strange's and the joint definition of critical requirements, "Essential conditions, resources and means for a critical capability to be fully operative" are acceptable.[48]

However, one can improve them by shifting the focus to the COG rather than the capability. Both definitions link critical requirements to capabilities which are verbs. However, since the COG possesses the critical capability, it is clearer to directly link the requirement to the COG. For example the capability of running does not require shoes, but a runner does. The question should be what does the COG require to perform the critical capability, not what does the capability require. This may seem like a small point but it keeps the focus on the tangible agent, the COG, which is targetable and the focus of planning efforts. The proposed definition of critical requirements is, "essential conditions, resources and means the COG requires to perform the critical capability."

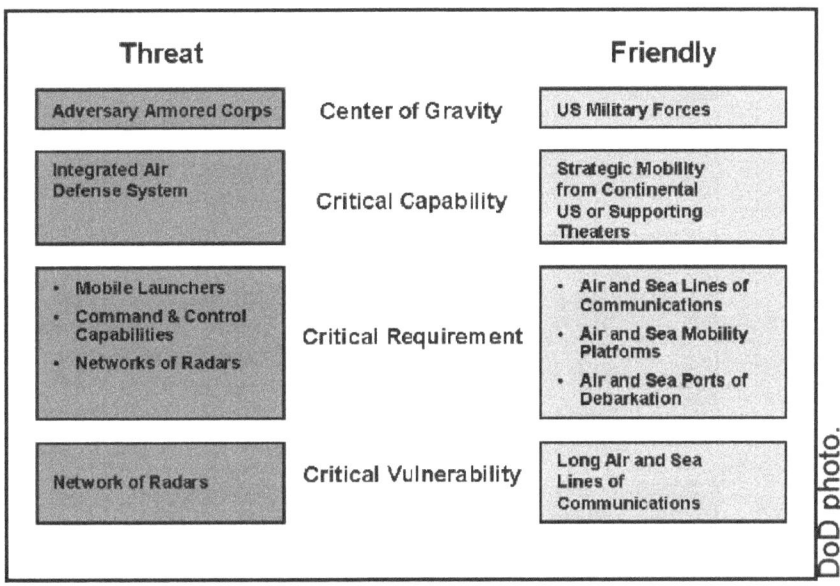

Figure 5. Center of Gravity Analysis Example.

Flawed definitions of the COG and critical factors result in flawed COG identification and analysis. Figure five from JP 5-0 illustrates poor reasoning and flawed center of gravity analysis that results from the current doctrinal definitions of center of gravity, and critical capabilities. No adversary objective or end state is given so one has to assume the identification of the adversary armored corps as the COG is correct. The critical capability, integrated air defense system, is not a capability at all; it is a thing which is perhaps a requirement. Provide air defense is a capability. Since one does not know the mission of the armored corps there is no way of knowing if air defense is a capability critical to achieving the objective. The critical requirements listed are requirements of an air defense system, not the COG. The radars may be vulnerable but the relationship to the COG is not clear so their relevancy to the COG is unknown. The example contains no logic, because the definitions lack logic. The result is an illustration in a doctrinal publication that contributes nothing positive and reinforces poor reasoning. Figure six illustrates an improved COG analysis based on the modernized definitions.

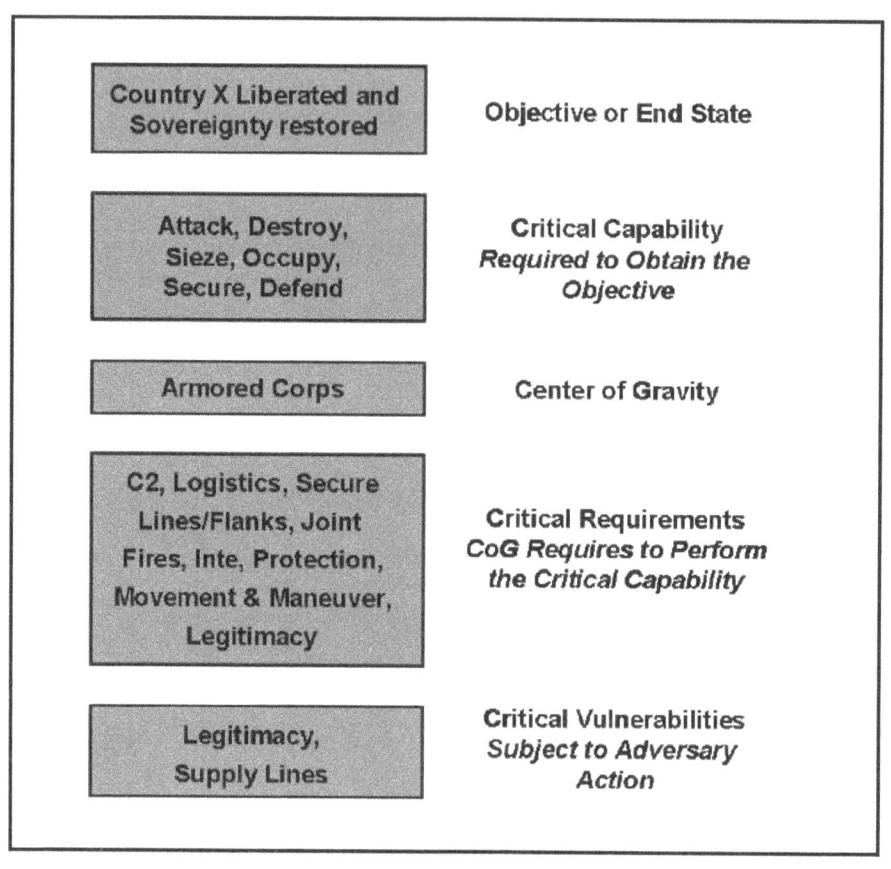

Figure 6. Revised Center of Gravity Analysis.

The modernized definitions resolve many of the valid criticisms currently associated with the doctrinal concept and definitions. Criticisms include; incompatibility with modern systems theory, a failure to account for dynamic environments, imprecise metaphors, and that COGs simply do not exist in the modern environment. The proposal is not only compatible with systems theory; it relies on it to provide understanding of the system. Since the proposed definition links the COG to objectives, capabilities and available means, it allows for changing COGs in dynamic environments where ends, ways and means constantly change. It does not rely on confusing and inaccurate metaphors that produce endless discussions on what is a source of power or a hub. Lastly, in the revised definition the COG is a tangible and targetable agent that performs an action and can be shown to exist. These characteristics are the new foundation for a modernized center of gravity concept. Fixing the definitions of the center of gravity, critical capabilities and critical requirements is the first step towards achieving the intent of JP 5-0. The second is a practical center of gravity identification method.

Identification of the Center of Gravity

Doctrine offers no practical method to identify the COG. It does suggest using a 'Systems of Systems' (SyoSy) approach combined with a nodal analysis to determine where the adversary derives its freedom of action or strength.[49] This analysis then allows analysts to, "visualize each COG's role/function relative to each of the various systems and subsystems."[50] In simple terms joint doctrine's COG identification process is; first understand the system through SyoSy analysis then "visualize" where the system derives its strength. Given the doctrinal COG definition's lack of precision and logic, "visualizing" isn't far from guessing but it may be the best doctrine can offer.

The SyoSy method is a tremendous tool to understand the environment and the adversary. It is also a necessary component for COG identification because it provides the data on a system's actors (nodes), relationships (links), functions, and tendencies/tensions required to identify a COG. However, as a stand-alone method for COG identification, it comes up short.[51] What is needed is a practical and easy to use method that builds on the understanding provided by SyoSy analysis but replaces the highly subjective "visualization" method.

Recognize that the best way to determine a center of gravity involves a systems perspective because without it, COG identification is just guesswork. However, the SyoSy covers a lot of ground, and it is easy to get lost in a system's networked forest of nodes and links and lose sight of what the target is. Arthur F. Lykke's strategic framework of ends, ways and means applied to a system offers a simple solution.[52] The framework's three simple questions; what is the system's desired end-state, how can it be achieved, and what resources are required—are the essential elements of systems thinking in support of COG identification and analysis. This is how it works. There are six steps, four to identify the COG and two for critical and vulnerable requirements. Using the environmental and situational information provided by the Joint Intelligence Preparation of the Operational Environment's (JIPOE) or other SyoSy analysis, do the following:

1. Identify the organization's desired ends or objectives.

2. Identify possible 'ways' or actions that can achieve the desired ends. Select the way(s) that analysis suggests the organization is most likely to use. Remember 'ways' are actions and should be expressed as verbs. Then select the most elemental or essential action(s)—that selection is/are the critical capability (ies). Ways = critical capabilities.

3. List the organization's means or resources available or needed to execute the critical capability. (In systems theory these are actors or nodes.)

4. Select the entity (tangible agent) from the list of means that inherently possess the critical capability. This is the center of gravity. It is the doer of the action that achieves the ends. (In systems theory this is the key actor or node.)

5. From the remaining means select those that are critical for execution of the critical capability. These are the critical requirements. (In systems theory these show links between the actors or nodes.)

6. Complete the process by identifying those critical requirements that are vulnerable to adversary actions.

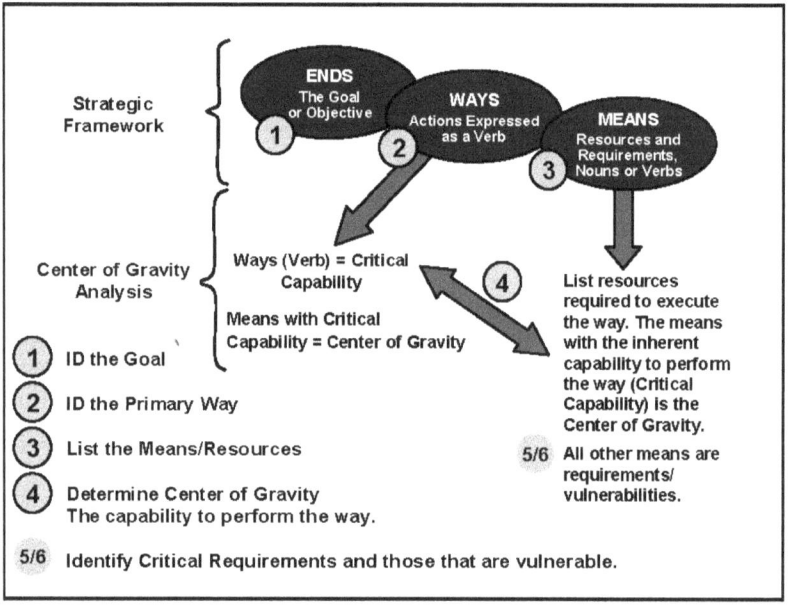

Figure 7. Center of Gravity Identification and Analysis.

Figure 7 illustrates the steps of the Ends, Way and Means method of Center of Gravity identification. This method provides a simple and clear process for COG identification and the ability to differentiate between a COG and other candidates that are actually critical requirements. This method with its objective rationale contributes to the intent of JP 5-0 by providing planners a focus point whose selection they can logically justify.

Validity Test: Supported/Supporting

Due to handicaps with the doctrinal definitions and identification methodology, validating a COG selection is very imprecise. To test a COG, joint doctrine recommends using a war game to determine if the defeat, destruction or weakening of the COG candidate causes the adversary to change courses of action or objectives.[53] If it changes, according to doctrine you validated the COG selection. However, what this actually validates is that the candidate is merely a critical node in the system. Logically if everything considered critical can be a COG there will be a plethora of COGs which brings into question the utility of the concept. Doctrine needs to replace the current war game validation system with one that not only tells us what is critical but what the COG is. The 'supported and supporting' test meets this criterion.

The 'supported and supporting' test verifies the center of gravity selection and distinguishes it from critical requirements and vulnerabilities by asking two questions. First, does the candidate perform the primary action (critical capability) that achieves the objective? Or is it supporting, used or consumed in the execution of the action? If the candidate is the 'doer' or supported and performs the primary action it is the COG. If it is used or consumed by another entity to execute the primary action it is a 'supporting' requirement. Entities that contribute to, but do not actually perform, the critical capability are requirements, not centers of gravity, no matter how critical their contribution. For example Winston Churchill, regardless of how critical and inspirational to the British people during World War II, was not the center of gravity because he could not defeat Nazi Germany. He was not the 'doer' or supported entity. The Allied military force was the 'doer' or supported entity that possessed the critical capability to defeat Nazi Germany. Winston Churchill was needed to create, lead and motivate an Allied force thus he was a 'supporting' critical requirement.

Here is an example of center of gravity identification, analysis and validation using SyoSy and the Ends, Way and Means method. Our subject system is a railroad. Intelligence analysts using a systems perspective and analysis reveals that the railroad company's objective is to make a profit (step1). They also provide a systems analysis of the railroad complete with a network analysis diagram that shows the actor/node relationship linkages and functions.

Analysts determine that the way to make a profit is *to move* freight from point A to point B (step 2). To move is the verb or critical capability. The list of means and resources (nodes) required include: tracks, fuel, freight, cars, operators, a support staff, locomotives, command and control systems and a financial management system (step 3). From the list of means analysts determine which has the inherent capability to move freight. They conclude that the locomotive had the inherent capability 'to move' and identify it as the COG. They then validate their selection (step 4) using the supported and supporting test.

The subjects of the 'supported and supporting' questions are derived from the systems analysis diagram or they contribute to building the diagram. Means or resources become the actors/nodes which have a function and relationship with other nodes in the system. The idea is to determine which nodes do the work and which nodes contribute. The working nodes posses the critical capability and the contributing nodes are the critical requirements. The fundamental questions to ask are who or what performs the critical capability (to move) and who or what contributes to that capability? For example:

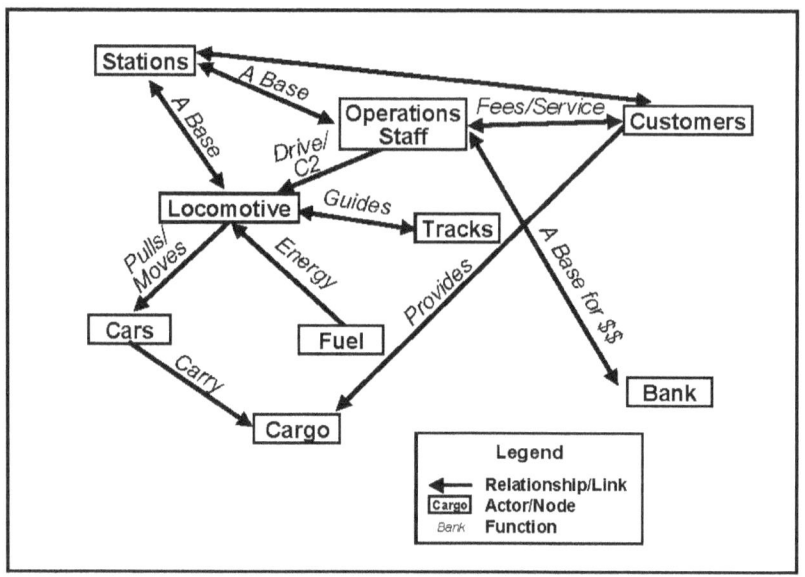

Figure 8. Systems Analysis, Netwrok Analysis Diagram.

Tracks do nothing by themselves other than support and guide the train. They are used by the train. Fuel does not move anything it is used or consumed by the locomotive. Cars are used by the locomotive to move freight. The cars only hold freight. Operators and staff are critical but do not have the inherent capability to move freight. Clients pay freight charges and are a motivating force but they don't move their own freight. The locomotive is the doer and is supported; it has the inherent capability to move. However, it cannot do so without the other means. Therefore the other means are identified as 'supporting' critical requirements that the center of gravity requires to function.

Some will argue that the locomotive it isn't the COG because in fact the railroad has seeral locomotives and they are dispersed in a network. Since there is no single locomotive or hub of locomotive power there is no center of gravity. Their argument is that COGs do not exist in networked systems. This argument is the result of Clausewitzian based center of gravity definitions and is a reason to redefine the center of gravity. The proposed definition allows COGs to exist dispersed across networked systems. The COG does not have to be concentrated or be a 'hub' and can exist dispersed across a system. The modernized COG concept allows planners to see and understand a system, determine what actions and agents accomplish the objectives and the critical relationships between the primary agent and other actors/nodes in the system. The concept does not say attack a COG directly; an indirect attack through critical vulnerabilities is an option. The concept does allow planners to analyze a system, identify key nodes, understand the relationships and identify critical points that they can attack or defend.

Having validated a COG selection, analysts determine critical requirements and what components of those are vulnerable (steps 5&6). Based on their ability to affect the critical vulnerabilities and the COG, planners determine which is more efficient, attacking the COG directly or attacking indirectly through critical vulnerabilities. Having identified a center of gravity and its relationship to other elements, campaign planners have a better understanding of how the system works and what and how to attack or protect.

Joint doctrine is clear on the concept's purpose and utility. The proposed set of definitions based on clarity, logic, precision and testability, combined with the logical ends, ways and means identification method and the validation test provides campaign planners a real analytical tool that fulfills doctrine's intent and works in the 21st century operating environment. The recommendation is, adopt the modernized concept.

Modernized Concept

The center of gravity concept has always generated questions for discussion and debate. Is it useful? Is it compatible with systems theory? Can there be multiple centers of gravity? Do they exist at each level of war? Can the center of gravity change and if so how? Many theorists have attempted to answer these and other questions,but the Clausewitzian based answers never seemed to satisfy. The following is a discussion of these questions based on the modernized concept and hopefully provides more satisfying answers.

Is the Center of Gravity Useful?

Some argue that the Center of Gravity concept is only an academic construct that has little practical utility in the 'real planning world'. Joint doctrine disagrees and clearly states it. "This process cannot be taken lightly, since a faulty conclusion resulting from a poor or hasty analysis can have very serious consequences, such as the inability to achieve strategic and operational objectives at an acceptable cost."[54] I agree with doctrine having participated in and witnessing firsthand the utility of the COG concept and the impact of COG determination on a campaign plan. In March 2005 the Multinational Forces – Iraq (MNF-I) staff was conducting a 'campaign plan review'. I was serving as a strategic planner in the headquarters' Strategy Plans and Assessment Division (SPA), As part of the review I conducted a COG identification and analysis using the ends, ways and means method while my counterpart in the Campaign Plans section used the more traditional and doctrinal method. I concluded that the population was the COG or 'doer' that would decide the outcome of the insurgency. My counterpart determined that the Iraqi government was the COG as it was the 'source of power'. Both proposals were briefed to Major General Steven Sergeant, Chief of SPA and Colonel Bill Hix, Chief of Strategy and the two of them agreed with my 'population' designation but decided to present both to the MNF-I Commander for a decision. The Commander after hearing the merits of both proposals decided to keep the Iraqi government as the MNF-I Campaign center of gravity and focus of effort.

A year later the Samarra Mosque attack in February 2006 marked the outbreak of increased insurgent and sectarian violence at levels yet unseen in the war.[55] Despite Iraqi and Coalition efforts to stem the violence it continued with civilian casualties peaking at a new high in July 2006.[56] This suggested that the MNF-I's campaign strategy was failing and we were losing the war.[57] In response to the deteriorating situation a 'New Way Forward' was announced in January 2007 and General David Petraeus took command and brought a new population centric counter-insurgency strategy. The success of this approach was born out in 'the awakening' movement which saw significant elements of the population turn against the insurgents resulting in Coalition and Iraqi security forces rolling back the insurgency.

My conclusion was that getting the center of gravity right makes a huge difference. The Iraqi government center of gravity strategy failed while the later population center of gravity succeeded in focusing the coalition's efforts where they had the greatest impact. So is the center of gravity useful? If based on sound reasoning and logic the answer is yes.

Is the Modernized Center of Gravity Compatible with Political and Systems Theory?

A colleague offered the following argument why COGs do not exist. "The COG is theory and opinion, and it is under-theorized and insufficiently buttressed. ... There's nothing like it in all of political science, international relations, and the practice of war and politics such that all agree."[58] Just because something is "under-theorized" or lacks complete agreement does not mean it does not exist. It only means it is not understood, perhaps due to under-theorization. Given the center of gravity's history, and current definition it is easy to see why understanding and agreement is lacking. However, a lack of understanding is an argument for dropping the Clausewitzian foundation and contributing to the "theorizing" and "buttressing" of the concept with a new course of action. It is not an argument for declaring the concept dead; rather it is an argument to fix the concept.

The center of gravity is a military planning concept, not a political science concept. It has existed in some form in military literature since the publication of *On War*, and in US military doctrine since 1986. Operational level plans since Operation Just Cause have included it.[59] An assertion that civilian political leaders, national security experts at the strategic level, political science professors and international relations experts do not use or cite the concept is not evidence of nonexistence. It only suggests that they do not read or use military doctrine in their domains.

Another argument for non-existence is systems theory. Networked systems proponents argue that there is no 'hub of power'. They claim organizations disperse capabilities and requirements across a net- work to reduce vulnerabilities. The very idea of a network is to eliminate or reduce single points of failure (hubs or centers of gravity). Some will argue that dispersed, networked organizations do not 'mass' or come together and form a hub and therefore there is no center of gravity. For example a School of Advanced Military Studies (SAMS) graduate stated that insurgencies do not have centers of gravity because insurgents do not mass.[60] Dr. Ryan a SAMS faculty member said in the context of a Clausewitzian definition that, "In a complex system, there may be no "center". Control and cohesion can be distributed. Then, identifying a COG attacks the system at the wrong scale, like a boxer swinging at a swarm of bees."[61] These arguments have merit if one clings to the mechanical metaphor of a hub or center. However if one is open to non-Clausewitzian models such as the proposed definition, *The Center of Gravity is the primary entity that possesses the inherent capability to achieve the objective*, then the arguments are moot. The primary determinant of the COG's existence should be the ends, way and means construct, not the organization's structure.

The fact is the current doctrinal concept is well grounded in systems theory. JP 5-0 and JP 2-01.3 both discuss systems perspectives and a system of systems approach to identifying and analyzing COGs. The idea of a center of gravity and its critical factors are nothing more than different terms for what systems' theorist Peter M. Senge calls, "high leverages of change".[62] However, doctrine could further strengthen the concept's linkage to systems thinking by deleting the Clausewitzian based phrases such as "sources of strength" and replacing it with terms like "systems". For example JP 5-0 could then say, "The COG construct is useful as an analytical tool to help JFCs [joint force commanders] and staffs analyze friendly and adversary *systems* for weaknesses and vulnerabilities."[63]

The modernized concept is not only compatible with systems theory, it also supports systems thinking. The definitions, the ends, ways and means identification method and the validation process together produce an understanding of a system's purpose, key nodes and critical linkages. It not only describes a system, it identifies critical factors that suggest 'points of leverage.'

For example, malaria is a decentralized system of networked parasites, vectors (mosquitoes), hosts and numerous environmental requirements. Its objective is propagation; the way is to reproduce in humans. There is no single parasite, vector or host to act as a source or hub of power, they are dispersed yet connected. These connections are critical requirements some of which are vulnerable. A mosquito net breaks the connection between a potential host and the vector. Changing the mosquito's environmental requirements breaks the connection between the parasite and the potential host. Understanding the malarial system and focusing on the mosquito as a COG with requirements and vulnerabilities provided insights on how to combat malaria despite it being a complex networked system.

Can There Be Multiple COGs?

The question always arises; can there be more than one COG? Doctrine acknowledges that multiple COGs can exist but recommends focusing on one. The proposed definition and identification method allows for multiple COGs if a system chooses multiple but distinctly different approaches to achieve its objective. There can be a COG for each approach. For example a nation confronting a crisis may choose to pursue both diplomatic solutions and military solutions. In this case there would be a diplomatic COG and a clearly separate military COG. The key is that the capabilities be sufficiently unique as to require different skill sets.

For example, at an operational level an insurgency generally has two COGs. There is the political COG that attempts to exploit then meet the population's needs or grievances. The other COG is the militant element that attempts to secure the population's support, while attempting to counter the adversary's COGs. These dual COGs (carrots and sticks) are why most insurgencies have both political wings and military wings. Think of the civil COG as a shovel to fill the population's pot hole of grievances and the militant COG is the guard that breaks the other guy's shovel while protecting his own. Since insurgences have two distinct approaches they have two distinct COGs that co-exist at the same time. What determines the number of COGs is the number of distinct capabilities required to achieve the objective. This also applies to multiple but distinct objectives.

Are There Centers of Gravity At Every Level of War?

The issue isn't whether or not COGs exist at each level of war. They do. COGs exist everywhere there is a system that has an objective, whether it is a nation or plant or something as small as a parasite. The real question is, is there utility in the center of gravity concept at all levels of war.[64] The answer is no. Generally, the simpler the problem or system, the more obvious the answer is and a COG study is not needed. For example a weed has a COG but you don't spend time analyzing its systems and requirements, you just pull or poison it – the direct approach. Malaria on the other hand is a complex system and a center of gravity identification and analysis of sorts was useful in the identification of the mosquito as a COG and standing water as a critical requirement that was vulnerable to abatement action – the indirect approach to attacking malaria. It is all a matter of system complexity, the greater the complexity the greater the utility in the concept. Because of the complexity-simplicity issue the Army says the concept is not relevant at the tactical level.[65] It isn't saying COGs do not exist at the tactical level, just that they are not useful.

The strategic and operational levels of war deal with "what" type questions. What is the adversary or friendly aims or objectives? What options are available? What resources are available or needed? What can obtain the objective? What is deficient? What must be protected or attacked? Answering these questions is the essence of strategic and operational level planning. The utility of the center of gravity is that it provides insights into answering these 'what' questions. Tactical levels deal less with 'what' questions and more with 'how' questions and therefore the center of gravity concept has less relevance.[66]

Can COGs Change in Dynamic Environments?

Clausewitzian based COGs can change, but it isn't clear how or why because there is no connection to purpose or logic. It seems the ability to change was an effect of the planner's flexibility rather than anything inherent in the concept. This led some to argue that the COG was not dynamic and could not accommodate rapid changes in the modern environment. Many cited the shift from conventional to insurgency operations during Operation Iraqi Freedom as the COG concept's failure to change in a dynamic environment or a failure for the concept to include a feedback mechanism. However, traditionalists would argue that in fact the COG could and did change especially as ends, ways or means changed. The problem was planners were not clever enough to see this environmental change. The proposed concept with its built in logic avoids this debate altogether and assists planners in seeing change by providing three areas or indicators of change – a feedback mechanism.

By tying the COG to objectives, capabilities and requirements rather than sources of power or hubs, the COG becomes more sensitive to environmental changes. This makes the concept more flexible and useful in dynamic environments. The proposed definition's three components; objective, capability and possessor of the capability – ends, ways and means- not only help identify a COG, they are indicators of changes in the environment. Planners identify changes in the environment by asking has the objective, ways or means changed. An advantage of the method is that it also provides clues on how to favorably change the environment by affecting critical vulnerabilities, requirements and COGs.

Ends, ways and means are interconnected: a change in one affects change in the others. Monitoring these changes provides the feedback necessary to adapt to a changing environment. In conflict the idea is to force an adversary to change their objective, normally by affecting a COG's critical capabilities. Change is induced by directly attacking the COG or indirectly by attacking critical requirements. The goal is to protect your objectives and COGs by guarding your means while forcing changes on the adversary that he can't adapt to.

In the context of military plans any change of end state or capabilities required during a phase, a major operation or a campaign can change the COG. Typically during phased operations there is an end state and a COG or main effort and supporting effort for each phase. When a phase changes due to attainment of the previous phase's end state the COG may change due to the capabilities required to attain the new phase's end state. The same also applies to major operations and campaigns.

What is a Better Relationship: Adversary or Objective?

Understanding the correct relationship between the COG, the objective and the adversary is critical to sound COG understanding and identification. Unfortunately the relationship is misunderstood.

Current doctrine and those relying on Clausewitz focus the relationship on the adversary while giving the objective little consideration. Joint doctrine claims COGs, "are formed out of the relationship between adversaries, and they do not exist in a strategic or operational vacuum."[67] In other words COGs only exist if there is an adversary. Dr Strange and Colonel Iron, relying on Clausewitz, also support the adversarial context saying, "…a center of gravity is relevant only in the relation to an enemy. It is not an isolated concept."[68] Use of the word "relevant" implies existence but no utility. However, they go on to say the COG is "not an isolated concept" suggesting it cannot exist outside the adversarial context. Following this logic, if a system has an objective, strength and means to achieve it, but no opposition, it does not have a COG or 'doer'. Doctrine suggests the adversary, based on his capabilities, is the determinant of the other's center of gravity. This ignores the role of the objective in COG identification.

This is not to say that the adversarial context does not have a role in center of gravity analysis. It can. If an adversary is present, and in most cases it is, then it is part of the environment and must be factored in. The adversary is one determinate of the capabilities required to achieve the objective. However, it is not an essential element for a COG to exist. On the other hand an objective or purpose for a system is essential. It must be present and the COG does not exist without it. For example if my objective is to be at work on time, I need a capability to get there. The means I chose with that capability is my car. It is my COG and I did not need an adversary to determine that.

This adversarial context potentially creates confusion by putting the primary emphasis on adversarial capabilities and not on attaining the system's objective. Another flaw is that emphasis on the adversarial relationship reinforces symmetrical thinking and mirror imaging which can be a detriment in the current environment. This is not to say there is no relationship to the adversary, there is, but only that it is insufficiently explained in doctrine and that it is a subordinate relationship to the COG-Objective relationship.

The objective and adversary are two sides of the same coin, but the COG identification process begins on the objective, not the adversary side. Adding the objective to the relationship and reducing the adversary to a secondary relationship make more sense. The adversary is relevant in selecting the ways to achieve the objective and the determination of one's vulnerabilities. But the objective remains the center of gravity's 'reason d'etre.' This is why Dr. Milan Vego of the Naval War College argues that the objective, not the adversary is the prime determinate of the center of gravity and this relationship is superior. Dr. Vego states, "It is the military objective that provides the larger framework within which the respective center of gravity is determined."[69] The end, ways and means COG identification methodology is such a framework. He goes on to state, "One should always bear in mind that it is the objective and the situation that determine a center of gravity, not the other way around."[70] In COG identification the objective is most critical and the adversary is a secondary factor because attaining the objective is the prime purpose.

Is the 'Ends, Ways, Means' Methodology Too Scientific For Operational Art?

Some argue that the rules or logic of the ends, ways and means methodology constrain 'creative' thinking by producing black and white answers in what is a grey world. Critics claim the methodology produces objective answers leaving little room for subjectivity; it is just too scientific or Cartesian for operational art. But the evidence discussed suggests the current 'art' and highly subjective 'visualization' method isn't satisfactory. Rules or 'science' is the foundation of art and art without science to serve as guidelines is a jumble of elements without form or purpose. While the current center of gravity has purpose, it lacks form, hence the concept's requirement for a more 'scientific' approach. The ends, ways, and means methodology purposely leads to more objective or 'scientific' answers which provides form to the concept and better focuses the application of operational art.

In the 'Arts' composition is synonymous with 'rules' or the science of art. Operational art has its elements of 'composition' of which the center of gravity is one. In panting the elements of composition are rules or guidelines regarding shape, perspective and color. The same is true in sculpture, music and writing, they all have their science. These rules or constraints on creativity are what separate the creativity of successful painter from the creativity of a three year old scribbling with crayons. Science is answering what "is". Art is the application of the "how to". Identifying the center of gravity is science in support of art. How to use the center of gravity is the art. The purpose of the ends, ways, and means methodology is to help produce more successful operational artists and decrease the number of 'three year olds' scribbling operational level plans.

Summary

Because of its basis in logic and clear definitions rather than metaphors, the modernized center of gravity concept should generate fewer questions and more answers. This improved situation should contribute to reasoned thought which in turn should enable strategists to focus their plans aided by the concept rather than being distracted by it.

Part Three: Using the Modernized Center of Gravity Concept

The following section discusses the role of the center of gravity in operational planning. Specific topics include, operational art, operational design, the operational approach and selected elements of operational design including decisive points, lines of operation and effort and direct-indirect approaches.

When FM 100-5 reintroduced the center of gravity concept it claimed it was the "essence of operational art"[71] Today a claim can be made that 'operational design' is now the essence of operational art.[72] Nevertheless, the center of gravity concept is still the powerful analytical tool doctrine describes. It now has an expanded role in the application of operational art, operational design and the expression of an operational approach. Therefore the issue isn't operational design versus the center of gravity. One just needs to understand where and how the center of gravity fits in operational art, operational design and the operational approach.

Center of Gravity's Role in Operational Art

Operational art is an umbrella term for a cognitive process used by commanders assisted by the staff to "describe how the joint force will employ its capabilities to achieve the military end state."[73] Operational design is joint doctrine's methodology to conduct and apply critical thinking and reasoning necessary for the application of operational art. It is the practical, 'how to' of operational art. Operational design helps commanders by providing a method to reduce the uncertainty of complex environments, provide understanding of the nature of the problem and enables them to construct an approach to solving the problem and achieving the end state. The end result of a commander's use of operational art assisted by operational design is an operational approach which is a broad description of the actions forces must take to achieve the desired end state.[74] The operational approach is the commander's initial intent and planning guidance to the staff that begins the detailed planning process. In simple terms operational art (conceptual planning) uses operational design, a method to produce an operational approach.

The center of gravity is the link that enables the commander to connect his situational understanding derived from operational design to the practical, 'what are we going to do about it' in the operational approach. While operational design assists in the identification of the problem, the center of gravity concept provides insights into how to remove the problem. Together, the problem identification and how to remove it are the essence of the operational approach.

Center of Gravity and Operational Design.

Operational design has three components; understanding the environment, defining the problem and producing an operational approach. Commanders and planners can analyze each component using a series of four basic questions. The answers to these questions provide understanding, identify the problem(s) and point the way to an approach to solving the problem. The four questions listed here are the essence of operational design.[75]

1. "What is going on in the environment?" This question prompts planners to capture the history, culture, current state, and future goals of relevant actors in the environment. This is part one of understanding the environment.

2. "What do we want the environment to look like?" This is part two and prompts planners to review higher level intents and missions and posit a desired future state of the environment. Knowing how the current environment operates by using a systems perspective and how we want the environment to be provides understanding of the environment and the information needed to answer the third question.

3. "What is the problem(s) that is preventing movement from the current state to the desired end state?" The answer to this question tells planners what the problem(s) is and where -conceptually- they should act to achieve the desired state? Problems can be thought of as obstacles or adversaries that stand in the way of achieving the end state. <u>The problem(s) is not the center of gravity; rather it defines the adversary and sets up the center of gravity identification and analysis process of that adversary system.</u> Planners and analysts using a systems perspective study the adversary/problem's system to determine its COG.

4. "How do we get from the current state to our desired state?" This prompts planners to envision what combinations of actions address the problem(s) through its COG(s) and related critical factors and help achieve the desired end state.

Center of Gravity and the Operational Approach.[76]

Once commanders and planners agree on the problem they need a way to address it. The operational approach is the broad outline and provides the commander's guidance on general actions usually expressed as missions or tasks that will produce the conditions that define the desired end state. Think of it as what needs to be done, not how to do it.

The operational approach is a conceptualization that starts by asking what action will solve or manage the problem/adversary. The center of gravity and critical factors analysis of the adversary will suggest requirements and vulnerabilities that offer possible solutions or courses of action. This analysis feeds the details that shape the commander's guidance and intent.

As with the other components of operational art there are no prescribed formats. However, joint doctrine suggests that the operational approach should include a concise description of the environment, a clear statement on what the problem or problem set is, an approach to resolve the problem and lastly any other specific guidance.[77] Developing an operational approach requires a continuous dialogue between the commander and the staff starting at the initiation of planning and continuing through mission analysis. It also requires data and analysis from the staff that includes termination, end state and centers of gravity.

A technique for developing an operational approach is to:

1. Identify the problem or problems set and then view it as an adversary system.

2. Determine the system's center of gravity (COG).

3. Identify the COG's critical requirements then critical vulnerabilities.

4. Create lines of operation or effort based on the critical requirements and critical vulnerabilities

5. These lines of operation or effort can become actions, missions or tasks.

Center of Gravity and Decisive Points.

Decisive points are typically- "a geographic place, specific key event, [center of gravity's] critical factor, or function that, when acted upon, allows a commander to gain a marked advantage over an adversary or contributes materially to achieving success."[78] For planners decisive points suggest the when, where and what actions to take. These points then become effects, objectives or tasks for subordinates.

(NATO doctrine uses the term "decisive conditions."[79] For most planning purposes the terms are synonymous.)

Keep in mind that a decisive point provides a 'marked advantage' or conversely for the adversary a marked disadvantage. An advantage is a step towards the objective or end state. While many things can be considered decisive points the challenge is to select those points that can be realistically addressed and from them to select the most critical or productive. This is where center of gravity analysis with its critical factors (critical requirements and critical vulnerabilities) becomes a useful tool in the identification of critical or productive decisive points.

The center of gravity analysis is a tool planners use to determine potential decisive points. Planners study centers of gravity, critical and vulnerable requirements to determine if they suggest or are potential decisive points. These decisive points are then arranged along lines of operation or effort. The logic is that denying an adversary's critical requirement weakens his COG thus providing you, and denying him a marked advantage. Conversely successfully defending your own critical requirements can be decisive points. It is important to note that decisive points are not limited to COG analysis and can include other events or functions. However in planning, especially during conceptual planning, COG analysis and listing critical requirements and critical vulnerabilities can serve as a start point for determining decisive points.

Center of Gravity and Lines of Operation (LOO) and Lines of Effort (LOE).

Lines of operation or effort are physical or conceptual paths that a force must take to reach its objective or end state. They lay out and arrange in a logical sequence actions, tasks, requirements or decisive points that create effects that in turn achieve the objective. They also serve to orient the force in terms of time, space and purpose in relation to the objective or adversary.[80] Commanders use combinations of lines of operation and effort as tools to visualize actions and sequences required to achieve the operations' end state or objective and to articulate their operational approach.

Lines of operation are geographic in nature and show paths from a base to an objective location. Physical geography combined with force capabilities, requirements and diplomatic or political factors determine the options for lines of operation. Lines of operation connect a series of decisive points, often based on critical requirements or vulnerabilities that lead to control of a geographic objective. Critical requirements that are geographical in nature such as lodgments, bases of operations and route infrastructure often determine a line of operation.

Lines of effort (LOE) are conceptual and link related actions to purpose and effect when geographical reference is not relevant. Lines of effort link decisive points with the logic of purpose. Determining lines of effort requires sound analysis and the ability to see how potentially-decisive events throughout the campaign or operation link together. The center of gravity analysis of critical requirements and vulnerabilities is a useful tool for determining areas of logic or purpose. For example critical requirements for command and control and logistics can become lines of effort to attack or protect. When determining and portraying LOEs, the staff should follow these steps:

1. Understand and portray the critical initial conditions in the environment.

2. Understand and portray the desired environmental conditions and the timing of achieving those conditions.

3. Understand and portray the objectives (phased over time as needed) to achieve the desired conditions.

4. Array decisive events (actions, functions, requirements, vulnerabilities etc) for adversary and friendly efforts.

5. Examine the decisive points and group them into unifying patterns.

6. Collect and organize the patterns into lines of effort that run throughout the operations or campaign.[81]

Graphics and or narratives are used to depict these lines of operation and effort and convey the logic and sequence of actions. Lines of operation are typically displayed on a map or schematic while lines of effort use a chart or matrix. Regardless of form, the aim is to assist commanders and planners to visualize the operation from start to finish and to enable them to construct a concept of operations or operational approach that will be used to develop courses of action. Figure 9 is an example of lines of effort chart using the COG analysis, critical requirements and critical vulnerabilities as a framework.

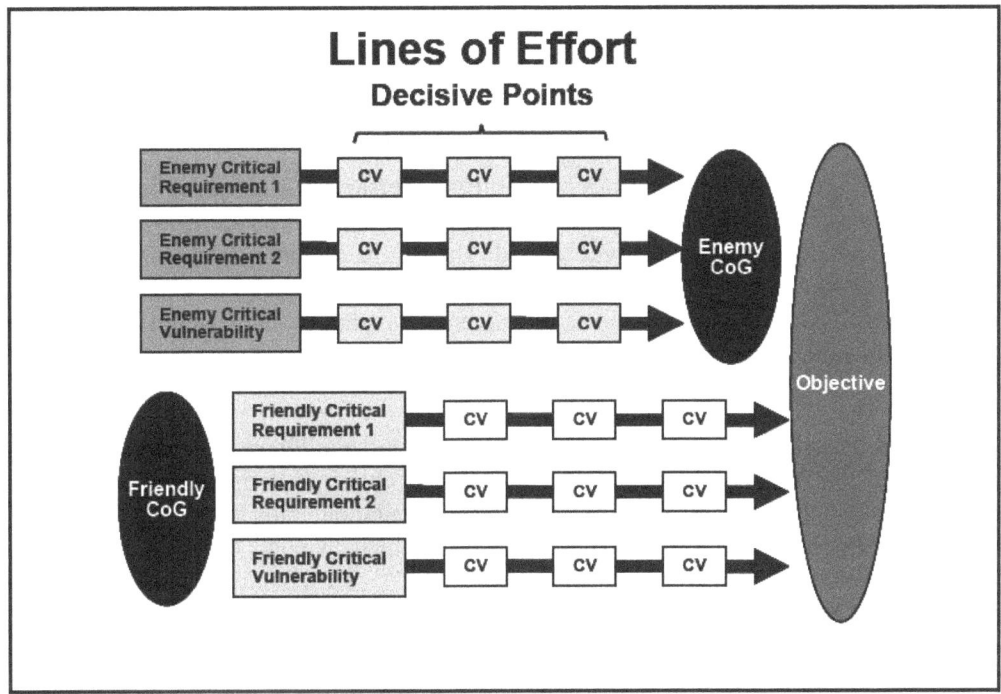

Figure 9. Lines of Effort.

Center of Gravity in Direct or Indirect Approachs.

There are two options for attacking a COG, directly or indirectly. In a direct approach one attacks the COG directly seeking to defeat it. This approach may have the advantage of being less time consuming and is appropriate when a force has overwhelming superiority over its adversary and risk is low. An indirect approach seeks to exploit an adversary's vulnerabilities while avoiding it strengths. It is an attack on a COG's critical requirements or vulnerabilities. This approach denies the COG the means it requires to perform a critical capability. With this approach a COG may still physically exist, but is unable to attain its objective. An indirect approach is appropriate when a force lacks the strength to attack a COG directly or is otherwise constrained from doing so.

Part Four: Comparison of Other Center of Gravity Identification Methods

This section's focus is on center of gravity identification methods, which is not the same as center of gravity analysis. This is an important but often overlooked distinction.

Identification focuses on selection of the COG. Analysis assumes a correct COG selection then looks at the COG's relationship with critical factors, (critical capabilities, critical requirements and critical vulnerabilities). Below are summaries of the main elements of center of gravity identification methods found in joint doctrine and the writings of Dr. Joe Strange, Dr. Milan Vego, and Dr. Antulio Echevarria. This is not detailed discussion of each method or how they are applied. The intent is to provide a basis for understanding and comparison.

Joint Doctrine.

Manual JP 5-0, *Joint Operation Planning,* does not provide a methodology; rather it explains who is responsible for the enemy center of gravity identification. It states:

> Joint force intelligence analysts identify adversary COGs, determining from which elements the adversary derives freedom of action, physical strength (means), and the will to fight. The J-2, in conjunction with other operational planners, then attempts to determine if the tentative or candidate COGs truly are critical to the adversary's strategy. This analysis is a linchpin in the planning effort. Others on the joint force staff conduct similar analysis to identify friendly COGs.[82]

To find a method one has to go to JP 2-01.3, *Joint Intelligence Preparation of the Operational Environment.* It states, "JIPOE analysts continuously assess the adversary's leadership, fielded forces, resources, infrastructure, population, transportation systems, and internal and external relationships to determine from which elements the adversary derives freedom of action, physical strength, or the will to fight."[83] "JIPOE utilizes a macro-analytic approach that seeks to identify an adversary's strategic vulnerabilities and COGs."[84] JP 2-01.3 then identifies the method saying, "The most effective method for JIPOE analysts to identify adversary COGs is to visualize each COG's role/function relative to each of the various systems and subsystems."[85] The 'visualization' method is a holistic view of a system and discerning where its strength comes from:

> Strange. Dr. Strange's method relies on a modified Clausewitzian definition of the center of gravity. Strange defines the center of gravity as, "Primary sources of moral or physical strength, power and resistance."[86] He then recommends listing the sources of power and to find the primary source of power using a "process of critical analysis".[87] Strange does not prescribe specific techniques for 'critical analysis'.

> Vego. Dr. Milan Vego, believes a center of gravity is a source of strength or leverage.[88] He advocates that, "An analytical construct should be used to determine the enemy and friendly centers of gravity…" Then, "…the judgment and wisdom of the commander's and their staffs are the keys to determining the proper center of gravity…"[89] The 'analytical construct' includes the *objective*, which is the principal factor, the *military situation*, and the *critical factors.* The military situation includes tangible and abstract military and non-military elements, more simply the operating

environment. Vego's critical factors are critical strengths, critical vulnerabilities, and critical weakness and are considered the essentials for the accomplishment of the objective. Using this three part construct to provide a holistic view and understanding, commanders and planners determine the source of strength. A method for determination is not prescribed.

Echevarria. Dr. Echevarria places the emphasis, not on strength but on cohesion and replaces the center of gravity metaphor with "centripetal force" that holds the force together. He also suggests that the concept is best suited for war seeking the complete defeat of an enemy, and has less utility in limited wars. He then lays out a three step process for COG identification.

1. Step 1: Determine whether identifying and attacking a COG is appropriate for the type of war [total defeat or limited] we are going to wage.

2. Step 2: Determine whether the adversary's whole structure or system is sufficiently connected to be treated as a single body. [concentrated or dispersed]

3. Step 3: Determine what element has the necessary centripetal force to hold the system together.

He also recommends redefining the COG as focal points that serve to hold a system or structure together and that draws power from a variety of sources and provide it with purpose and direction.[90] Note that this definition has three elements; holds a system together, draws power, and provides purpose and direction. One must assume that a COG candidate must possess all three elements.

A survey of center of gravity doctrine and articles show that the most common method of COG identification is 'critical analysis' and its partner 'visualize' and use of an 'analytical framework' summed up as 'critical reasoning.'[91] None of these 'methodologies' describe a process for their application. One of the few exceptions is Antulio Echevarria's 'Center of Gravity Recommendations for Joint Doctrine' with its three step process.[92] A criticism of these methods is that they lack practical 'how to' techniques for planners on how to apply them and leaves planners scratching their heads. The 'ends, ways and means' methodology answers this criticism. It is nothing more than a codification of the application of critical reasoning that provides an 'analytical framework' for step by step center of gravity determination methodology. Not only is the 'ends, ways and means' methodology compatible with the other methods (Echevarria excepted) it provides a simple and logical technique for applying critical analysis or thinking.

Summary

To make the center of gravity concept the useful 'analytical tool' that doctrine intended it to be, doctrine should adopt the modernized definitions based on the intent of doctrine, modern systems thinking and the criteria of clarity, logic, precision and testability. Doctrine should then adopt the six step 'ends, ways, and mean' center of gravity identification methodology. Should doctrine accept these proposals then planners could stop debating what the center of gravity is and get on with using it, Figure ten.

	Basis	Context	Method	Application
Joint Doctrine	Source of Power	Adversarial and System of Systems	Visualize	Levels of War
Strange	Source of Power	Adversarial	Critical Analysis	Levels of War
Vego	Source of Power	Objective and Situation	Analytical Framework	Levels of War
Echevarria	Provides Cohesion	Type War and Force	3 Step	Selective
Eikmeier	Attains the Objective	Objective and System of Systems	Ends, Ways, Means	Universal

Figure 10. Center of Gravity Sources.

Modernized Definitions

1. Center of Gravity. *The primary entity that inherently possesses the critical capabilities to achieve the objective.*

2. Critical Capabilities. *Primary abilities essential to the accomplishment of the objective which merits a Center of Gravity to be identified as such.*

3. Critical Requirements. *Essential conditions, resources and means the COG requires to perform the critical capability.*

4. Critical Vulnerabilities. *Critical requirements or components thereof which are deficient or vulnerable to neutralization, interdiction or attack in a manner achieving decisive results.*

Center of Gravity Identification Methodology

1. Identify the organization's desired ends.

2. Identify 'ways' or actions that can achieve the desired ends. Select the way(s) the organization is most likely to use. That selection is/are the critical capability(ies). Ways = critical capabilities.

3. List the organization's means or resources available or needed to execute the critical capability.

4. Select the entity from the list of means that inherently possess the critical capability. This is the center of gravity.

5. From the remaining means select those that are critical for execution of the critical capability. These are the critical requirements.

6. Identify those critical requirements that are vulnerable to adversary actions.

Notes

1. Dr. Joe Strange and Col Richard Iron, "Understanding Centers of Gravity and Critical Vulnerabilities, Part 1", online at www.au.af.mil/au/awc/awcgate/usmc/ COG1.pdf pp.1 (accessed 15 December 2011).

2. Dr, Alex Ryan, email to LTC Celestino Perez, Command and General Staff College, Fort Leavenworth, Kansas, passed on to Dale C. Eikmeier, 13 October 2011.

3. Carl von Clausewitz, *On War,* editors and translators, Michael Howard and Peter Paret, Princeton, NJ. Princeton University Press, 1984. 485-486. And Department of the Army, *FM 100-5 Operations*. Washington DC, May 1986. pp.10, Appx B, 179-180.

4. Department of Defense (DoD), *Joint Publication (JP) 5-0 Joint Operation Planning* (U.S. Department of Defense Washington DC 2011), III-22,23.

5. *On War* 485-486.

6. Carl von Clausewitz, *On War,* editors and translators, Michael Howard and Peter Paret, (Princeton, NJ: Princeton University Press, 1984), 485-486. And Department of the Army, *Field Manual (FM) 100-5 Operations*, (Department of the Army:Washington DC,1986), 10, Appx B, 179-180; Department of the Army, *FM 100-5 Operations*. Washington DC, May 1986. pp.10, Appx B, 179-180. Department of the Army, *Field Manual (FM) 100-5 Operations* Headquarters, Department of the Army:Washington DC,1986),10 Appx B, 179-180. and Mark, Cancian, "Centers of Gravity Are a Myth", *Proceedings* September 1998, 30.

7. LTC Celestino Perez Jr. PhD, email to Dale C. Eikmeier, Command and General Staff College, Fort Leavenworth, KS,30 September 2011.

8. DoD, JP 5-0, III-22,23.

9. Discussions at Fort Leavenworth, Kansas during the winter and spring 2010 among Command General Staff College instructors, and the Deputy Commandant's Initiative Group on the implementation of 'Design' in the US Army's FM 5-0 *The Operations Process.* The issue was whether or not the design methodology and its "problem frame" would replace the center of gravity.

10. Paraphrased from Stephen D. Brookfield, *The Skillful Teacher,* 2nd Edition, (Jossey-Bass, San Francisco) 2006, 13.

11. Dept of the Army, FM 100-5, 10, Appx B, 179-180.

12. Author's conclusion based on the changing definitions and descriptions of the center of gravity in both US Army and Joint Doctrine from 1986 through 2011 (FM 100-5 1986/1993, JP 5-00.1 2002, JP 5-0 2006/2011) and the number of articles and critiques on centers of gravity (Strange, Echevarria, Vego, Eikmeier).

13. Dr. Christopher Bassford, online at http://www.nndb.com/people/676/000087415/ (accessed 5 December 2011).

14. B. H. Liddell Hart, *Strategy,* (Meridian: New York, New York, 1991), 344.

15. Presentation by Lars Falk, Swedish Defense Research Agency, "Centers of Gravity and Clausewitz's Model of War" 2nd Annual Conference on Terrorism and Global Security, Washington DC, Ambivium Institute on Security and Cooperation. 14-15 September 2011, http://www.ambivium.org/events.html.

16. Author's experiences as a student and instructor at the Army's Command and General Staff College, the School of Advanced Military Studies, as an instructor at the Army War College and as an operational level planner. The mechanical meaning of center of gravity would have to be explained so use of the metaphor could be understood. If a metaphor has to be explained the use of a metaphor is in appropriate to begin with.

17. Milan Vego, "Clausewitz's Schwerpunkt: Mistranslated from German Misunderstood in English", online at http://findarticles.com/p/articles/mi_m0PBZ/is_1_87/ai_n27135952/ (accessed 10 January 2012). and Antulio J. Echevarria II, "Clausewitz's Center Of Gravity: Changing Our Warfighting Doctrine—Again!" (Carlisle Barracks, PA, Strategic Studies Institute September 2003), 6.

18. Milan Vego, *Joint Operational Warfare Theory and Practice,* (Newport, RI, US Naval War College, September 2007), VII-37 –VII-48.

19. Colonel J.J. Graham's 1874 English translation of *On War,* 144, 151, 331, available as an ebook at www. Gutenberg.org.

20. Dr. Christopher Bassford online article at http://www.clausewitz.com/bibl/WhichTrans.htm (accessed 5 December 2011).

21. Dr. Joe Strange and Colonel Richard Iron, *Understanding Centers of Gravity and Critical Vulnerabilities,* National Defense University 2003,online at http://www.au.af.mil/au/awc/awcgate/ usmc/ COG1.pdf .7 (accessed 15 December 2011).

22. Email and phone discussions between Dr. Milan Vego, U.S. Naval War College, Newport, Rhode Island and Dale C. Eikmeier, US Army Command and General Staff College, Fort Leavenworth, Kansas on 13 February 2012

23. Strange and Iron, 10.

24. Dennis Prange, Munich Foundation, discussions with the author at the 2d Annual Conference on Terrorism and Global Security, Washington DC. Ambivium Institute on Security and Cooperation. 14-15 September 2011, online at http://www.ambivium.org/events.html.

25. Dept of the Army, FM 100-5, (1986), 179.

26. Department of the Army, Field Manual (FM) *100-5 Operations.* (Headquarters Department of the Army: Washington DC 1993) GL-1.

27. Dr. Joe Strange. Perspectives on Warfighting Number Four Second Edition , Centers of Gravity & Critical Vulnerabilities, (Quantico, VA: Marine Corps Association, 1996), ix .

28.Discussions with Dr. James J. Schneider, School of Advance Military Studies, Fort Leavenworth, Kansas, 1998.

29. Department of Defense (DoD), Joint Publication (JP) 1-02, *Department of Defense Dictionary of Military and Associated Terms,* (Department of Defense, Washington DC, 23 March 1994), 63.

30. Department of Defense (DoD), Joint Publication (JP) 5-00.1, *Joint Doctrine for Campaign Planning,* (Department of Defense, Washington DC, 25 January 2002), GL-3.

31. Department of Defense (DoD), Joint Publication (JP) *5-0 Joint Operation Planning,*(Department of Defense, Washington DC, 26 December 2006,) IV-8 and Department of Defense (DOD), Joint Publication (JP) 5-0 *Joint Operation Planning,* (Department of Defense, Washington DC, 11 August 2011), III-22.

32. NATO, *Allied Joint Doctrine AJP-01(D)* (Headquarters North Atlantic Treaty Organization Brussels, Belgium, 21 December 2010), Lexicon-5.

33. NATO, 5-15.

34. See Center of Gravity articles by Dr. Joe Strange and COL Richard Iron, Dr. James Schneider, Dr. Antulio Echevarria II, Dr. Milan Vego, and COL Dale Eikmeier, just to name a few.

35. Dr. Ryan email.

36. JP 5-0 , (2011) GL-8.

37. JP 5.0, III-22.

38. JP 5.0, III-22.

39. JP 5.0, III-23 figure III-11.

40. JP 5.0, III-24.

41. JP 5.0, III-23.

42. The use of the word "primary" is attributed to Dr. Joe Strange. Dr. Joe Strange. *Perspectives on Warfighting Number Four Second Edition*, ix.

43. JP 5-0, (2011) III-22.

44. JP 5-0, (2011) III-24.

45. JP 5-0, (2011) III-24.

46. Strange. *Perspectives on Warfighting Number Four* Second Edition, ix.

47. JP 5-0, (2011) GL-8 ,IV-12.

48. Strange. *Perspectives on Warfighting Number Four* Second Edition, ix, and DoD, JP 5-0, GL-8 ,III-24 .

49. Department of Defense (DoD), Joint Publication (JP) 2-01.3 *Joint Intelligence Preparation of the Operational Environment*, (Department of Defense, Washington DC, 16 June 2009), I-3,4, II-44,45,46, III-13.

50. JP 5-0, 2-01.3, II-65.

51. Author's personal experience as a planner and strategist at the tactical through strategic levels in Operations DESERT SHIELD/STORM, IRAQI FREEDOM and ENDURING FREEDOM and as an instructor at the US Army Command and General Staff College, the School of Advanced Military Studies, and the US Army War College.

52. Arthur F. Lykke Jr., ed., *Military Strategy: Theory and Application* (US Army War College, Carlisle, PA, 1998).

53. DOD, JP 5-0, (2011) III-24.

54. DOD.

55. Council on Foreign Relations, Timeline for the Iraq War, online at http://www.cfr.org/iraq/timeline-iraq-war/p18876?gclid=CICBsszE46wCFRAq7AodXRgpnw (accessed 13 January 2012).

56. Timeline for the Iraq War.

57. Associated Press, "Senator Reid says the War is Lost", April 202007, online at http://www.msnbc.msn.com/id/18227928/ns/politics/t/reid-iraq-war-lost-us-cant-win/, (accessed 13 January 2012).

58. LTC Celestino Perez Jr., email to Dale C. Eikmeier, Command and General Staff College, Fort Leavenworth, Kansas, 30 September.

59. LTG David Huntoon, XVIII Corps planner during Operation Just Cause, email to Dale C. Eikmeier Command and General Staff College, 30 October 2011. Author's personal experience as a planner in the 1st Infantry Division's G3 section during DESERT STORM and DESERT SHIELD; as a J3 planner at USCENTCOM Fwd, Camp As Sayliyah, Qatar, Operation ENDURING FREEDOM, January 2004; and as a strategist in Multinational Forces Iraq, strategy, Plans and Assessments Division, Baghdad, Iraq, Operation Iraqi Freedom, 2005.

60. Discussion in a meeting on center of gravity at the Command and General Staff College, Fort Leavenworth, KS, October 26, 2011.

61. Dr. Alex Ryan email 13 October 2011, provided to the center of gravity meeting at the Command and General Staff College, Fort Leavenworth, Kansas, 26 October 2011.

62. Peter M. Senge, *The Fifth Discipline*, (Doubleday: New York, 1990), 114-126.

63. DOD, JP 5-0 (2011) III-22,23.

64. Department of the Army, *FM 3-0 Operations*. February 2008, (Headquarters Department of the Army, Washington DC), 6-8.

65. Dept of the Army.

66. Dept of the Army.

67. DOD, JP 5-0 (2011), III-22.

68. Joseph Strange and Richard Iron, "Center of Gravity: What Clausewitz Really Meant", *Joint Forces Quarterly,* Summer 2003: 24.

69. Vego, *Joint Operational Warfare Theory and Practice,* VII-24.

70. Vego.

71. Dept of the Army, FM 100-5 Operations. (1986) 10.

72. DOD, JP 5-0, (2011), III-2.

73. DOD, JP 5-0, (2011), III-1.

74. DOD, JP 5-0, (2011).

75. Celestino Perez, "A Practical Guide to Design: A Way to Think About It, and a Way to Do It," *Military Review*, (March-April 2011).

76. The term "Operational Approach," depending on its context, can have two meanings. In the context of Design it is a concept of how to solve a problem or commander's vision. When discussing the "Elements of Operational Design" it is either a direct or indirect approach to attacking a center of gravity.

77. DOD, JP 5-0 (2011), III-14.

78. DOD, JP 5-0 (2011), III-26.

79. Allied Joint Publication -01(D), 5A2.

80. DOD, JP 5-0 (2011), III-27,28.

81. Department of Military Strategy, Planning and Operations, *CAMPAIGN PLANNING HANDBOOK AY 11,* (US Army War College, Carlisle Barracks, PA). 62.

82. DOD, JP 5-0 (2011), III-23.

83. DOD, JP 2-01.3, xx.

84. DOD, JP 2-01.3, I-4.

85. DOD, JP 2-01.3, II-65.

86. Strange. Perspectives on Warfighting Number Four Second Edition, ix.

87. Strange, 18.

88. Vego, VII-13.

89. Vego, VII-14.

90. Antulio Echevarria II, "Center of Gravity Recommendations for Joint Doctrine", *Joint Forces Quarterly,* issue 35.

91. Strange. 18: DoD, JP 2-01.3, pp. II-65; Vego, VII-14.

92. Antulio Echevarria II, "Center of Gravity Recommendations for Joint Doctrine."

Figure 5. "Center of Gravity Analysis Example," Joint Pub 5-0, Joint Operation Planning, 11 August 2011, page III-25, figure III-12. CGSC Copyright Registration Number: 12-1073 C/E.

www.ingramcontent.com/pod-product-compliance
Lightning Source LLC
Chambersburg PA
CBHW050500110426
42742CB00018B/3321